W9-BXH-293

DATE DUE

MAR 21 '94			
JAN 0 4 2009			
DEC 0 7 2011			
JAN 0 4 2012			

HIGHSMITH 45-220

✶

To Keep and Bear Arms

✶ ✶ ✶ ✶ ✶

KF
3941
•D38
1969

✳ ✳ ✳ ✳ ✳

TO KEEP

AND BEAR ARMS

✳ ✳ ✳ ✳ ✳

Bill R. Davidson

Tennessee Tech. Library
Cookeville, Tenn.

ARLINGTON HOUSE   *New Rochelle, New York*

300733

Copyright © 1969 by Arlington House, New Rochelle, New York.

All rights reserved. No portion of this book may be reproduced without written permission from the publisher, except by a reviewer who may quote brief passages in connection with a review.

Library of Congress Catalog Card Number 75-93455
SBN 87000–064–0

MANUFACTURED IN THE UNITED STATES OF AMERICA

Deliver us from privileged leaders of grand aspirations whose studied accents, staged gesticulations, or great wealth do not necessarily make them fit to tell anyone how to do anything. They succeed only in fostering more crime, losing more lives, and deluding more fools.

Contents

✷ ✷ ✷ ✷ ✷

CONTENTS 8

✳

To Keep and Bear Arms

✳ ✳ ✳ ✳ ✳

Introduction

✳ ✳ ✳ ✳ ✳

"The British are more interested in umbrellas than guns."—Scotland Yard official

THE WORLD IS FULL OF EXPERTS, AND LATELY AMERICANS HAVE been exposed to a full-tilt charge by the most dangerous type of all: the gilded, persuasive, and high-class nonexpert who gets people killed. The motive, oddly, is supposed to be anti-killing—humanitarianism. But all through American history, those of pacific bent or humanitarian motive have usually accounted for the deaths of more citizens than either our jingoists or those who advocate solid preparedness and direct methods.

The "ban all guns" mentality has been gaining momentum in the United States since someone—who and for what reason are immaterial to this book—took a rifle and shot President John Kennedy. Just lately the dead President's brother Ted has vaulted into his silver-mounted hero saddle to lead the charge. He contends that young Americans no longer need to be taught rifle marksmanship, that rifle accuracy is out of style, that such training only adds to internal disorders. He has a spontaneous or at least willing claque of other politicians, newspaper editorialists and columnists, television and radio commentators, and magazine writers. The Kennedy family's holdings and influence in the information media are well known. This probably goes far to explain how and why they have mustered loud and persistent support. It happens, however, to be a miserably misinformed support and may even be intentionally misdirected.

After an Arab fanatic slew Bobby Kennedy, the cry for "gun controls" was raised louder than ever. The press, television, psychiatrists, and others went on a four-star orgy of trying to persuade the public that guns were responsible for all our violence. The National Rifle Association, which had spent most of its time and treasure for years trying to preserve the Second Amendment—the right to keep and bear arms—against such onsets, was assaulted as one of the great villains in our society. Ted Kennedy was joined by the full cult of anti-gun Senators—Joe Tydings, Tom Dodd, Joe Clark, and others—in seeking to find guns at fault. It was the cheap, easy, quick solution.

Dodd converted the second Kennedy killing into a forum for nationwide gun registration, which he had piously opposed before in a posture of humility trying to get his mail-order control bill enacted. Tydings, who had originally identified himself as a hunter (specifically, shotgunner after ducks, with his children, around Chesapeake Bay), used the occasion to drum up demand for severe federal as well as state controls. A year later, facing reelection, he circulated a picture of himself and his sons in duck-shooting regalia.

The fact remained that neither registration nor mail controls nor any of the panaceas Dodd, Tydings, or others (including Lyndon Johnson) sought would have deterred any of the major killers whose bloodletting triggered "demand" for such action. Neither Lee Harvey Oswald nor anyone else of that peculiar, disturbed, driven breed would have been foiled by any such provisions.

And the skill with guns these legislators condemned and vilified, in the attempt to cash in on such occasions, remained a far more vital asset to the nation than the short-term, quickie solutions they pressed for.

The probability is that marksmanship—proficiency with small arms—will be required in *increasing* degree for young men and other citizens, in this the world's most powerful country in its most difficult period. Nothing in war, right into the middle of 1969, has shown anything to refute this. Perhaps the specific techniques and skills may change. For example, long-range, high-precision shooting has declined in a staggered spiral since the Boer War. But the fundamental need for skill with small arms is one of the few constants in war and human self-defense. Even sniping, the highest skill in precision shooting, staged a comeback during the later 1960's; the Marine Corps started cultivating military sniping again and by 1966 had provided one platoon per regiment of those genuinely expert shots in the field in Vietnam. But while one facet or another of the shooting skills may have periodic ups or downs, the basic tool of the United States soldier or any soldier, regular or reservist or citizen militiaman, will continue to be some kind of shoulder or hand-fired weapon (or both of them) capable of accurately expelling a number of lethal projectiles easily carried on the person. And the more Americans there are who know how to use such weapons readily, the stronger will our (and their) chances be for survival in a world which has come to shrink from personal killing but develops weapons of mass destruction in escalating degree.

The expertise of those who preach that guns are out of date in war is easily challenged. Ted Kennedy served his Korean war stint (1951–53) as a military policeman in Western Europe, a long way from where the pro-marksmanship professionals of the Marine Corps and Army were reacquiring the old rifle skills on Korean hilltops. The late Bobby Kennedy spent two years in the Navy, culminating in destroyer service (1944–46). Someone once said Ted "doesn't know which end of the gun the bullet comes from." That is only a slightly unfair description. In his political and emotional zeal to discredit guns, Ted disparaged all the evidence from the battlefields (battlefields that he had never seen, except perhaps afterward on carefully guided tours), all the expert testimony of people who know war and shooting and history. He helped launch a sort of holy politico-propaganda war against the

National Rifle Association because its people—who *are* experts—
have had the temerity to stand up and challenge a Kennedy, when
Kennedys have ordained a crusade, and the crusade has not quite
jumped off on schedule.

A great many questions have been posed since the presidential
assassination and other outbursts of criminal vindictiveness, passion, and insanity. Reason dictates a reasonable legislative course,
certainly, to keep the criminal, the mentally disturbed person, the
narcotics user, the serious alcoholic, and the juvenile (except with
proper supervision) from freely and easily obtaining guns. But a
great effort must be made to insure that such legislation does not
interfere with the entirely valid, in fact vital, role of firearms in
our national defense, in helping resist crime, in bettering our international marksmanship reputation, and in the recreational
hunting which pays the bill for most of the wildlife everybody
enjoys.

How far can gun legislation go on a constitutional level? Will
any of it work, and if so, how much? Has it worked in areas where
it has been tried with great stringency? Would it hurt this country
if the marksmanship program of the government and of subsidiary
groups were reduced? How consistent with a free, democratic society is arbitrary control over human pursuits?

This book is an attempt to answer these questions by a writer
who has been a newspaperman and magazine reporter, a police
officer, a competitive shooter, a hunter—all in different states and
regions of the United States. The writer has also been an ardent
student of the history of this country and the world and in particular of the wars we have fought, in abysmally unprepared fashion,
at great and always avoidable cost. He is firmly convinced that the
course many seek in firearms control legislation is really prohibition, as total, blighting, and morally stupid as was the attempt at
Prohibition of alcoholic beverages from 1919 to 1933. There is
something ironic in the crusade against firearms, because it is
mounted by urban sophisticates who would be repelled by com-
parisons with the hard-shelled rural bigots who marched out of the

19th century and foisted Prohibition off on us. Yet there is a common denominator of puritanical intolerance and greed to reform between the anti-gun bigots and the anti-liquor zealots: between Carrie Nation and Carl Bakal. The proponents of fire-arms "controls" have a psychological rapport with and use similar tactics to the people who promoted Prohibition. Both seek to commit wholesale abrogations of the Bill of Rights and ordinary, common-sense living in a free nation. The disarmers, while prid-ing themselves on liberal and humanitarian motives, are pretty much theoretical heirs of the puritanism that consumed the Drys— transplanted from some Scottsboro lynching ground to Broad-way.

It has been in the Northeast, remember, that the impetus for stiff gun laws has grown. And while the judicial or police or legis-lative leaders of the big northeastern states (many of which have no state Bill of Rights provision guaranteeing the basic right to bear arms) deny firearms to citizens, citizens are robbed, mugged, assaulted, raped, and killed—ignorant of how to defend themselves and prevented from doing so by a system that is increasingly solic-itous of everybody except the victims of such crimes.

It is time the citizenry had a chance to look at a few facts of life—and to learn that there is indeed a case for guns, at least until Utopia gets here. They should know that the United States homi-cide rate by gun is actually declining, not soaring due to the al-leged ease of murder with guns; that accidental deaths from the use of guns decrease most years now, with improved training tech-niques, and that they are safer out in the hunting field with a gun than in their bathtubs or at their dining tables or swimming.

As someone said, a free people which abdicates its rights as well as its responsibilities pretty quickly ceases to be free. Supreme Court Justice William O. Douglas has spelled out the method:

"We have a Bill of Rights designed to keep government out of private domains. But the fences have been broken down; and machinery to restore them has been denied. The Bill of Rights— with the judicial gloss it has acquired—plainly is not adequate to protect the individual against the growing bureaucracy. He faces a formidable opponent in government, even when he is endowed with funds and with courage. The individual is almost certain to be plowed under unless he has a well-organized, active political group to speak for him. The church is one. The press is another. The union is a third. But if a powerful sponsor is lacking, individual liberty withers—in spite of glowing opinions and resounding constitutional phrases."

Nicolò Machiavelli, Florentine diplomat and cynical commentator on his times, was about as far from Douglas's idealism as you can get and still be in the same human race. But from his late 15th-early 16th-century vantage point, Machiavelli noticed some things that should give idealistic Americans and other breeds long, hard thought:

".... It is more difficult to bring a republic, armed with its own arms, under the sway of one of its citizens than it is to bring one armed with foreign (mercenary) arms. Rome and Sparta stood for many ages armed and free. The Switzers are completely armed and quite free."

Almost 500 years later, "the Switzers" are still completely armed and quite free.

Machiavelli had one flaming moment of idealism (in retrospect, he might have called it weakness). He tried to organize a citizen militia in Florence and indeed all over Italy, to drive out foreign and home-grown tyrants and subdue their mercenaries. He failed. Italy was not ready for nationalism in 1500. But it is worth citing that the most astute and cynical diplomatic commentator of his time saw the great value of an armed citizenry—as valid in his country as in Rome or Sparta. And as valid in ours.

There is a distinct possibility, if not probability, that part of World War Three will be fought within the United States' contiguous 48 states as well as its two outlying ones. Almost anyone who has paid attention to military developments in the last 50 or 60 years is aware that whether we know or wish it or not, the American Atlantic frontier prior to 1940 was guarded in large part by the British Navy. The British served our purposes for their own reasons, of course, being (until recent aberrations raised doubts) a courageous and hard-headed race; they helped enforce the Monroe Doctrine in the 19th century not from admiration for us or the Doctrine, but because our goals happened to coincide with theirs in the Western Hemisphere. They didn't want German, Austrian, French, or Russian imperial activities expanding in Latin America. Nor did we. And in the two world wars, the British fleet was a great shield that absorbed and fended off the blows of Continental military power while we decided whether we would get involved. We got involved. And after being literally bled white in the gross military stupidities of 1914–18—the British officer (i.e., potential leader) casualty rate was strikingly higher than that of its allies and enemies—Britain found itself bereft of leadership and short of money. It possessed a certain reserve of courage, however, exemplified by Winston Churchill; it held Nazi Germany in check until Russia became involved and the United States hauled itself out of the Depression and entered the war. We were literally bulldogged into war by Japan, but once the role of world leadership was thrust upon us, we had no choice. We still have none. In the postwar world we had the troops, and money, to rule as Britain had done but could no longer do. Very reluctantly we assumed the role imperial Britain had played. Where there had been several great powers in the world, there were after 1945 only two: the United States and the Soviet Union. China, for all its immense defensive capacity in an Asian land war, lacked the capability to deal out nuclear, worldwide destruction the way the United States and the U.S.S.R. could. Just how much longer China will be without this capability is good only for short-term speculation. China will become increasingly menacing because, while its arsenal may overtake ours only in lurches, its strategic mentality doesn't seem to have changed much from the time of the Korean fighting. The idea of accepting 300 million nuclear-war casualties deters the Chinese Communist hierarchy no more now than it did when Mao Tse-tung uttered it years ago.

The point is, when major war next materializes, it will come first and most fiercely to the United States—without warning, the diplomatic niceties, or time to make special preparations. The period for making special preparations has already largely elapsed. It started in 1953, when the United States government learned that the U.S.S.R. possessed a hydrogen bomb. A long list of American presidents have been guilty of moral ineptitude and political cowardice—call it criminal negligence and apply it with nonpartisanship—by failing to gird the nation for what will come, sooner or later. They vacillated between lack of initiative to take up a controversial cause and that peculiar liberal, hope-for-the-best altruism that often dominates American and British political thinking. The tremendous scientific and construction capacities of the nation—to develop and manufacture the shelters and other aids that might help insure survival—were never called into play. The situation was a good deal like that of the Pennsylvania legislature in the 1760's, when a pacifist majority refused to appropriate funds for the frontier militia to get guns, lead, and powder because, it was felt, this would provoke the Indians. Meantime, of course, the Indians were committing unspeakable cruelties along the frontier, and a few associates of those pacifist gentlemen in Philadelphia were peddling guns and ammunition and alcohol to the hostiles. (Only a forceful reaction by the citizen militia—menacing the legislature—procured the required appropriation.)

We have no workable master Civil Defense plan that provides for all the contingencies. There are fragments and sketches of plans here and there. Some CD officials recommend a sort of "everybody's-on-his-own" approach to disaster. Individuals—rather clear-headedly, it is conceded—are told they'll have to protect their own families and themselves as best they can in the chaos and panic certain to follow nuclear exchange. Other CD officials don't even show this much foresight. (They are fascinated with the intricacies of directing traffic, however.) The Department of Defense, assigned overlordship of Civil Defense by the Kennedy administration, is preoccupied with controlling vehicles in movement (though there may well be no vehicles to move anywhere, nor roads over which to move) and radiology, but is not much interested in the basic tasks of maintaining order, restoring reasonable control, and girding for recovery. Nor is it much concerned in dealing with subversion or enemy infiltration. Correspondence between the author and various Defense Department functionaries is convincing on this point. The Department is not at all interested in a militia program (even though in all hard fact the states have little or no militia). The Department is deeply committed, however, to what is politically expedient, popular, or noncontroversial.

The standard Department of Defense attitude was spelled out in a letter dated August 17, 1967, from Hubert A. Schon, Acting Director of Civil Defense under McNamara, to the author: "The concept of a 'civil defense militia' is not compatible with the purposes of civil defense, as set forth by Congress," Schon said. He did not add that Defense sought no strengthening of CD in this respect—nor did he need to, since McNamara for half a dozen years steadfastly opposed any such ideas. CD had been placed under Defense early in the Kennedy era—and interred there.

Defense spokesman Schon indicated no dissatisfaction with the nakedness of the nation. The states could be left to work it out, he implied—odd thinking from an administration dedicated to more and greater centralization of authority and effort. "Since a state militia-type force is subject only to state authority, its organization, training, and employment is subject to the sole discretion of state authorities. Any civilian marksmanship program tied to a militia system would, therefore, be a matter for individual state decision."

The Civil Defense Act of Congress on which Schon and Defense rested their case (in 1967, five years after the Cuban missile flare-up, and a dozen years after the Russians first made public their possession of hydrogen bombs) was enacted in 1950!

Schon said that duties of civil defense were to be: " (1) to minimize the effects upon the civilian population caused or which would be caused by an attack upon the U.S., (2) to deal with the immediate emergency conditions which would be created by any such attack, and (3) to effectuate emergency repairs to, or the emergency restoration of, vital utilities and facilities destroyed or damaged by any such attack."

The definition is absorbingly inclusive for the rather non-existent capabilities and training. Now, almost two decades after the act was passed, how many CD units have been trained to meet such awesome assignments? By the federal government *or* those suddenly potent state elements on which Schon professes to rely?

Widespread urban riots the last several summers have shown what part of World War Three may be like. The tactical bumbling of United States police and much of the military in dealing with a handful of not-too-good snipers (a much misused word) indicated the contempt for really good small-arms skills which most of our police and political chiefs share with some of our military leaders. A few skilled sniper-spotter teams, trained to cope with rooftop and window gunmen, could have made the streets safe much faster and with less loss of innocent life. They would have applied casualties where casualties belonged: to the gunmen. As it was, half-trained Guardsmen and police sprayed entire buildings with semi-automatic or fully automatic weapons. Innocent women and children were needlessly killed. The gunmen (calling them snipers confers on them a skill they did not possess) slipped away. It might have worked in close-up jungle fights, but it was not intelligent, controlled application of small-arms fire in touchy situations requiring both judgment and ability. No governor or mayor had the courage to call for and apply the right techniques. Most didn't even know of the existence of such skills. Major Robert Russell, a Marine Corps expert who brought about the resurrection of the sniper program in his service, could have provided the sniper-spotter teams. So could the civilian rifle clubs in the affected communities. But while Guardsmen sprayed buildings broadside, Senators Ted Kennedy and Stephen Young ridiculed marksmanship. Governors (led by New Jersey's Richard Hughes whom nobody can beat to the panic button) panicked. Mayors vacillated. The Guard and police caught hell for the ineptness of their political masters, and for their masters' failure to prepare them to deal with the urban crisis's ugliest manifestations.

In war, you don't really blame the troops who panic and run away from a battle; not if you want to do better next time. You blame the people who put them there unprepared or undisciplined. Thus, the National Guard and the police can hardly be held accountable for the riot-control failures of 1967. The original sin lies with their political masters. Unawareness, a refusal to face reality, a disdain for the nuts and bolts chores in training men— these were the trademarks of United States politicians in handling the urban crisis when violence erupted.

There is an old Mexican proverb about how revolutionaries always raise the cry "Death to the rich!"—but it is always the poor who get killed. We, in our apathetic tolerance of politicians who won't spell it out, who won't act, have gotten far more citizens killed than we would have with more direct measures and more forethought.

What people in free and open societies like to forget is that in war there are only a few brutal constants among innumerable puzzles and unwelcome shocks. One of these very few constants was aptly put by the Korean-era chief of United States Army ground forces, General John R. Hodge: "Every man must be trained to fight as an infantryman first."

Training a man to fight as an infantryman entails primarily teaching him to shoot well with his small arms—his personal weapons.

In America, almost everybody wants to be a pilot, a sailor, a button-pusher in clean white tunic, or a medic. But in war most people end up having to be infantrymen. There is never a surplus of young men who shoot well.

Field Marshal Lord A. P. Wavell warned the British army in the 1930's to "prepare for war, not *a* war."

Former Chairman of the Joint Chiefs of Staff General Lyman L. Lemnitzer said: "In any type of military operations, one thing that has not changed is the importance of the soldier's mastery of his individual weapons, fundamentally the rifle. . . . This importance has increased. One of the basic requirements of modern warfare is the greatly increased dispersion of units. In order to minimize the effectiveness of the enemy's firepower, our units will be dispersed over a much larger area than ever before. . . . They will have to be more completely self-sustained and their members will be called upon to exercise an even bigger degree of individual self-reliance."

This is the sort of war our leaders believed (and our people were told) had gone away at Hiroshima in 1945. Periodically they pretend it has gone away. But it has not, and if you will not accept that, then stop right here. Go off and read something soothing, like that doughty nonexpert on infantry war, Teddy Kennedy. The resultant coma will be cozy, if brief.

Chapter 1

Lessons Right and Wrong—
Israel and the Riots

*****

"As of November 1, 1965, out of about 4,000 responses
to the Director of Civilian Markmanship's civil
rights directive, only 17 clubs elected to drop from the
program rather than sign the compliance agreement
[barring racial discrimination in NRA gun clubs]."
—the Arthur D. Little Report

"Pikes, or to be accurate lengths of iron tubing with
bayonet-like blades at the end, were issued in bulk to
many Home Guard units; they were officially recommended as 'balanced instruments particularly useful
for street fighting.' "—Peter Fleming (in *Operation
Sea Lion*) on the lack of small arms for the British
Home Guard awaiting the expected Nazi invasion

THE SUMMER OF 1967 PROVIDED TWO OUTSTANDING EXAMPLES OF
behavior pertinent to any discussion of a militia for the United
States. One was Israel's lightning, efficient response to menace by a
supposedly overwhelming assembly of enemies. This was a collective response, but it was based on a system putting high value on
individual preparedness and aptitude for that commonest of all
human drives, self-preservation. The other was the criminal mis-
handling of the Newark and Plainfield, New Jersey riots by that
state's erratic and sometimes irrational governor, Richard Hughes.
National Guardsmen and police drew much criticism for their

roles in the disorders; that was an understandable, but not too rational condemnation of collective authority when the real, prime guilt was Hughes' for committing one error after another in trying to cope with insurrection. Hughes literally blew his cool. Governing a state in high disorder by emoting before TV cameras, by alternately overusing and withdrawing force, by panic, and smear apparently cost him greatly in subsequent state legislature elections. But it cost others a lot more.

Americans grasped for lessons out of Israel's sudden success against the ganged-up Arab forces in June 1967. Many found the answers elusive, as answers usually are. Others read wrong, even silly lessons into the victory. Miraculous answers to problems involving war don't exist. What lessons are to be learned are really old ones that require relearning. The strategies of Moshe Dayan and his Israeli commanders were eminently successful against Arab forces that were in part an undisciplined rabble without leadership. Americans seeking parallels they could apply in Vietnam were deluded. The Sinai and other desert terrain are not Vietnam. The desert country where Israeli armor and mechanized forces flowed so brilliantly is not the jungle. Israel had the option of quickly routing its weaker foes on one front, the Egyptian one, while pressing head-on against its toughest enemy, Jordan (some would dispute this and claim Syrian forces are potentially more formidable), and holding against a third, Syria. This is quite different from Vietnam, because the Viet Cong and the regular North Vietnamese Army are not Arabs. The enemy in Vietnam is usually well led and highly motivated, as Moshe Dayan saw in his tour of our fighting areas, and as he said later in a TV commentary.

Only in weapons are the Arabs to be equated with the Hanoi and VC forces. The Vietnamese of Communist persuasion does not run away and abandon his hardware helter-skelter, except under the stiffest pressure. And even under such pressure many times he stands and fights unless orders dictate otherwise.

People like one Midwestern Congressman who suggested we trade Israel materials for Dayan are overrating the Israeli general and grossly insulting the quality of United States command in Vietnam.

The lesson furnished by Israel is readiness, not just generalship. Israel was totally prepared. It exerted good leadership, ruthless planning, extra-good organization, a high degree of success in execution. The state was mentally and physically ready to fight. As one admiring Pentagon observer told an NBC-TV newsman, "Every Israeli had a gun and knew exactly what to do with it." The same lesson, to a somewhat less refined extent, was obtainable from Israel's 1956 Sinai triumph in the Suez campaign, if anyone had cared to look for it. Some military people did find the lesson, then as in 1967. But it was not and still is not at this writing expedient to say so out loud in Washington.

All-out preparedness, peculiarly, is okay with the American political establishment as long as it's confined to some friendly smaller nation, like Israel. That beleaguered country, we are told, lives under the gun. It is daily, hourly, menaced by hostility and hatred. Look, the establishment argument unfolds, at 1956 and 1967. A garrison-state mentality in Israel is not paranoid, it is reality. But if anyone suggests that something even approaching the Israeli preparedness level is indicated for us, *this* is paranoia!

Yet, look at reality: Israel survives by preparedness, by reasoned militancy. It is a nation peopled more than any other by those who have learned the mortal peril of pacifically trusting to the goodness of man. It trusts only its own people with ideas or arms, because the builders of the state are those who somehow escaped Hitler's death chambers or Russian pogroms and anti-Zionism. Even so, all its readiness is adequate only to keep Arabs in line. Israel would be overwhelmed by a major power. The one real force that kept the Soviet Union, the new handmaid of Allah (however temporarily), from intervening to destroy Israel in 1967, was the United States. Without the possibility of American retaliation, the Soviet Union would have engineered the destruction of Israel in the same remorseless way it ravaged Eastern Europe.

But those in this country who read the right lesson in that 1967 campaign are daily branded extremists or neo-fascists or something else equally far-fetched. It is quite a feat to connect Israel's reasoned militancy with neo-fascism, since the militancy was deliberately created by the survivors of fascism's worst excesses. But then the link between the battlefield and the cocktail circuit on the New York–Washington–Hollywood axis is a tenuous one. Most sophisticated Americans bought Ladybird Johnson's crusade against automobile junkyards, but missed the message in a heap of burned-out Egyptian tanks.

The same leverage that keeps Israel alive in the Near East, applied on a much broader scale, keeps the United States and the entire free world alive on the global plane. "We live in the bullseye," John F. Kennedy told the United States during the October 1962 Cuban missile crisis. Yet we have done almost nothing to cope with this fact since 1962 except strive for nuclear status quo. Other peoples are forging new weapons and making new plans. It is happening right in Israel's backyard. Anyone on the Bosporus these days who can see and count must be aware of the intrusion of the Russian naval power in the Near East, with all that this means for Israel and us "next time."

If Washington were to accept the lesson of Israel, it might undercut the socioeconomic goals of the last half-dozen years, but it would not *have* to do so. If the Vietnam war has drained away many of our resources that would be spent otherwise on social welfare, housing, education, rehabilitation, and other remedial programs, it will not always be so. Certainly when Vietnam costs less, as it will when the war ends, sooner or later, funds will be available to implement an intelligent militia program. Funds *should* be available now. But it will be inexcusable if they are not provided once Vietnam costs us a little less. This would still leave

a great deal more money than is now available for internal prob-
lem-solving.

Worse than spending or the lack of it, however, is the peculiar
emphasis put on guns in the administration's recent "crime control" programs. The Johnson administration's 1965–68 crime-fighting legislation contained some elements of destruction for many
thousands of young Americans as well as other citizens. Each year's
package included measures to restrict drastically the ownership
and use of firearms, even sporting firearms with which people
hunt and learn to shoot. It made one wonder if the administration
actually realized what basic tool its troops were using in Southeast
Asia. The Arthur D. Little Company Report (January, 1966) to
the Defense Department flatly stated the value of the marksmanship program (usually called DCM program, for Director of Civilian Marksmanship), which allows young Americans and others to
familiarize themselves with firearms. The report argued vigorously
for the program's broadening and popularization.

The Little Report was ordered by the Defense Department because a few misinformed or intemperate, perhaps frightened,
people in Congress had been led to suspect the DCM program was
in error. Some felt its providing arms and ammunition to approved rifle and pistol clubs was obsolescent. Others suspected
there was not adequate surety that arms and ammunition always
went only to the right clubs and individuals. Some others frankly
used the fears of the first two groups to help discredit citizen
marksmanship. The Little Report easily found all these fears and
motives groundless. It was difficult to accuse the report team of any
pro-Defense bias, certainly; the team was headed by retired Lieutenant General James Gavin, who left the Army because of frequent and deep differences with Defense Department thinking.
Sycophancy with Defense is a sin Gavin is least likely to commit.
Perhaps for this reason, the report was largely ignored by Secretary
McNamara, who seemed preoccupied with sophisticated weaponry
(little of it practical in Vietnam or other brushfire wars). Mc-

Namara rejected the notion that the totally prepared soldier is the key to winning wars, *any* kind of war. The marksmanship program, which the Little Report showed helps keep young men alive in combat, was reduced as an "economy" measure. Its supporters called the economy false and said the real reason the DCM program was scotched was political revenge on the National Rifle Association and others for steadfastly opposing administration gun legislation.

It was felt in some circles that crimping the DCM program by withdrawing Army financial support, especially for the colorful National Matches at Camp Perry, Ohio, would force the NRA to give in on the administration gun bill. The opposite proved true. NRA initiated plans to support the National Matches with its own financing. NRA membership topped one million. It campaigned to show that the real reason for failure to get a reasonable gun-control bill through Congress was a refusal to compromise by some supporters of the administration attitude: Attorney General Ramsey Clark, Senators Bobby and Ted Kennedy, and their some-time stooge, Senator Tom Dodd.

Nonetheless, Defense has continued to ignore the words and the impact of the Little Report. The citizen shooting program survives because of the dedicated volunteer interest of a handful of rifle and pistol club leaders (the Little Report called them "quite conscientious and responsible people").

The report added, for those who find menace in the program: "Shooting clubs differ from most other sports organizations in that they have a greater overriding concern for safety and for avoiding involvement in incidents which would place them in an unfavorable light in their community." (The major conclusion and recommendations of the Arthur D. Little Report are contained in Appendix A.)

The attitude that accepts paranoid criticism of the marksmanship program shows up in finer detail in the recent controversy over our M16 service rifle. This shows best the ignorance of most Americans about the staple weapons of war. An article in the May

1967 *American Rifleman* briefed the pros and cons of the M16 dispute in expert form. It was written by Army Captain Presley W. Kendall, both a Master-class rifle competitor and a Vietnam combat veteran. The mass-circulation media were in a spasm of "news" reports on the rifle. But no one paid any attention to Kendall's account, one of the few accurate, professional examinations of the gun. Later, the NRA's presiding ordnance expert, retired Colonel E. H. Harrison, wrote a more detailed and illuminating two-part series on the M16 (*American Rifleman*, January and February 1968). He raised important technical questions and advocated that the adoption of the rifle and its 5.56mm. (.223 caliber) light, high-speed cartridge was not nearly as meticulously conducted as should have been the case. There has been no survey of the M16 controversy by the mass-distribution media that even approaches Colonel Harrison's. Most of the TV and wire service reporters discussing the rifle are woefully ignorant, even afraid of small arms. They know nothing about ballistics. They further mislead an already misled population. A strong course in reading such informed publications as *Infantry*, the NRA's *American Rifleman*, the *Combat Forces Journal*, the publications of the American Ordnance Association, and *Army* magazine would help. You don't get gun expertise by studying journalism at Columbia or Northwestern, and there are very few knowledgeable shooters among the wire service and network reporters.

Already, in this urbanized and peculiarly balanced society, mothers and their consorts—husbands is overcomplimenting the breed—rear their youngsters to fear firearms (firearms homicides are almost halved per capita since 1930) but not the automobile (casualties: 50,000 killed annually). Network television avoids showing the killing of game by sport hunting, even though this rather tame outlet provides the revenues that keep almost all wildlife management programs in existence. But every day and night television shows flagrant, stupid misuse of guns. Cowboys and Indians, marshals and badmen, Blue and Gray, spies and counterspies, American and enemy soldiers point, shoot, hit, miss, jab, and dab at each other with firearms. The way most of this is done would give legitimate gun users—target shooters, properly trained hunters, police officers, collectors—the worst kind of fits. And does, as the writer can testify. But hyper-tuned congressmen seldom hit this sort of misuse a lick; serious, basic marksmanship training, the sort the Little Report described, is seldom shown, and hunter-safety firearms training classes, advocated and conducted by the NRA and most conservation agencies, are never shown on anything except local programs. The national finals of every sport from bigtime football and baseball to shuffleboard, pingpong, and surfing are faithfully depicted on sports programs. Not the National Matches at Camp Perry. *Yet more basic, worthwhile lore on national and individual survival is disseminated at Camp Perry each year than in all other major sports events combined.*

No national event deserves more exposure; none gets less. This may be another nagging symptom of the refusal to accept that lesson out of Israel. Somehow the public image is shaped in the fantasy that the United States can go on avoiding nuclear war by fighting limited wars, yet does not even have to prepare its people to fight limited wars. Some people want to substitute the rifle for the big bomb, understandably; yet they don't believe in teaching how to use it.

Governor Hughes' querulous response to Newark and Plainfield was an example of the leadership cited here. His main reaction was to condemn citizens who had bought or kept guns to defend their homes. Hughes jumped into the Newark riot and applied force wholesale—at first. It was not necessarily undue force in the beginning, but rather force not tuned up with the proper training. National Guardsmen and police were not armed or equipped to control the sources of trouble. Riot guns wouldn't reach rifle-armed hoodlums on roofs or in windows; those equipped with semi- or fully automatic rifles often were not trained to use these weapons safely in a crowded, urban environment where careful fire was the only sensible solution. If troops and police failed, it was their training, and those who were supposed to direct it, from the political top down, that failed. The men didn't fail; they only did what they had been partly trained to do. The same happened to elements of the United States forces sent to Korea in June 1950. In neither case did nearly enough political heads roll.

In Plainfield, a large number of semi-automatic rifles were stolen, presumably by rioters, from a small factory where such rifles were rebuilt. Hughes launched a wide search that deteriorated into stormtrooper tactics against uninvolved citizens, some of whom kept hunting rifles or shotguns. When this sparked public indignation, Hughes didn't alter tactics—he simply withdrew protective forces, ordered his police and troops to quit firing back at hoodlums, and blamed it all on "guns." This he emoted on CBS TV's "Face The Nation" in spite of New Jersey's having one of the strictest gun-control laws in the United States. A major Jersey daily paper commented: "The same state officials who sponsored the gun-control legislation stopped the search for the still-missing guns when it became politically undesirable to press it."

If it had been pressed right from the first, without reducing Negro citizens' homes to rubble and without seizing their inoffensive deer or bird guns, the search might have prospered. Most of the seized weapons had never been used in any offensive action, nor against any authority. They were the property of uninvolved citizens, like their furniture and bedding and other items torn apart in the search. It's no wonder to anyone that American Civil Liberties Union suits followed. The amount of private property wrongfully grabbed was far bigger than the number of illegal weapons discovered.

Yet Hughes and his political allies would be the first to object to a responsible, centrally controlled citizen militia. It's difficult to say why. With minor variations, what occurred at Newark and Plainfield has occurred in several other cities; in others, riots were less destructive. The President's Commission on Civil Disorders found that misuse of firearms was far less widespread than newspaper or TV accounts implied. Most of the victims of gunfire in several major riots were individuals who got in the way of irresponsible or inaccurate shooting by protective forces. Nothing in the report argues more strongly for sane, controlled marksmanship, directed where it should be and applied to the guilty—not to women and children cowering in the line of fire. Vigilantism, that pet hoodoo of the feverish, was almost nonexistent. Few citizens killed each other. The causes of urban violence are elsewhere, lurking somewhere between economics, sociology, and our tolerance of a dual standard.

Our own history shows how a militia evolved as a successful instrument, as long as it was used in guerrilla Indian war. Charles W. Thayer in his *Guerrilla* (Harper & Row, N.Y.) relates how early American history was one long militia-guerrilla war. It was counter-guerrilla when not guerrilla. Like the early Tartars, the Anglo-Celtic-Teutonic American pioneer society was mobile and warlike (but not military). Its men, like the Boers later on, lacked the discipline and training to stand firmly against regular soldiery. That was for the Continental Line so successfully trained by Prussian Baron von Steuben. To consolidate and win the American Revolution, the colonial troops required the steadiness of their British opponents. This they acquired and went on to win the consolidating campaigns, with French help. Our militia, skulking in the bushes and forests, hurt Britain mightily at times and prevented its winning the war. While it could never have won this war by itself, the militia played a great role in our history. It extended the postwar United States frontier from the Alleghenies to the Mississippi River and later to the Pacific. Militia guerrilla war was the standard formula for success in opening up the Old Northwest (now Midwest) and to a lesser extent was instrumental in settling much of the trans-Mississippi West. Americans adapted to it in a way seldom equaled in history.

Thayer and correspondent-novelist Robert Ruark showed how a Western-oriented manhood, once committed to guerrilla war, adapted so well to it that the troublemakers wished they'd started something else. Ruark has shown in *Something of Value* (fiction imposed upon factual basis), that Western men, when prodded, can win in guerrilla war against a far more primitive and cruel culture. The British settlers in East Africa, after they concluded it was the only course, out-Mau-Mau-ed the Mau-Mau. They adopted terror and calculated bestiality in a manner much surpassing anything the Kikuyu tribesmen, the core of the Mau-Mau, could develop. The American pioneer between 1600 and 1900 did much the same. He out-Indianed the Indian. Even our regular troops, in the latter half of the 19th century, fought what was essentially guerrilla war in destroying the last Indian resistance within the United States. General George Crook accomplished this twice with the Apaches in Arizona. Colonel Ranald MacKenzie did an even more thorough job on the larger, more mobile Comanche tribe of the Southern Plains.

In World War Two, Marine Lieutenant General H. M. (Howlin' Mad) Smith, one of the pioneer students of amphibious war, said this about island war in the Pacific: "Despite all the steel and explosives we poured on island bastions like Iwo Jima and Tarawa, it was riflemen who had to go in and do the job."

Time correspondent Robert Sherrod, who reported several of the invasions, cited superior American marksmanship with small arms as a key to Pacific victory. Sherrod also observed how deluded American society had become in the 1930's, thinking that basic grappling on the ground among troops was somehow passé. The Marines, unlike some Army units, went to war convinced that the way to win was to be "tougher than hell and kill Japs wholesale," and they achieved noteworthy success with this simple formula. Marksmanship played a powerful part in all this, from Guadalcanal to Okinawa. We had all the logistical supremacies—steel, explosives, air, shipping, food—but it kept getting down to the Grunt with his rifle, according to a Marine veteran of a later war who is quoted elsewhere in this book.

There are eminent military and political thinkers who believe most war henceforth, for quite a while at least, will be one form or another of guerrilla war. To those who say Americans or other

Westerners cannot adapt to such war, one need only look back to World War Two, in the Pacific or Burma. Or to the Boers in their 1899–1902 war with Great Britain.

The Boers provided a classic example of how to frustrate a great empire, possessed of staunch regular troops and all the logistical advantages. In the first months of their war, the South African white farmers, organized into informal guerrilla units, confounded the best professional troops in the world. They were aided by fumbling British generalship (later succeeded by competent command from Lords Roberts and Kitchener). But the Boer farmers on horseback with Mauser rifles were guerrillas, certainly. They wore farm clothes, rode stout Basuto or other African horses, and moved like the wind on demand, ambushing and outshooting (far, far outshooting!) Guards and Highlanders and Hussar and Lancer units who for months could never get close with their cold steel. It astounded the world and led Britain to reappraise much of its training of troops. Boer marksmanship taught Britons the value of skilled shooting; in 1914, a handful of British regulars accounted for an astonishing number of Germans marching through Flanders and France.

Many thinkers have wondered at the difference between our own war of independence and the losing try made by the two South African republics. The difference was that no foreign power came to the aid of the Transvaal and Orange Free State. There was no Bourbon France, out for vengeance against England, to intervene massively with men, ships, and munitions. Foreign aid to the Boers was scattered and timid. The Boers waited in vain for Germany to intervene or the United States to intercede. But they set new patterns in war, which were as appropriate in their veldt habitat as were those of the Vietminh in Indochina when the French were squeezed out in in the 1950's. But the Vietminh had China across the border and the Soviets in the wings, as well as Frenchmen doing their work in Paris.

It has been more than a hundred years since American civilians were exposed en masse to war at home. People forget because they wish to forget and are led or allowed to do so. They can hardly be blamed. In a permissive, free society, forgetting is easy. It is our leaders who should be blamed for not making us remember. They should not let us forget Czechoslovakia, for example; we should bear in mind what happened there in 1938, 1939, 1948, and 1968.

A surprise assault on North America, unlike Nazi and Soviet aggression in Eastern Europe, would have to involve nuclear weaponry. It would not even register without it. The attack would have to destroy our retaliatory capabilities. It would also be directed against major communications, transport, industrial, and population centers. The accompaniment would be terrorism induced in as many ways as possible. This would include the use of surviving enemy agents (the Communist mentality doesn't call for advance warning to spare rank-and-file help), to initiate and spread the wildest, widest possible panic, and disrupt all normal activity. Agents would have been briefed long before, without knowing if and when an attack would take place, on disrupting communications, attacking police centers, destroying power plants, arsenals, and everything on which great cities rely, seizing radio and television outlets to disseminate false information and much, much more. Water would be polluted, with germ warfare undertaken or rumors of it circulated. Agents in various police and military units would try to confuse orders and disrupt command. Anything to slow or stop cohesive response would be likely. Police and military leaders would be assassinated (the usable ones might be kidnapped). Airports would be put under siege, missile pads assaulted, trains derailed, highways and bridges blown up. Sacrificial airborne units would be dropped to assault key positions that infiltrators and subversives couldn't handle. The mere presence of even a few "throwaway" airborne troops would add tremendously to the panic. These would be well-motivated, top-quality troops, knowing that in all probability they could not be reinforced or relieved. At first and for a while afterward, these troops might be more effective than any regular forces put against them.

The same sort of attacks would be aimed at main United States bases overseas, and at those of our allies—at least those allies with the capacity and will to respond. This would probably wipe out many of our front-line military people, since a high proportion of the best troops are usually based overseas. The first task within the United States would be to restore order, destroy enemy forces and agents, and stop panic. Surviving federal and state forces and police simply would not be up to the assignment without extra help. There wouldn't be enough personnel, but a good militia program geared to auxiliary military and police duty—realistic duty, not directing vehicle traffic—would help enormously. The aftereffects, of terror (humanly and materially induced), would be enormous. Existing forces and plans and present public morals are not up to even part of such an emergency.

Here is a capsule of how specific areas (but by no means all) of the nation's life might be affected:

PANIC

American cities, populated to a high degree by persons psychologically unprepared for real disaster, physically soft and excitable, would be the fattest targets possible. Few urban dwellers have any experience at all with the shock of modern war. Most have been encouraged to rely on the police or other agencies or services for almost all solutions. City dwellers who survived initial attacks would probably pose some kind of mass psychiatric problem; they would almost certainly be unmanageable for a time. Surviving elements would have to be rounded up and restored to normal life as well as possible under severe emergency conditions, once police and fire and other agencies were able to function. Residents of smaller cities and rural areas, if away from main nuclear blasts, would tend to survive at a high rate. Some rural elements of the population are still used to living off the land, if only on hunting and camping trips. Their great problem might be dealing with crowds of victims wandering out of stricken cities. Life for at least the first few days, if not weeks, would be on an everyone-for-himself basis.

DISEASE

Even the results of conventional attack would pose a problem. But mass death from nuclear assault would present multiple problems. And a thorough-planning enemy (what other kind can you count on?) would probably wage germ warfare, delivered in different ways. Hospitals and clinics would be sabotaged. As already mentioned, water would be contaminated. There would be the rising problem from unburied bodies. Mental disorders brought on or accentuated by the attack would be overwhelming.

FIRE

Like police protection, this service would be disrupted, much equipment destroyed, much personnel killed or hurt. Fire forces might not be able to recoup for several days. Here as with the police, a militia trained to meet most responsibilities would be invaluable. In fact, the militia should be the most versatile element in the society, with at least a minimum of training in all basic "recovery" techniques—riot control, health, fire, police, guerrilla and counter-guerrilla action, transportation, and communications.

SERVICES

Water, power, gas, and other services would be nonexistent in most areas. Sabotage by enemy agents, air-dropped or shore-landed, would take out most of the facilities not originally hit by resident agents. Many segments of the public would have no heat if the attack came during winter; others, dependent on power to pump water, would be without any to drink in a short time.

COMMUNICATIONS

Most communities would be on their own. There would be little or no shipment of supplies, probably no direction from Washington and most state capitals. With television, radio, telephones, telegraph lines, and everything else except perhaps amateur radio out of operation, it would be easy for enemy agents to spread more panic, doubt, disorder, and confusion. The seizure of the broadcasting stations for accomplishing this is an old tactic. The average American's attachment for, indeed subservience to, television and radio would expedite the confusion.

SABOTAGE

Our long coastlines, many isolated landing strips, and historic inability to cope with espionage are all against us. Bootlegging in Prohibition times, the narcotics traffic in recent years, our casual attitudes toward security are barometers of how great a problem sabotage would present.

United States troops fighting in Asia have learned that in fluid guerrilla and counter-guerrilla war, the front covers a 360-degree circle. In the next war, the front may sweep right through your own backyard. This is another excellent, positive argument for a capable militia.

Chapter **2**

Organizing a Militia

✱✱✱✱✱

"Wherefore the citizens ought to practice war—not in
time of war, but rather while they are at peace."
—Plato

THE IDEA OF A MILITIA—FOR CIVIL DEFENSE, MILITARY, OR POLICE
use in one or another kind of emergency—has occurred to only a
few Americans until urban riots caused more to consider it.

But riots are far from the only indication of the need for a
militia. The more pressing problem is (or should be) what would
happen if the National Guard and organized military reserves
were elsewhere—already called up and on duty far away—when
some serious crisis erupted? While riots may force a reconsidera-
tion of a militia, the far likelier and more dangerous prospect is
for nuclear attack combined with subversion and perhaps limited-
purpose invasion. An all-out attack on the United States would
almost certainly destroy a large part of our existing military and
police forces. Combined with well-planned subversion and invasion, even invasion knowingly sacrificing troops just to create disorder and panic, it could leave us in a state of chaos almost beyond
imagination.

A militia would play a significant role in containing and combatting all of the panic, disorder, subversion, and helplessness that
would follow such an attack. Properly conceived and trained, it
would be almost priceless. But a hardheaded look at these pros-

pects and others like them makes it quite clear that for political reasons and lack of courage, the federal government has not come to grips with the problem. Our leaders have not bought the concept of providing an emergency militia, mainly for reasons that do not exist. They are afraid of the idea. Yet there is a deep and growing sentiment in the public for better provision for coping with serious disorders—not orderly demonstrations but riots—for more personal involvement in halting the rise in felonies, and (among the farther-seeing) for ways to help insure restoration of order if nuclear attack occurs.

When a May 1967 editorial in the *American Rifleman* magazine sounded some of these thoughts, a few people, prone to quick judgments had fits. Some political and journalistic pundits deliberately misinformed people about what the editorial said. All sorts of improbable and ridiculous implications were read into it. But the *Rifleman*'s intent was simply to suggest that in major and multiple disaster, with the National Guard and service reserve already occupied or riddled along with all else, communities and states would require a militia. The citizen is and should be the natural militiaman, the ultimate reservist. The *Rifleman* suggested, and many who think about such matters agreed, that the time had come to develop such thinking.

No one was advocating private armies or vigilantism. The only strong tendency to private armies discernible now is among those extremists of the farther left who seek to overturn the republic. The racial extremes of the farther right have become increasingly discredited since public indignation overwhelmed them in the early 1960's. The Ku Klux Klan, in reality, has not been significant since then. It receded from a national into a regionalized movement, and while regionalized movements can be obnoxious, even dangerous in isolated places, they do not pose an over-all threat to the nation.

The militia idea has for the time being been effectively blackballed by people who are still fighting the corpse of white racism, by those who see stormtroopers in their dreams, and by a few people who genuinely seek to keep the United States weak and to reduce its ability to cope with disaster. The impetus for a militia died in the whirring computers and political calculations of the Defense Department under Robert McNamara. It will take considerable political courage and leadership to revive the idea, sound as it is.

The idea of a militia would have to earn the confidence of a great majority of the public. It can hardly do so with a government reluctant even to discuss it. A militia would need to be efficient, well trained, and highly responsible (unlike most American militia in history). It would have to meet all kinds of demands, including many not faced before even by regular troops. It should be an adjunct to police, military, fire, public health, and other elements. Riot control, counter-guerrilla and guerrilla war, sanitation, radio and other communications, demolition, sabotage and counter-sabotage, supply, transport, even the conversion of enemy equipment—vehicles, weapons, other tools—would be a part of its training. Language training would be important in areas of the United States bordering on or near those where French (as in Canada and part of the Caribbean) or Spanish (Latin America) is spoken. As long as the Caribbean–Central America area holds pockets of anti-United States power and is a springboard, training ground, and potential missile and troop base for policies hostile to this country, there will be a very real menace to the United States. This will be particularly strong along our Mexican border, because when you strip away all the diplomacies, Mexico is a vacuum insofar as military power is concerned. And an alliance between an ultra-nationalist, separated Quebec and Castro or Castro-like elements in Central America and the Caribbean is far from impossible.

Another role for a militia would be rural. There might be a strong need for help in harvesting crops, rebuilding rail, water and power lines, and other non-urban work between or after emergencies. While the major tasks facing most militia units might remain where population is clustered, keeping the country fed and linked would be as important as maintaining order, power, communications, transport, and so on.

Legally and technically, we probably have had no militia since 1933. We are repeatedly told that the National Guard of the 50 states is "the militia." The strong legal likelihood is that this is not so. In 1916, the National Guard of the states became by law a component part of the national peacetime establishment, subject to call to duty as part of the Army of the United States, according to Robert A. Sprecher in his prizewinning essay (Part 2) in the July 1965 issue of the *American Bar Association Journal* (Sprecher argued for revitalization of the right to bear arms, under the Second Amendment to the United States Constitution, as an aid in national defense and curbing crime).

Following up the 1916 move, the National Guard of the United States was created by an act of Congress in 1933, and became a part of the Army of the United States at all times. Thus there has apparently been no organized militia in the true sense of the term for the past 35 years. The home-guard units of the World War Two era fell into discard afterward. Only recently a few were dismembered at the instigation of the more excitable elements in the civil liberties movement who saw great menace in a handful of reasonably competent fellow citizens helping regular police and military forces in time of crisis. As usual, vigilantism was the argument. As usual, a serious examination of facts and motives showed the fears were groundless.

There has grown up much confusion about "vigilantism." Responsible contribution to public protection under adequate controls is hardly vigilante action. A well-ordered police or sheriff's reserve or a home-guard militia under reasonable control is not vigilante activity. But the passion for permissiveness has gone beyond smearing the militia concept as some kind of fascist repression; indeed, buying a gun to protect one's family *within the home* is branded as extremism. People are urged to "get involved" to help curb crime, but the pleas come from the sources that seek gun-control legislation to disarm the citizenry.

Many police chiefs and sheriffs like Cook County, Illinois' Sheriff Wood maintain reserve units. But when Wood sought a "posse"—an unfortunate word choice but not necessarily a bad idea—he was balked by Chicago-area politicians in massive array, most of them fearing or misunderstanding what he sought. The press helped compound the excitement. Sufficient political leverage was exercised to persuade a judge to order Wood to stop recruiting and training men. The key to this was that he had already started *training* the 1,000 men he wanted, and only after recruiting them on a fairly selective basis. No one was collecting an armed mob. This was a responsible effort to get together a large, selected number of reasonably able men to assist in predicted disorders—and to train these men. But fearful politicians almost tore Wood's head off, abetted by the press and television. The final verdict is by no means passed on this. A few weeks later one of the high priests of restraint and piety about Wood's "vigilantism," Chicago Mayor Richard Daley, was berating his police chief for not following through on orders to kill arsonists and shoot-to-wound looters.

In many states and towns, sheriff's or police reserves are the *only* militia-in-being or other utility force behind the formal police and military. If organized forces were subjected to great strains and many calls, these reserves would in essence become a militia by default.

A militia would have to be gathered from all segments of the society, with fair representation for groups which feel slighted by society: minority groups. This would require the strictest possible fairness—not just to gratify some frantic screeching for instant redress, but in the long-range interest of gaining wide public respect for an institution of a democratic state. A broad cross section of ethnic groups would contribute to acceptance. This is what Wood sought in Cook County; and he got a good turnout of the most affected minority, Negroes. What he also got then, and Daley got later, was misunderstanding, based on publicity full of scare words on television and in newsprint. Both were vigorously con-

demned by the Justice Department and other officials whose notion of a riot remains the time the Princeton boys tore down the
goal posts at Franklin Field.

One of the best ways for the military to head off the growing
disaffection between the public and itself might be to cultivate
the militia—not fight the idea of amateur soldiers as so many
career professionals are wont to do. Modern war has pretty well
shown that even the strongest military establishment is eventually
helpless if it faces prolonged public antipathy. Franco Spain had
to muster much more than miltary support to endure and conquer
the Madrid Republican government. And many forget that Hitler
originally attained political power in Germany with the military
divided between hostility and apathy toward him. None of the
so-called fascist states of Europe was as militaristic as Japan in
1941—yet Japan was essentially not a fascist state. Similarly, the
Russian Revolution was finalized by a conglomerate of mutinous
sailors, former Czarist troops (mostly enlisted men led by former
noncommissioned officers), and a mixture of industrial workers
(quite a large number, relatively) and peasants (not as many—
despite subsequent Communist gushings to the contrary).

Mao, Castro, and others, some not as flagrantly undemocratic
as the Red paragons, have shown that a popular militia often
achieves much more with the public than even the snappiest
standing army. The Communists—and we can all learn from foes
as well as friends—have proven rather conclusively what will unfold from other sources in this book as well: Most new war is and
probably will be guerrilla or anti-guerrilla in essence, and
guerrillas are essentially more or less popular militia.

A United States military establishment that cheerfully seeks
identification with the public militia reserves is very likely to
enjoy wider public acceptance of its goals and needs than is the
present politically isolated, increasingly unpopular establishment—the so-called "military-industrial complex" that appears to
be the new nemesis of the liberal left (which, in its groping for
a left-oriented isolation that retreats not only from confrontation

but responsibility, would probably have had to invent the miltary-industrial complex if the idea had not been suggested by President Eisenhower).

It would be a formidable task, even for a demagogue bent on disarmament, to trim the budget or damage the image of a military establishment that commanded the voting allegiance of millions of other Americans because of firm local-level personal relationships—through a militia. Moreover, a closer personal link to the military would give many citizens an insight into just what programs and plans of the military were justifiable or necessary and which ones were fat. The right to bear arms can still be, and rather emphatically should be, the palladium of a free people, as much so as when the idea first was formed in ancient Greece.

Political confusions aside, the history of militia in our wars has not been good. The main message obtainable from studying American militia at war is that under conventional battle conditions it is not adequate to deal with regular forces. This is true of almost all militias in virtually all wars. The colonies had no chance of winning the Revolution and becoming a nation until they developed trained, disciplined regular forces which could meet the British on even terms in the open field. Militia was adequate to conduct guerrilla operations in the interior, but winning the war required skilled, disciplined forces to take and hold key positions in the major theaters, and this has been just as true in Vietnam as it was in our Revolutionary War, 1775–83.

But because of the cumulative lessons in how *not* to use militias, too many people, when they finally saw the message, vaulted all the way to the opposite conclusion—that militia is no good at all under any circumstances. This of course is as far off-base as was the old colonial-era notion that a militia was the solution to all military requirements.

While nothing failed worse for us than our Revolutionary War, War of 1812, and Civil War militias (our record of trying to use militia against the British and Canadians in 1812–14 may be the most miserable episode in our military history), most of the errors and sins committed by militia resulted from *misuse*. History has indicated that militia can successfully operate to control guerrillas, or if forced to do so, can become guerrilla itself. It can defeat regular forces in guerrilla war. It can maintain order, control riots, do all the essential nuts and bolts jobs a community, state, or nation requires—always provided it has expert tutelage and supervision. These abilities persist in a militia, real or potential, because a militia is simply a collection of citizens called together to protect or preserve the state in any way that will work. It is or would be a collection of diverse skills, not a band of men formally schooled for years to do a specific military job. It could do many jobs fairly well, but it could not be the Fifth Marines or the 173rd Airborne Brigade. But while it could not defeat the 173rd Airborne in open battle, it could chop up and finally kill such a regular unit granted the right conditions for a militia.

Paradoxically, when we needed trained regulars the most, in 1775 or 1812, we vastly overrated militia; today when we desperately need a good militia, we ignore the real role and possibility of a militia. The overconfidence in militia of 1775 is no more ridiculous than the 1968 notion (politically motivated, as was the 1775 thinking) that militias have no role in our society or strategy. One delusion is as dangerous as was the other.

How do you recruit a militia? The goal should be the best possible people—not simply the most well-to-do, certainly, nor the best educated, nor the most militantly patriotic people. What is desired are the best-rounded, most responsible individuals, genuinely concerned with aiding in the protection of their community or state. There are ways, some of which will be sketched here, to recruit reasonable, responsible people and keep out the predictable assortment of lunatics, grudge-holders, and the frustrated.

Training should be started as quickly as possible, along with some basic indoctrination in the goals of the militia program and the laws and history of the United States. The history of volunteer armed forces shows, time and again, that idleness breeds more discontent, undiscipline, and absenteeism than anything else.

Controls should be spread out. Such equipment as would be needed (basic uniforms, weapons, vehicles, radios, other gear) should probably come from federal stores declared in excess of current military requirements. Direct control should be exercised from the state capital, as with the National Guard when the Guard is at home. Militia officers should be subject to the orders of, first, the state governor, then whatever local officials they would be called up to assist. The presumption is that a militia would not be activated unless seriously needed—that is, in a crisis.

Training militiamen in the use of enemy materials, especially weapons, vehicles, and radios, should be a requisite. The United States Army has been fighting enemies using Russia's basic AK47 assault rifle since the 1950's, yet only in 1968 were regular troops widely instructed in the AK47's use. The order to effect this was issued by General William C. Westmoreland after his return from Vietnam to take up Chief of Staff duties. A militia expected to cope with Communist agents and airdropped troops would need to know a fair amount about all of the more common Soviet-bloc arms as well as basic vehicles and communications gear. All would be useful.

Men should receive per-diem pay plus government equipment and food, medical care, and other standard service benefits when on active duty. Training pay, such as the Guard and reserves draw, would be desirable. A purely volunteer force in which men serve for no pay and must even defer their own equipment expenses is not conducive to the self-respect an effective militia needs. Too many cities and counties require their police reserves to serve with no pay and provide their own equipment. This is asking rather too much of conscientious and devoted citizens and has an adverse effect—it tends to collect mostly men with above-average incomes and makes it perhaps a little too easy for the frustrated badge-flasher type to find a home. The relatively minor expense of outfitting militiamen with what are virtually surplus weapons and equipment and paying them an on-duty pittance is well worth the return. Most important of all, paying militiamen—however small the sum may be—puts a certain disciplinary leverage on them that helps insure better attendance and performance. The experience of totally unpaid sheriff's and police reserves has not been good in these respects.

In training, a reasonably high degree of physical fitness and proficiency with weapons should be the goals. As with the infantryman, the citizen militiaman's prime tool would be his firearm. Other training and exposure to different equipment could follow. The weapons of militia units would probably not need to include heavy ordnance—perhaps the mortar, but probably not the crew-served machine gun. The militia should be trained, equipped, and mentally tuned to travel light and fast, across town, between cities, or however indicated. Personal, individual weapons should be the key—semi-automatic or fully automatic rifles, semi-automatic carbines, submachine guns, riot shotguns, ordinary bolt-action sporting rifles with telescopic sights for special purposes. The bolt-action rifle is no longer a mass-issue military weapon, but with a scope it is an excellent sniping tool because of its usually higher degree of accuracy. Lever-action sporting rifles and carbines are better general-combat weapons in today's warfare than are bolt-action rifles, but they are inferior to semi-automatic weapons for most fighting. The semi-automatic rifle or carbine is almost certainly the best basic tool for a militiaman, combining reasonable accuracy with reasonable rate of fire. It is usually the easiest weapon with which to teach marksmanship, once safe-handling fundamentals are mastered. The fully automatic rifle or carbine is probably overrated, is fairly difficult to teach to masses of men, and is wasteful of ammunition.

Handguns (pistols and revolvers) are probably much more worthwhile tools for a militia (operating in disorders, as guerrillas or against guerrillas) than for regular forces. There should be more emphasis on the handgun than in formal infantry training or other full-time formations. Militia troops, to fulfill the mission of being lightly equipped and mobile, should not be saddled with weapons beyond the size of individual ones, that is, light automatic rifles and mortars at the most.

The notion that the handgun is not applicable to modern war is unsupportable by fact. There is a certain basis for arguments that the United States service model .45-caliber pistol is not very practical, but the main reason behind this is that few service personnel have been properly trained with the demanding old .45. Perhaps less fiercely recoiling .38 Special, .357 Magnum, or 9mm. pistols would be easier to train men to use (this is not the place to conduct such a discussion). But once adequately trained with the .45 Model 1911 pistol or any other reliable handgun, a militia-man or regular serviceman can be very formidable up to 50, 75, 100, or even 150 yards—depending on his own skill.

An article by-lined Norman Sklarewitz in a recent *Wall Street Journal* discounts a great deal of the fiction that the handgun is useless in today's primarily guerrilla war: "The .45 has come into new favor with the military because of its short-range effectiveness. It is well suited to the type of fighting going on in Vietnam."

The same article tells how a Marine sergeant named John J. McGinty saved his decimated platoon from being cut off and annihilated in an action in Quang Tri province, South Vietnam. Even though wounded, McGinty killed five Vietcong with his .45. He was awarded the Medal of Honor. Not very close to where such matters were being decided with a handgun, a paid staff official for the National Council For A Responsible Firearms Policy was advocating the abolition of private ownership of handguns. A post-battle conversation between McGinty and the anti-gun office-holder at the very least would be interesting.

Most of those who argue the handgun has no role in war are either preaching for propaganda effect or are woefully misinformed.

Marksmanship should be of a high order, as the 1967 riot experience clearly showed. Training along this line is probably best obtained from civilian rifle clubs that have large-bore (military-type) rifle target matches. The best concentrated source of training in military rifle skills, aside from regular-forces special marksmanship units whose training would probably not be available to a militia at any time, peacetime or otherwise, is in such rifle clubs. Other sporting clubs active with .22-caliber rifles and shotguns (trap and skeet) could also help. This sort of training leadership is the main mission of civilian gun clubs, which are able to exist at least in part through the Civilian Marksmanship program and its assistance to clubs. For general military purposes, the militia would probably get its training from what few regular-forces personnel were available, supplemented by a large number of retired service personnel with appropriate backgrounds. Retired regular-service officers and sergeants live in virtually every American community. Most are interested in, deeply concerned, with the good of the country. Those with Military Police, Air Police, Shore Patrol, Infantry, Marine, or other combat experience would be useful in training militiamen. Many would still be physically able to serve in the militia themselves.

Selecting applicants would vary according to size and kind of community. In smaller towns and rural areas where most people know each other, the choice process would be pretty easy. In urban areas, notably those with populations of 50,000, 60,000, or more, much more detailed selection would probably be indicated. Police checks of applicants would be mandatory. Neighbors, fellow employees, and others close to applicants should be at least briefly interrogated. A questionnaire for applicants, calling for both commonsense and general knowledge responses, is an excellent aid in eliminating undesirable people (questionnaires of this type are in use now by many police agencies). Also quite good is an oral interview by a panel of concerned citizens. People with personality problems, grudges, or genuinely aberrant political ideas would have to be eliminated. Some kind of psychiatric examination might be indicated. So would a polygraph test. Some of these testing processes might be impractical, too time-involving, or expensive. But almost all are in use and highly valued by major security and defense agencies. Using as many of these tools as possible would be a safeguard against accepting undesirable applicants.

A probation period for new personnel is indicated by general experience in similar organizations. How long? Sixty to ninety days are probably enough, though some state police forces and the Border Patrol require a year. During the probation period, new personnel should be evaluated by experienced senior officers. One main goal should be to put particularly skilled persons where they can do the most good. Brief fitness reports should be made on individuals and on militia officers holding commissioned or noncommissioned rank. But record-keeping and clerical work should be kept to an absolute minimum. Too much clerical work defeats the lightness-and-mobility concept, and experience dating all the way back to the Revolution shows that nothing frustrates citizen-soldier efficiency more than an overbalance of boring paper work and impractical drill. Disillusionment with part-time or emergency service is usually proportionate to the amount of work or drill not related to fighting or learning to fight.

All applicants should be fingerprinted and photographed and the results checked with federal and state police as an extra protection against undesirables. Too many reserve and even regular police outfits have been embarrassed by failure to make these basic checks. More than one agency has suddenly discovered that one of its officers had a police record.

Selection of higher officers for a militia should be left to the qualified professionals who will be training and overseeing the unit. Some reserves have been allowed to elect their own officers. This usually produces the same chaos that the election of militia officers did in our early wars. Results ranged from very lucky through ludicrous to downright disastrous. Officers appointed by politically or personally motivated superiors or elected for reasons of personal or political popularity (often the same thing) tended, with a few exceptions, to be the architects of most of our military debacles. Even in police reserves controlled by serving regulars there is always high risk in naming men to lead other men. The best approach might be to have the highest ranking supervisory officers name all militia officers. Or they might be passed on by some small local evaluating panel. It might include representatives of local government, labor, business, and perhaps other institutions—churches and shooting clubs, for example. Officers should be chosen with no regard whatsoever for race or religion or other non-essential points. Emphasis should be put on respect, leadership, controlled aggressiveness, response to discipline, and like qualities. Personality traits commanding leadership are vital. In a volunteer unit, authority or discipline can be overdone and lead to great problems. But overly permissive leadership—*non*-leadership—can be just as harmful and is probably more prone to occur in local-level volunteer units. One of the great contributing factors in our military disasters in the early part of the Korean fighting was the Army's tolerance of permissiveness and failure to assert leadership requirements on the lower levels of command, as more than one study has shown. This lack of leadership can be especially ruinous in the fluid, free-flowing fighting that guerrilla and counter-guerrilla war has evolved into in the last few years. Small-unit team-work and reliance on personal skills and hardihood assume enormous importance in such wars.

Is an intelligence test necessary? Probably not. Militiamen would need to be able to read and write English and to handle ordinary arithmetic on about a sixth-grade level. Beyond that, good judgment and practical skills would be at a premium. In training, certainly, both peacetime (criminal, civil) and military law should get some attention. A militia would doubtless have to help administer both kinds. When to use force and how much, and when not to use force; search and seizure; arrests, and so on—these are all likely to be important matters for a militia operating under civilian law, in situations when martial law is not invoked. The difference between felonies and misdemeanors and how to proceed with each kind of case are important.

There is tricky, touchy material in all of this. Individuals with subversive purposes will try to join a militia, for rather obvious reasons. It will not be easy to detect all of these people. The more intelligent and persuasive ones will squeeze in to create dissension or confusion, exploit minor internal problems, commit sabotage, or prevent fast reaction to emergencies. Some such people, when exposed, will try to make court tests to force acceptance or prevent their ouster, in spite of their loudly proclaimed intent to do all the harm they can. It is difficult to foretell how some of these cases might be decided by this era's courts. But the more dangerous and expert subversives are those who have spent much of their lives submerging themselves in the middle-class "mainstream" (to apologetically use a word much overtaxed by politicians) of our way of life. It is not the Peace Front New Leftist who will pose a great problem to the militia, except for noisemaking; it will be the quiet, easy-going fellow in the same block who has spent half his life fitting in as a lawyer, welder, or bartender—who learned his real trade in some espionage school in the U.S.S.R. or its bases abroad.

Responsible citizens are needed with abiding concern for the nation and the community—people wanting to help "do something" in a responsible, controlled way spelled out in the procedures of an orderly and free society. It will not be easy to attract such people. But it is possible. If such motives as responsible patriotism, concern for society and one's own family are properly presented, the right kind of citizens can be recruited from all economic, social, and ethnic elements.

As to age, physical qualifications, and health, reasonable lines may be drawn. It is much more of a problem to detect and turn away the mentally unbalanced than to eliminate people not up to the job physically. The old colonial militia standard—16 to 60—is a little too broad. But young people 16 or 17 might well be accepted. Militia service prior to induction into regular service would be an asset. It would also give concerned youths a chance to contribute to community and nation in a practical way. It would be a check against the excesses juveniles commit through idleness or parental neglect in this disturbed and affluent society. A good, hard workout cures much cussedness. So do pride and purpose.

Physically it might be wise to accept almost all except those incapable of learning to carry out militia duties. Those with no serious disorder or handicap, even if not physically up to immediate service, can be gotten into condition. Most Americans are not unhealthy; they're just in poor shape. Most of this can be rectified by conditioning. Other citizens with specific but not major handicaps might be used in limited assignments if they have useful skills—communications, transport, ordnance, and so forth. Certainly a man who has a minor disability can be used in some job at which he excels if the militia has a function for it. A one-armed linguist, a physical training instructor who has lost an eye, a skilled demolitions man who has an ulcer—these are a few examples. All these and many more would be useful.

Physical training should be geared to accommodate individuals as much as possible. Older men should not be forced to shape up at the pace demanded for the trainees at Fort Bragg or Parris Island. There must be stress on fitness, but it should be graduated. Recent developments in fitness training for office employees and military clerical personnel are excellent starting points. Overweight is probably the top enemy of the kind of man likely to be recruited in a militia. The irretrievably fat will have to be rejected, at least until they get their bulk down within limits allowing mobility and decent health. It's probably unfortunate (because a few inordinately fat men, like ten-foot alligators, can move quite fast), but grossness in body destroys public confidence in police or troops more than any other physical failing. And public confidence is exactly what the militia must have and keep.

The availability of a large pool of draft rejectees who are not too unfit was shown in a recent *Time* magazine article (March 15, 1968). The Army studied 1.5 million men called up for preinduction examination between 1960 and 1962 and reported that 25.4 percent were rejected for medical reasons. Many were re-

fused for minor or at least not severe organic disorders: musculo-
skeletal difficulties (stiff arms, trick knees, flat feet, loss of a minor
member) ; many were overweight or underweight. Others, turned
down for reasons like acne or being too tall or too short would
certainly be eligible for a militia. As *Time* said, the Army's approach in 1960–62 was, "When in doubt, reject." American induction examiners have tended to do this most of the time, even when
Eisenhower's European theater was finding itself very short of
riflemen in France and Germany, 1944–45.

A suggested physical program is offered in the Appendix. Gradually increased calisthenics, jogging, combinations of various exercises, and agility exercises are the prime ones. A program of static
workouts, like weight-lifting, probably has its advantages for some
other purposes but for a militia program, exercises combining
agility with running are probably the best ones.

Should women be considered? The wartime experience of almost every nation faced with close menace—Britain, Germany,
Russia, others—argues strongly for it. Women can handle a great
many of the communications, transport, and other noncombat
functions of a militia. They can help regular medical personnel.
In some countries and crises, women have served as snipers, saboteurs, and with crews on heavier ordnance. The United States has
never faced the absolute emergency that dictated this practice, but
if it does, some women can adapt to killing and can be so used. For
militia purposes, if women are to be accepted, only those without
pressing family commitments should be considered. Women with
minor children at home should *not* be considered, but they will
still be young enough after all their children are reared, in many
cases. Marital status is not as pertinent as actual family responsibilities.

Arms for a nation defending itself against industry-shattering
nuclear attack might become pretty primitive. Planning for a
militia should include devoting thought and research to what we
now call primitive weapons—perhaps black-powder guns and even
longbows and crossbows. From a source-of-supply standpoint, the

most practical firearms ever used in the United States were those firing black powder with flint as the sparking agent. Flint is widely available in the United States and many other countries. Flintlock guns had distinct disadvantages—unreliability when wet or oily, fragility, slowness in detonation. But black powder can be manufactured under conditions where smokeless powder could not be made—even, given an ingenious person with some knowledge of chemistry, at home. And flint can be found in many rock formations.

Smokeless powder cannot be home-manufactured under present conditions. And the detonating agent for modern firearms, a primer, is impossible for most ordinary citizens to manufacture. This is also true for percussion caps, which evolved after flintlock weapons but before modern priming and one-piece fixed cartridges. Caps have to be manufactured. The wide availability of flint and the simple chemicals that make black powder argue strongly for scientific consideration of an improvement on these materials, so that if ordinary sources of modern cartridges and the components that go into cartridges are destroyed, there will be a readily available weapon with ammunition that makes at least a partially acceptable substitute. Flint-powder detonation as we knew it when it went out of use, between 1820 and 1860, approximately, was not too reliable. But it would seem modern science could rectify many of the flaws in the old system.

Lead for bullets for black-powder guns will remain easily available and can be melted down for molding on almost any kind of hot fire. Lead would probably not be a problem even in a survival crisis. But those who think they would remain stocked with modern ammunition because they can reload cartridges themselves should bear in mind that they have to buy most of the components for reloading—smokeless powder and primers in particular. These would not be available after a series of all-out attacks. The same plants that manufacture cartridges turn out components, and all would be gone.

The .22 rimfire cartridge and the rifles and handguns firing it are by most reckoning the best for survival uses. The ammunition, even the highly efficient .22 long rifle hollow-point cartridge, is very light and handy to carry. A carton of .22 long rifle shells (500 of them) weighs little. A family, militia unit, or individual with a .22 weapon and carton of shells per person could do well living off the country, granted any luck at all. The .22 long rifle hollow-point bullet is accurate to 150 or even 200 yards under good conditions; it will kill deer-sized animals with well-placed shots, and it will easily fill a lot of stew-pots or Dutch ovens with smaller game. The .22 handgun is easier for the novice to learn to shoot well than any of the big centerfire handguns. A woman can learn to handle a .22 pistol very well if she has good motivation and decent training. A couple of boxes of cartridges (100 shells) will hardly crowd a pants pocket or lady's tote bag. While the bigger military rifle and handgun calibers have many more positive advantages for military or police uses, the .22 remains the likeliest choice for a survival situation.

Chapter 3

The Constitution and Politics

✳ ✳ ✳ ✳ ✳

"Fear of assassination often produces restraints compatible with dictatorship, not democracy."—United States Supreme Court Justice William O. Douglas, 1963

THE QUESTION OF WHETHER THE SECOND AMENDMENT TO THE United States Constitution insures the right to keep and bear arms to an individual has never been thoroughly settled by our federal courts. Several cases involving the amendment vis-à-vis the individual went to the United States Supreme Court between 1876 and 1939. No decision really settled the controversy. The 1939 decision involved a sawed-off shotgun, which in 1939 did not appear to be a militia weapon. The Second Amendment says: "A well regulated militia being necessary to the security of a free State, the right of the people to keep and bear Arms, shall not be infringed."

But what does this mean? Does it imply, as some argue, that only the "people" collectively have this right? Or does the right extend to the individual citizen as the ultimate reservist, as others insist?

Two serving Justices of the United States Supreme Court have expressed views which tend to reinforce the Second Amendment as applying to the individual citizen if and when some new test is posed. Justice William O. Douglas, writing in the *New York University Law Review* (Vol. 38, page 233), said: "The closest the framers [of the Constitution] came to the affirmative side of liberty was in the right to bear arms. Yet this too has been greatly modified by judicial construction." And Justice Hugo Black has written in Black, "The Bill of Rights," *New York University Law Review* (Vol. 35, page 865, 1960), "Although the Supreme Court has held this amendment to include only arms necessary to a well-regulated militia, as so construed, its prohibition is absolute." The word "absolute" is interesting. Because the pet argument of those who like to convince the public that the right is only a collective one is that the Second Amendment conveys no absolute right. From these justices' writings and other opinions and statements, it is difficult to agree with those who seek to persuade Congress and the public that enactment of repressive firearms laws would be upheld by the Supreme Court.

Nonetheless, the political climate has been turned against firearms insofar as a large segment of opinion shapers can manage it. The training or arming of citizens with guns has been equated with extremism. Our troops have been sent into what is essentially a small-arms war with small arms of dubious quality. Even the tragic lessons of Korea, led by its premium on accurate marksmanship, are expediently forgotten or downgraded. The fact that each individual's responsibility is to defend the nation—and particularly the imminent responsibility of young men—is paralleled by a government responsibility to supply adequate training and incentive—this fact is completely overlooked. So is the concomitant fact that the primary way to defend the country is, has been, and probably will continue to be with small arms. The primary small weapon involved will be the rifle, in one form or another, for quite some time to come.

The national government has failed to meet such obligations and discourages states, communities, or organizations which do. People who do not like the hard course expedite this failure. So do political leaders who prefer the cheap and easy ways out, and those whose ends are best served by discouraging the defense responsibility. Some even fear a citizenry in arms—perhaps for the reason that there is hardly a case in history where a citizenry in arms has been tyrannized or even seriously misgoverned for very long.

All of this could be swept away, and should be swept away, if we contemplate survival, by listening to the forthright advice of the men off the battlefields—those who know. Instead we have paid great heed to people with close access to the bigger information media, people who have masters and purposes of their own to serve. The goal of a determined minority in Washington was and is to discredit lawful ownership and use of guns with facts, half-facts, or untruth, applied with smears and innuendoes. It is a massive propaganda effort that has largely succeeded. It was initiated after John F. Kennedy was killed with a mail-order rifle. Michigan Congressman John Dingell, a liberal Democrat and staunch advocate of conservation causes and shooting sports, summed up the entire anti-gun argument in one apt word in a recent talk before the House of Represenatives: "Phony."

Dingell has reason to know. He called the interests seeking stiff gun curbs, led by Senators Thomas Dodd and Teddy and Bobby Kennedy, charlatans and purveyors of snake oil. It was harsh language to use on respected political figures of the same party, and it undoubtedly cut those with the conviction of their own destiny and grand aspirations. But when the Dodd-Kennedy "case" on gun legislation is examined, Dingell's terms are almost polite, compared to the reality. The American Bar Foundation turned up one sterling example. Its parent organization, the American Bar Association, has for several years backed the administration (and Dodd-Kennedy) approach to federal gun legislation. The approach involves first stopping all or almost all interstate firearms sales, then applying powerful incentives to the states to regulate guns as closely as possible to further discourage their use—even, apparently, in legitimate sports shooting. Yet when the Bar Foundation made an extensive survey of free access to guns and its effect on crime, it simply could not show a case for such a link, and said so. The prime conclusion stated that there is probably no way gun laws can materially affect our crime rate. There are many sociological and other factors that *do* play a part in crime. But a comparison of crime rates in states and cities having severe gun-control laws with those areas having less regulation shoots the gun-control proponents' case out of the saddle.

The prevention of political assassination as a plea for stiff gun curbs simply does not wear well, in the analysis of history or in reality. None of the proposed gun-law panaceas would have deterred any of the assassins whose deeds revived the "crusade" against guns. Neither registration nor the Dodd-Kennedy approaches would have saved John or Bobby Kennedy or Martin Luther King.

The Roman Senate in its heyday had strict prohibitions against members entering with arms. Yet a group of Senators converged with daggers on Julius Caesar, and the Senate was overturned many times in the republican as well as the imperial era by armed men—Senators, plain citizens, and troops.

The important lesson of all historic attempts to curb the misdeeds of men by weapons laws is that such statutes invariably affect or are observed only by those who have no need of such statutes. They entirely miss the target—that breed of subhuman which uses violence, calculated or aberrant, to gain its ends.

An eminent University of Pennsylvania sociologist, an admitted believer in very severe gun legislation who set out to show a guns-crime link, came up with pretty much the same result as the Bar Foundation. Dr. Marvin Wolfgang probed a large number of Philadelphia homicides over a lengthy period. He reluctantly concluded that there was no solid relationship between violent crime and access to guns. He remained anti-gun but, unlike most of those who agree with him philosophically, had the integrity to admit the relationship did not exist.

Alan S. Krug, an economist formerly with Pennsylvania State University, published a detailed survey of jurisdictions with stiff gun laws compared to those with lenient ones. His study showed:

1. Crime is caused by socioeconomic problems, not by firearms.

2. Firearms are involved in only 3 percent of all crimes in the United States, "therefore, firearms licensing laws, even if highly effective, would not be likely to cause any appreciable decrease in the over-all crime rate."

Also, Krug discovered, as Wolfgang had, access to guns doesn't equate with crime. Higher homicide rates in the United States than in England, where access to guns is much more controlled, don't necessarily mean that gun-control laws are desirable or even indicated for the United States.

Wolfgang wrote: "Several students of homicide have tried to show that the high number of, or easy access to, firearms in this country is causally related to our relatively high homicide rate. Such a conclusion cannot be drawn from the Philadelphia data— The hypothesis of a casual relationship between the homicide rate and proportionate use of firearms in killing is, therefore, rejected," he summed up.

Krug said New York City's experience revealed "that criminals are not deterred in their quest for firearms by firearms laws, and . . . such individuals persist in carrying weapons regardless of any law which has so far been enacted." All this testimony and much more like it does not get reported by the major network television "news" reports nor by the top metropolitan press, save in a few exceptional areas. But those pressing for stiff gun laws depend inflexibly upon such distorted writings as Carl Bakal's *Right To Bear Arms*, which has easily been challenged as to both content and purpose. Some critics have hinted that Bakal's book was in part subsidized by a politically interested antagonist to an armed citizenry.

Bakal, who was never directly in combat service during World War II and Korea, actually knows very little about firearms. "Yet his Army service has been played up as if it had endowed him with a special knowledge of guns," the *American Rifleman* for September 1968 commented. "Limitations on the author's knowledge of firearms are reflected in such ways as his unqualified reference to a proposed 1926 handgun regulation covering 'any firearm with a barrel length under 12 inches.'" The *Rifleman* added, "Bakal quotes with apparent endorsement a statement that such a regulation 'could be completely evaded by having a pistol 13 inches in length.' So it could, if the statement referred to barrel length. But no manufacturer regularly produces handguns with barrels longer than 12 inches. Yet Bakal apparently did not know that."

Bakal would have had trouble learning such material in his Army stint. He was in a rear-guard element in the Philippines *after* World War II ended; the Korean conflict, Bakal spent a year in a Signal Corps Depot in Germany (a long way from Korea's lessons in marksmanship, but the same noncombat school of gun expertise that Teddy Kennedy attended, obviously) as a *scenario writer*. The Hollywood–Washington–New York news-managing, column-grinding, and belt-it-out entertainment axis pays an undue heed to gun-inept ex-scenario writers and young Senators who never heard a shot in combat.

Bakal's distorted or slanted figures have been cited by most foes of private gun ownership. When chided for using some of these, Assistant Attorney General Fred Vinson, Jr. replied he knew they were unofficial, but said he liked them anyhow. His chief, Ramsey Clark, even tried to tell the Senate the National Rifle Association received "cannons" and shells from the Defense Department's civilian marksmanship program. Clark was not much upset when called to account by Senator Roman Hruska for this misstatement, all too unfortunately common to the efforts to discredit gun ownership at every level.

The civilian marksmanship program of the Defense Department, implemented with NRA cooperation and coordination, has been a particular target for the Kennedy-Dodd interests. The notion has been planted that pre-induction marksmanship training, through responsible gun clubs, is somehow menacing to the republic. Among other things, this is an insult to the public, and in particular to young people, white, black, and otherwise, who need to be taught to shoot as part of a prospective national service obligation. But more vital, the argument that such training is obsolete is deliberately to ignore the kind of war young Americans have been called on to wage since 1945.

Concurrent with the attack on marksmanship has been a major effort to enact gun-licensing laws at state and local levels in line with the New York Sullivan Law. More than a half-century ago, New York political boss Tim Sullivan rammed through his state's legislature what was until recently the nation's most oppressive gun-control statute. It has, as one prominent shooting sportsman told Congress, been contributing to crime in New York and to the disarmament of ordinary citizens for nearly 60 years. Its contributions along this line will be examined in a separate chapter on crime and police. The law has been duplicated in even stricter degree by the states of New Jersey and Illinois and the cities of Philadelphia and Chicago. The basic thrust of Sullivan and laws like it allots to the police the almost unlimited authority to decide who can or cannot own a gun (under the Sullivan law proper at this writing, only handguns are affected; however, New York City has moved to cover *all* weapons, including sporting rifles and shotguns, and Governor Nelson Rockefeller is urging similar legislation statewide).

The police in some jurisdictions (again, New York City is an outstanding example) abuse this authority and wield it with a literal life or death power. Citizens who are refused permits for no valid reason, yet arm themselves anyway, frequently are more punitively prosecuted than those who assault or rob them. The police maxim under Sullivan-type controls is: "You don't need a gun; we'll protect you." This of course has no application for those who wish guns for hunting, target shooting, or other outdoor pursuits. But abusiveness is frequently the rule of police judgment even for sportsmen.

In 1913, the New York State Supreme Court ruled that the Sullivan Act was constitutional only because it did not apply to all guns. Apparently its saving grace was that it covered only concealable weapons. How this would be viewed today by a New York State Supreme Court is interesting. Even more intriguing is what would happen to the entire body of gun registration laws when they are challenged, even though Sullivan has been in effect since 1910. Its basic approach is certain to be tested in the reasonably near future because New York City has extended the coverage to rifles and shotguns—hardly concealable weapons in most cases.

The great danger in most current gun registration laws is that they grant to the police a judicial authority, yet the police are essentially an administrative and enforcement agency without the capacity or the background to make essentially judicial decisions. This authority to determine by departmental administrative decision whether one is allowed to have a gun, for hunting, target shooting, defense, or whatever, is seldom tempered by desirable appeals processes. Sullivanism in simplest terms tends to disarm the law-abiding citizenry without deterring criminals, as research has proven over and again. New York City's and New York State's crime rates hardly enhance the credentials of such legislation (see Chapter 8: "Crime, Police, and Guns," below).

There is a strong feeling among opponents of Sullivanism that the United States Supreme Court would not uphold the Second Amendment as a personal guarantee of the right to keep and bear arms if a law covering solely concealable weapons were challenged. This is the main reason why the Sullivan Act was not carried to the federal courts years ago. However, ever since 1942 there has been some doubt as to whether the constitution as now interpreted would allow prohibition of ownership of *any* firearms. The reason is a decision that year by the First United States Circuit Court of Appeals, which said in part: "The federal government can limit the keeping and bearing of arms by a single individual as well as by a group of individuals, but it cannot prohibit the possession or use of any weapon which has any reasonable relationship to the preservation or efficiency of a well-regulated militia." The court said in the same decision that the rule of the 1939 Miller case (covering prohibitive taxation and registration of fully automatic weapons—machine guns—and sawed-off shotguns) was out of date "because of the well-known fact that in the so-called 'Commando' units some sort of military use seems to have been found for almost any modern lethal weapon."

Chicago Attorney Robert A. Sprecher, whose essay defending the right to bear arms won the American Bar Association's 1964 Samuel Pool Weaver Constitutional Essay Competition, wrote: "The court also speculated that under the Miller rule Congress could not regulate the possession or use by any private persons not presently or prospectively members of any military unit, of distinctly military arms, such as machine guns, trench mortars, anti-tank, or anti-aircraft guns, even though under the circumstances surrounding such possession or use it would be inconceivable that a private person could have any legitimate reason for such a weapon."

The writer here hastens to add that neither he nor his evidence seeks to justify widespread private ownership of heavy ordnance or crew-served weapons. The quotation, however, serves to show that there are serious constitutional questions affecting the power of government to control ownership and use of arms by responsible, law-abiding citizens.

Judge Bartlett Rummel, a longtime Washington State jurist and former president of the National Rifle Association, agrees with the Sprecher interpretation. He thinks that the Supreme Court cannot continue to be selective and uphold only certain rights out of the Bill of Rights. The Fourteenth Amendment will be the authority, he thinks. "The Supreme Court of the United States is gradually getting around to holding that all the provisions of the Bill of Rights have been incorporated into the Constitution, as applied to the states, by the 14th Amendment," Rummel wrote in an exhaustive treatment of the question in the *American Rifleman* for June 1964. Thus the amendment that gave the court the power to require the states to live up to civil rights obligations will lead, Rummel feels, to the states' being compelled to stop infringing on the Second Amendment.

However, when the 1969 Supreme Court had a chance to expand on this, it declined. Reviewing an appeal against the New Jersey gun-owner licensing act, the court simply upheld the New Jersey state supreme court's endorsement of the bill. The top court said it was not able or willing—whichever it may have meant—to find "any substantial federal question." This tended to reinforce belief that gun-owner licensing laws, apart from gun-registration laws perhaps, are constitutional, or at least will be recognized as constitutional by the present makeup of the court.

The New Jersey bill, popularly named after its creator, Attorney General Sills, provides for hearings by gun-license applicants who are wrongfully rejected—or who feel they have been so mistreated. However, unlike some other gun-licensing laws, the hearing provisions have been regarded as weak or nebulous. That was one reason Jersey sportsmen and others appealed to the United States Supreme Court.

Sportsmen—some of whom do not object to more carefully drawn ID-card bills—have generally regarded owner-licensing statutes in Illinois and Massachusetts as less oppressive and more clearly written.

The New Jersey appeal was filed on the hard-to-define basis that it restricts the fundamental human right of self-defense. Nor was it challenged because of abuse by police. The appeal was on such abstract basis that the Supreme Court may have indeed felt there was no fundamental federal issue involved. Perhaps it felt the time was ill-advised to reach for a reason to void such a law; it is possible a direct appeal based on the Second Amendment may elicit a different response from a new court in the next few years. Or it is possible the court preferred to wait for a challenge based on police abuse of power conferred by the Sills Bill. It is also regrettably possible, however, that ideological thinking—sociology—led the court to uphold Sills. Certainly ideological,

rather than legal, thinking permitted the law to survive to reach
Washington. A *state* court less prone to sociological guidance or
political pressure would probably have voided the law or part of it.

Sprecher raised the highly interesting point that since the Congress in 1933 included the National Guard as part of the Army of
the United States "at all times," the high court would probably
find that the states in fact have no militias as such—all the more
reason for the armed citizenry, which the *Federalist Papers* show
was the intent of the militia provision in the Second Amendment.
Sprecher says: "With the urgent need for civil defense and particularly if the 'stand-by home guard' is ever incorporated into the
national army, is it not important that as wide a base of the citizenry as possible be armed and somewhat trained? Armed and
trained citizens may not prevent an atomic attack but they can
preserve internal order after one."

An examination of the writings of the Framers of the Constitution, notably the prolific writers Alexander Hamilton, a conservative, and James Madison, a liberal (in their era), shows the intent
of the Second Amendment concerning an armed citizenry.

In Federalist Paper No. 29, Hamilton wrote that while select
bodies of the militia (read National Guard) were to be gathered,
trained, and maintained, the rest of the public should remain
armed at home. "Little more can reasonably be aimed at, with
respect to the people at large, than to have them properly armed
and equipped," Hamilton said. He also tried to put to rest the
rather wild fears some Americans still have about an armed citizenry: "There is something so far-fetched and so extravagant in
the idea of danger to liberty from the militia [the average citizen,
remember] that one is at a loss whether to treat it with gravity or
raillery."

This bears weight because Hamilton was the principal architect
of post-Revolutionary America's conservative, centralist political
movement, the Federalist Party. Hamilton and his associates held
as a cardinal belief a deep distrust for "the mob," as many in those
days called the citizenry at large. Hamilton cinched up his belief

in a citizen militia as a safeguard against arbitrary rule and oppression by a standing army: "An excellent body of well-trained militia, ready to take the field whenever the defence of the State shall require it. This will not only lessen the call for military establishments, but if circumstances should at any time oblige the government to form an army of any magnitude that army can never be formidable to the liberties of the people while there is a large body of citizens, little, if at all, inferior to them in discipline and the use of arms, who stand ready to defend their own rights and those of their fellow-citizens. This appears to me the only substitute that can be devised for a standing army, and the best possible security against it, should it exist."

On many points, Madison eventually disagreed with Hamilton. He became a leading figure of the opposing Democratic-Republican Party. Yet on the role of the armed citizen, conservative and liberal here agreed. Madison put his belief in somewhat different terms which reach the same conclusion: He considered "the advantage of being armed" one of the significant bulwarks of the nation against both foreign invasion and domestic oppression. Armed citizens, Madison felt, formed "a barrier against the enterprises of ambition, more insurmountable than any which a simple government of any form can admit of." He added: "The governments [of Europe]. . . are afraid to trust the people with arms." This is far more true now than when Hamilton and Madison so wrote in supporting adoption of the Constitution. Of all the nations of Europe, only a few, led by Switzerland, have reasonable gun-ownership policies. England today has gun laws more repressive than those in the Soviet Union. The personal freedom of Britons, always highly vaunted, is subject to restrictions that can lead to the establishment of a police state. All that the Framers wrote tends to support the concept of the militia as the entire public, the final mass of defense.

Few Americans of any calling have paid more attention and wrestled harder with the problem of a militia than George Washington. Most of what he decided was also reflected in the writings of Hamilton and Madison—but he probably thought the matter through more from a purely military view, and less from that of a Framer of the Constitution.

Walter Millis, writing in *The Center Magazine* (published by the Center for the Study of Democratic Institutions) for March 1968, commented that "Washington (after the Revolutionary War and in making a peacetime army) would have cut the volunteer professional army to the bone, but he would also have retained the universal militia obligation to provide a general pool of armed and at least semi-trained manpower . . . He did not think of it as a combat force in itself. He would therefore have introduced between the regulars and the mass militia what we now call a 'ready reserve.' "

Millis, a noted military historian of liberal bent, was grappling with the Selective Service concept when he wrote this. But he provides some interesting insights into Washington's thinking— which is far from outmoded right now, and in fact reveals some clarities our modern Pentagon and political planners might review.

Unfortunately the Congress, when it enacted the Militia Act of 1792, dropped "the salient feature" of Washington's concept, Millis wrote—it did not provide for the ready reserve of militia-men. And "the great mass of the universal militia went unneeded, and the militia system atrophied," Millis added, "giving way to the volunteer state armies of part-time citizen soldiers."

The militia went untrained, miserably so, as its poltroonish performance against Canadians—mainly militia like our troops but of a far sterner mettle—and British in 1812–15 so starkly revealed.

Millis thinks Washington wanted the militia "brought to a high state of efficiency." He wanted all able-bodied males compulsorily enrolled. For he had learned that lack of discipline was the chronic curse of our militia. He believed in some kind of training, at the least, for all able males ages 18 to 50. The same idea has intriguing values today, however repugnant it may be sociologically to the people whose chief peacetime compulsion is to prevent preparedness.

Those who keep arguing for an all-volunteer army, whatever the reason, might talk to the more thoughtful veterans of our last fully volunteer army, the pre-1940 version. John Conlon, an Ohio student of military history and marksmanship, has no hesitation: "The idea leaves me cold, as I used to be in one of those things (volunteer armies), and we got less attention than the redheaded bastard at the family reunion.

"We couldn't have defeated anyone larger than Mexico, and it'd have been quite a strain on the forces."

A militia comprising both draftees and a ready reserve—with the at-home militia genuinely trained—is what Washington and his younger, more political associates sought. Nothing has happened or is likely to happen to diminish the value of such thinking.

Rummel said there is just one major case substantially upholding only the *collective* (or people as a whole) concept of the Second Amendment. It is not a federal case but a state one—*Salina v. Blakeley*, decided in 1905 by the Kansas Supreme Court. Several other high-court cases inclined to the opposite direction when the arms involved have clearly been those applicable to militia use.

Sprecher goes a bit farther: "Should we protect ourselves against . . . crime through the Second Amendment?" he asks. "Today, many states make it a crime for a citizen to defend himself or his home with a deadly weapon against the attacker or invader. The concern for the rights of the criminal has brought us to the rather horrifying situation that if organized crime decrees one's death, neither the law nor the victim can do much about it." Somewhat the same could be said today of the mob—the real mob, running Cairo-style through the streets.

Nor are Sprecher and Rummel alone in suspecting the Second Amendment will be upheld, will *have* to be upheld, as an individual instrument. Rummel quoted Norman Redlich, law professor at New York University: "As already indicated . . . most of the major provisions of the Bill of Rights have either been incorporated into the 14th Amendment or are likely to be in the near future."

Justice Douglas said in the *NYU Law Review,* "A Bill of Rights. . . is a reminder to officials that all power is a heady thing, and that there are limits beyond which it is not safe to go. A few provisions of our Bill of Rights, notably the Third Amendment and its prohibition against quartering of soldiers in private homes, have no immediate connection to any modern problem. Most of the other guarantees of governments are, however, as important today as they were when first adopted. Many of them are even more important."

There is significance in the fact that the Warren Commission, meeting in all hotspurred anguish and fear and doubt following John Kennedy's assassination, did not make any recommendation as to firearms legislation. The Warren Commission, unlike later crime, riot, and other commissions appointed by the Lyndon Johnson administration, was outstanding for both political balance and for having as its head an important, if controversial, *jurist,* Chief Justice Earl Warren. But the possible constitutional as well as common-sense barriers to gun controls did not deter those who failed to find incentive in the Warren Report. Senator Thomas Dodd, who had been offering a bill to control mail sales of handguns, abruptly switched to include all firearms in his proposal. This bill gathered momentum very slowly but was in a fair position to pass, with some amendments, when the Justice Department, in early 1965, offered its own much stiffer bill with broad, vague powers reserved for the federal government to "control" gun sales, including over-the-counter sales. The suspicion is that the Justice Department would have gone farther if it had felt it could constitutionally do so. As it was, the Justice bill touched off deep and wide opposition that Dodd's own *original* idea had not. Dodd abandoned his own bill to support the Justice version; so did the Kennedy brothers, and eventually President Johnson was persuaded by successive attorneys general, Nicholas de B. Katzenbach and Ramsey Clark, to back the Justice approach.

The more the Justice bill became embroiled and stalled, the more Justice tended to embellish it with stricter provisions. There is a certain tendency for delayed legislation to accumulate amendments, and in all probability the Justice Department's stiff-gun-bill fans felt that since eventual passage was very likely, making the legislation constantly more restrictive would eventually lead to enactment of a really severe measure.

Robert Kennedy, for his part, testified for more than even the Justice Department sought. He urged nationwide gun registration, or a fragmentary approach to it; his brother Ted kept referring to the Administration-Dodd bill as a "first step," all of which simply fueled the growing opposition with fears that there would be successively more stringent legislation unfolded if the Administration-Dodd measure was adopted. This would, its foes felt, lead eventually to confiscation or almost as severe controls, wholly beyond the bounds of reason or practicality. Nothing the Kennedys or their allies said allayed these fears, and indeed their language became more intolerant and uncompromising as time went by.

As late as 1968, a compromise between Dodd's old, original bill and the Administration-Dodd version could easily have been achieved had the Kennedys and other anti-gun principals been willing. Bobby Kennedy said, however, in terms no one could call soothing, "Show me a man who doesn't want to register his guns and I'll show you someone who shouldn't have any."

This compares strikingly with the reason Hamilton, Madison and others labored to persuade a recalcitrant nation to accept the Constitution, the inclusion of a Bill of Rights "to allay the fears our forefathers had toward a central government which might become tyrannical," Rummel explained. One might respond to Kennedy by paraphrasing: "Show me a political leader who fears the citizenry and I'll show you a leader who should not be trusted." Ted Kennedy's position, negating the Second Amendment, contrasts very strongly with his standpoint on other constitutional rights. Or is it that he has in him a streak of the same politics that agitated Tim Sullivan to procure the bill named after him in New York, which insured the disarmament of Sullivan's enemies and the continued arming of his own people?

The national media certainly have helped discredit the Second Amendment. The Kennedy-Dodd line is accepted gospel. Opposing positions draw sketchy and often facetious attention in news stories and are dealt with summarily by editorial writers. The same people are, however, busily guarding the First Amendment—freedom of the press—against "assaults" by jurists and attorneys seeking a better Sixth Amendment—right to fair trial. It's curious to observe the upholders of the First Amendment trying to preside over the demise of the Second; they get, rather oddly, considerable help from many attorneys who find the Sixth Amendment a vital buttress to our society, but who feel apprehensive about the Second Amendment. It all depends on whose right is being gored.

Both fail to recognize that whether or not, as Mao Tse-tung said, *all* power comes out of the barrel of a gun, the Second Amendment is the restrained, democratic, and reasonable nation's way of compelling the other freedoms they value. The implied threat of force, reasonably poised, is all a democratic system normally requires to insure order. Controlled violence keeps free societies alive. If the citizenry were genuinely prone to full-scale oppression and outraging of all rights and values, the First, Fifth, and other amendments would mean nothing. This is what Hamilton and Madison foresaw in approving the Second Amendment. It has perhaps as much impact now as it had when we were still embroiled with red Indians and had just banished Redcoats.

Perhaps a future United States Supreme Court would have to interpret the meaning of the Second Amendment as being akin to this—that a citizen has a right to keep and bear arms until he commits a crime with arms.

Certainly the basic reason for such a right, as a safeguard against oppressive government and its chief instrument, a "standing" military force, has never disappeared. It sounds alarmist, and it evokes angry denials in the army and from government, to suggest this in view of the long historic honeymoon that has been granted the United States—a military almost entirely free of major political involvement. But honeymoons end, as do benign political periods. One wonders what might have happened if Harry Truman's 1945–48 administration had not yielded certain basic, harsh wartime controls on the economy. Or what could have followed a head-on confrontation had Truman refused to accede to the Supreme Court's order to free steel mills that he seized in his second term. Or what would have been the result if Douglas MacArthur had indeed determined to come home and use all his great prestige and strategic brilliance to defy the politicians who relieved him from command? Or what if Dwight Eisenhower had been a man to convert his immense popularity into a regimentarian and paternal regime?

All of these possibilities point to the value of a citizenry capable of defending its own fundamental interests when they are threatened by oppressive government and the great forces that government can exert. Fortunately none of the leaders possessing such options exercised them—nor, doubtless, were most even tempted to follow such an arbitrary course. But the possibilities continue to exist, especially in a system of government tending towards greater and greater concentration of power in its executive branch. Absolute power corrupts just as surely now as when the phrase was coined. It would disturb many thinking Americans to realize that such an acutely observant student of democratic government as Winston Churchill (who was billed in our popular press as virtually a "czar" in wartime England) regarded the powers and options open to Franklin Roosevelt as very wide and great, as a sort of composite of the roles of king and first minister.

We are repeatedly told by critics of the right to bear arms that Hamilton, Madison, and the other Founding Fathers sought the Second Amendment as a protection against "Redcoats and Indians." And it is true that the menace of British reoccupation was in their minds—they had just completed a graduate course in oppression by British power, and Canadian and Indian bases were not far away. But many of the statesmen who drew up the early instruments of our government had never seen a live red Indian, nor were they concerned in a long-range way with hostile aborigines. The language used by Hamilton and Madison shows they regarded the right to keep and bear arms as a long-time investment in liberty. Redcoats receded, but the value of the right grew. And it appears to have more pertinence to the century we live in, with its constant trend to more centralized power and more arbitrary and authoritarian (if sometimes "benevolent") government—far more than Hamilton and Madison knew, but perhaps not more than they envisioned.

The conduct of the Federal Communications Commission is an intriguing exercise in selectively lopsided regulation. Television has been the worst offender against the Second Amendment. Almost no network-level television shows on gun legislation have done anything even remotely resembling an objective treatment. The standard network "report" reads like something ground out by Kennedy or Dodd hacks. The FCC, however, has been straining mightily to insure that anti-tobacco advertising proponents have a fair shake before the tube, all the while registering complete unconcern over fairness standards violated by network anti-gun shows. Tobacco has its pros and cons and a definite economic value within the nation, but destruction of the Second Amendment can relate to the future of the nation, to survival in war or disorder, and to the security of the individual, his family, and his home.

Much of the trouble, aside from the FCC's abdication of its responsibility, derives from the native habitat of those who control most of our top television and news-reporting establishments. They matured in a milieu where people thought guns and self-defense are only for the police or military, or (illicitly) for criminals. For lack of an apter phrase, this could be called the New York City Mentality. It has captivated the New York–Washington–Hollywood media axis. Mind shapers who subscribe to it wallow in a chrome half-world (perhaps ready to crash in on them) which defies the absolutes of history. The United States has not felt domestic war in a century, and even then only the South and a few border states were visited with it. People at large have no concept of what occurs with invasion or revolution, or both combined. Their acceptance of anti-gun, anti-preparedness preaching is understandable, if unreasonable; their culture and experience have not prepared them for anything else.

Many news reports call the gun-legislation fuss an argument between "reform" elements and a great lobby—the NRA and its allies. Or else a "confrontation" (a word politicians typically overuse) between urban and rural beliefs. The first charge is patently untrue. The second is nearly accurate.

It is difficult to say just where the line is crossed between lobbying and genuine public expression. Certainly the NRA, with a million members, and the National Wildlife Federation (two million) have vigorously opposed what they felt was unwise or unduly restrictive legislation. They have also backed what they felt was reasonable, workable legislation. The NRA has caught literal hell for imagined feats of obstructionism and virulent opposition that even a much bigger, fatter, and more sinister "lobby" would find impossible. The NRA and its cause would not succeed without broad public support. The National Wildlife Federation has fought almost as stubbornly against Dodd-Kennedy thinking. Somehow it has escaped the dragooning and opprobrium that anti-gun forces have aimed at NRA. So have other major groups which have fought hard against Dodd-Kennedy proposals: the Amateur Trapshooting Association, the National Skeet Shooting Association, the Izaak Walton League, the International Association of Game and Fish Commissioners, the National Police Officers Association, the National Grange, the American Legion, the game and fish department of virtually every state (including the home states of Dodd and the Kennedys), farm organizations, even archery groups who felt gun-hunting sportsmen were being unfairly persecuted for the misdeeds of a few criminals or assassins.

The NRA has been the leader and most effective opponent of Dodd-Kennedy federal controls. But it has not been the largest or the only major foe. This is something the administration gun-bill supporters do not discuss. It appears more profitable to try to single out the NRA and maneuver it away from its broad base of support by citizens and other organizations. But without wide popular support, NRA and its allies would have capitulated long ago. In 1965, mail against gun-control bills literally outnumbered all other mail to Congress, including letters written on the Vietnam war, civil rights, education, housing, and other issues.

One reason anti-gun elements have had great difficulty making their press-agentry smears stick to shooters and hunters is that their target represents a broad cross section of the country. NRA members, hunters, collectors, and so on, come from all sections, all ethnic and religious blocs, all segments of the economy. There is no one special philosophy. It is hard to drum up a poor image for shooters and hunters because the National Wildlife Federation, NRA, and similar groups include at least respectable proportions of Jews, Negroes, WASP, Catholics, Californians, Texans, Easterners, and so on. They include members of the police, civilians, the military, hunters who may be part-time pacifists, veterans who don't hunt, and many more. Two of the best recent defenses of gun ownership in the *American Rifleman* magazine were written by a Negro Army reservist who is an electronics specialist and a rabbi who had served in the Israeli air force before returning to the United States. It is a strenuous and frustrating task for Dodd's and Kennedy's press agents to tag the NRA a racist-extremist outfit in the face of such testimonials.

(The National Rifle Association's membership by the first quarter of 1969 counted 73 persons decorated for heroism in Vietnam, including two winners of the Medal of Honor, two Navy Crosses, 17 Silver Stars, 25 Bronze Stars, and 15 Distinguished Flying Crosses. It is quite doubtful that a total tally of all anti-gun organizations, overt as well as subterranean, would produce a total even approaching that—even including astronaut John Glenn, head of the Kennedy-backed Emergency Committee for Gun Legislation.)

The real split in gun-control philosophy lies between the big cities of the Northeast, the Great Lakes, and California on the one side and most of the remainder of the United States on the other side. It could almost accurately be called a seaboard vs. interior division, but it is not quite that. Nor is it entirely rural vs. urban, although this is nearly factual. The interior states have evolved a different philosophy on firearms, except for a few big cities like Chicago and others around the Great Lakes metropolitan belt. Western (except California) and Southern states, and most Midwestern states have resisted efforts for stiffer gun-control legislation; their representatives and people tend to feel that legislation which may work well or be desirable in New York or Washington can easily be ridiculous in Indiana or Wyoming. Assuming a need for certain controls in New York (and the Sullivan Act's history does not bolster that assumption), laws that may succeed there can be oppressive to Nebraska farmers, Texas ranchers, or small-town merchants in Georgia. And very few laws make sense to hunters, who find most legislation ludicrous in that it only hampers the law-abiding sportsman or other citizen but seldom thwarts assassins, armed robbers, murderers, or other violent, determined people. Those concerned with the future of hunting tend to gather in support of laws compelling much better education and training of citizens in the use of guns, and more severe penalties for their misuse. More of this is discussed in Chapter 6: "Hunting."

An *American Rifleman* survey of governors in early 1969—as most state legislatures sat—showed most governors were not interested in "controlling" guns and some had deep distrust of the constitutional and other aspects of an invasion of private rights.

Idaho's Don Samuelson wrote President Johnson a serious, probing letter after Johnson's administration came out strong for registration and licensing (in a particularly onerous form) in mid-1968:

"Mr. President, our people are concerned. Quite frankly, they fear that disarmament might be the ultimate goal . . . . They are aware of the enormous increase in criminal activities. They are concerned that disarmament will place them at the mercy of the criminal element.

"The volume of mail we have received on this subject is truly amazing. Almost without exception, the arguments submitted in opposition to federal gun controls have been highly articulate and reflect well on the basic intelligence and practical insights of our people."

"Axis" newsmen snorted that people from Idaho and other rural-state residents opposing the control proposals were howling wolf—that the great volume of crime occurred in cities where there was much less resistance to gun laws. They missed the finer point: Idahoans and other rural-state residents had elected to cope with crime in a more direct way, while urbanites as a group had surrendered not only the right but both the wish and the tools as well. Criminals or a mob trying to take over an average Mountain West small city or town might find the resistance more punishing than anything to be met from police in larger seaboard cities. The desire to defend oneself, however bewildering to network or metro-press reporters, persists in rural areas in the West, in some sections of the Midwest and even in that much-maligned section which has produced so many Medal of Honor winners, the South.

Governors as far apart ideologically as Samuelson; Georgia's Lester Maddox; New Mexico's David Cargo, and Texas' Preston Smith expressed basic agreement with Samuelson's constituents.

Smith said, in addressing Texas outdoor writers:

"When you take away guns from citizens, you take away liberty!"

The remark drew little news attention beyond Texas. If the converse had been said by a Kennedy, a Tydings, or a Dodd, it'd have received prime play across the country. It is a respectable summary of how many Americans feel about being disarmed in an increasingly unpredictable society.

A prime illustration of the breakdown on gun controls came in the Senate on August 22, 1967. Teddy Kennedy had introduced an amendment to the Defense Department appropriation to eliminate civilian marksmanship funds. The Director of Civilian Marksmanship program (also discussed elsewhere in this book) in essence provides support in the form of obsolescent Army rifles, pistols, ammunition, targets, and other supplies which help train people in gun clubs and foster interest in NRA-related military and international competitive shooting. Kennedy's idea was to strike out against the NRA, at least in part for its continuing resistance to what he deemed wise legislation for the United States. He lost by a 67–23 vote. Of the 22 senators Teddy persuaded to go along with him, only two (Inouye of Hawaii and Bartlett of Alaska) were from Western states. A sizable number of doves and lesser critics of the State and Defense Departments' policies voted to retain the civilian shooting funds in the appropriation. This included such dovish senators as Aiken of Vermont, Bayh of Indiana, Church of Idaho, Gruening of Alaska, Hartke of Indiana, Mansfield of Montana, McCarthy of Minnesota, McGovern of South Dakota, Morse of Oregon, and Percy of Illinois.

The Defense Department, with Robert McNamara still presiding, later ignored the desires of Congress and stripped most of the marksmanship funds away from the budget, including military support for the National Rifle and Pistol Matches at Camp Perry, Ohio, virtually a sport-shooting Olympus. This action ignored the 3-1 margin in the Senate and a similar preponderance (by voice vote) in the House of Representatives.

Bartlett's reasons for abandoning an almost solid Western phalanx on the vote are not known to the writer. Inouye's home state, while western geographically, is not Western in the historic or traditional sense and has a background of rather strict firearms controls. But Hawaiian Democrat Inouye's Republican opposite number, Fong, voted to support the citizen marksmanship program.

Three Southern senators, predictably doves Fulbright of Arkansas and Gore of Tennessee, with newcomer Spong of Virginia, voted with the two Kennedys. Two senators from a state with a vigorous sportsman-hunter vote, Michigan's Griffin and Hart, voted against marksmanship. Hart usually backed legislation favored by organized sportsmen in his state and tended to support their view on the main thrust of Dodd-Kennedy legislation where it affected rifles and shotguns. Hart's vote against the marksmanship program was almost the only surprise in the "anti" column. Senators Dodd and Stephen Young gave their predictable all to undermine the program. Party had little to do with the vote. Home-state sentiment counted for much so long as it was pro-shooting. Private passions ruled with Dodd, the Kennedys, Fulbright, Gore and, doubtless, most other senators who opposed the marksmanship program. Certainly few had a preponderance of mail urging defeat of the program, or urging passage of the administration bill which was locked up in committee and remained so (all this cannot avoid confirming the feeling that the marksmanship program was being assaulted because its greatest protagonist, the NRA, had succeeded in roadblocking the administration's "control" bill).

Dodd, a moderate-to-conservative Democrat, was aligned with liberal Republicans Javits of New York and Case of New Jersey; Arizona conservative Republican Fannin was arrayed with Morse, moderate Democrat Symington of Missouri, liberal dove Church, Bourbon Democrats Eastland of Mississippi, and Ellender of Louisiana. Joining that group in all its diversity were usual Kennedy ally Bayh and Maine moderates Muskie (Democrat) and Smith (Republican). And so on. It was a revealing cleavage that showed distinct, even deep divergence in regional sentiment.

Morse, who taught law in Oregon before getting into politics as the nation's most eminent maverick, told the Senate he was not sure that even mail-order gun controls were constitutional. He said the Senate would be "walking on thin constitutional ice" in approving a ban on mail-order gun sales. It was a point for deep thought by those who say Congress has all power to regulate weapons possession, to ban mail sales, and go beyond that to national licensing or registration.

The attitude toward guns on the part of the Justice and Treasury Departments during the Johnson administration indicated that if these departments felt they could go farther constitutionally than simply banning or regulating mail sales, they would do so. The language used by Ramsey Clark and many others made this pretty clear. The 1967–68 administration-Dodd gun-control proposals probably embodied all the interference and regulation that Justice believed it could get away with. The evolution of the bill into its 1967–68 form—from a fairly stringent beginning in 1965—indicates why Tom Dodd didn't press for his own moderate bill in early '65. He undoubtedly knew something better (that is, stiffer and more complex) was coming. A week after he made impassioned pleas for his own bill in February 1965, traveling the country on its behalf, he cast it aside and went to work for the stringent Justice approach. The results of that are still coming in and are still confused. But creating confusion about differences between the two bills, the mild original Dodd one and the Justice bill he suddenly squatted on like a guilt-ridden mother hen, was part of his purpose, as most of his press agentry has shown. Meantime, Justice almost certainly evolved the toughest bill it could and would almost surely have liked to go farther. But constitutionally could it? The fact that it did not seek to do so tells much.

It's also significant to the politics of the gun-law argument that there are fifteen states which do not guarantee the right to keep and bear arms in their state constitutions. Most of the more obnoxious gun-law proposals have originated or been adopted in these fifteen states. New Jersey, New York, Illinois, and California head this list. It is with these tendencies to legislate against citizen gun ownership that anticipated United States Supreme Court decisions will sooner or later have to deal. In the interim, the gun haters (most of whom don't know an M1 carbine from a blowgun without an NRA manual to tell them) will continue pressing for ever tighter legislation, on the pious if impotent premise that such laws will eventually banish guns and Evil simultaneously.

How well this philosophy has succeeded in New York and other jurisdictions where the public has bought it is demonstrated in Chapter 8: "Crime, Police, and Guns."

Chapter 4

Marksmanship

✳ ✳ ✳ ✳ ✳

"Soldiers are rarely fit to rule—but they must be fit to fight."—T. R. Fehrenbach (in *This Kind of War— Korea: A Study in Unpreparedness*)

An Associated Press story out of Hue, the embattled old imperial capital of Vietnam, led off with a basic precept that American strategists, political leaders, and voters should ponder: "Planes bomb it. Navy ships offshore and big guns on land shell it. But a United States Marine says: 'It still comes down to the Grunt and his rifle.' "

A few thousand years in the evolution of military hardware, from bronze hacking instruments to atomic weapons, haven't altered this fundamental of war. People who survived World War Two, especially in the Pacific, Burma, and Italy, absorbed this lesson with remorseless clarity. But for others it was easy to forget. Our society prefers ignoring facts that are brutal or grubby.

Yet the world's most modern example of lightning war, the short Israeli conquest of Pan-Arabia's massed but inept troops in June 1967, contained no new truth. When CBS-TV newscaster Mike Wallace asked military expert Brigadier General S. L. A. Marshall (retired) for the key to that amazing triumph, Marshall said, "Marksmanship"—with all weapons. It was appropriate for Wallace and CBS to hear; in a domestic news environment, he and CBS had set some kind of record in anti-gun television reports. His network had done more than any other major U.S. news medium to disparage sensible use of guns and the training of American citizens with them.

Neil Sheehan, a Vietnam correspondent for the *New York Times* (which has also waged a strident anti-gun campaign in its once-accurate news columns), helped undermine his daily's pious position by reporting: "The American serviceman in Vietnam is proportionately engaging in a good deal more basic infantry combat than his elders did in World War II and Korea." Statistics tend to back this up. The Vietnam war in late 1966 had produced a much higher wound toll from small-arms fire than its two predecessors. Small-arms bullets caused 18 percent of wounds in 1941–45, 27 percent in Korea but 35 percent in Vietnam.

Nor has the Army learned much, or its political masters permitted it to implement what it has learned, about the persistent shortage of basic riflemen that has plagued our military system for years.

Time magazine for March 15th 1968 said: "In all the talk about possible mobilization to meet America's needs in Vietnam, one nagging question inevitably arises. With 3,426,680 men in uniform, why should the U.S. have to call up reserves and expand the draft in order to give General William Westmoreland the 206,000 men he needs?

"The answer is that the armed forces are seriously short of riflemen. Nearly half of the nation's fighting men are in the Air Force (904,062) and the Navy (748,762).

"It is the Army (with 1,477,019 men) and the Marine Corps (296,837) that need new muscle. As of last week, both services were stretched thin, at home and abroad."

Not just as of last week, *Time*. As of the last 30 to 40 years. To repeat, there is always a shortage of young men who shoot well. The computerized humanitarian who presided over Defense for Presidents Kennedy and Johnson ignored history in his passion for packaged multi-use products and for helping the Johnson administration and the Kennedys get a "gun bill" enacted. He procured instead the F111 (with its penchant for crashing in various vaguely defined jungles), a dismemberment of the old reserve system (bad as it was, it was better than the confusion he left), and elite troops who could not shoot. McNamara thus proved that what fails in Detroit—Edselization—can also fail in Washington and around the globe.

It was in Korea in 1950–53 that the United States Army rediscovered its old faith in marksmanship, which led to at least a marginal improvement in our small-arms fire for a decade afterward. The pointless and unnecessary casualties among poorly prepared troops in Korea, especially in 1950, restored marksmanship to eminence with an Army and world which had decided atomic proliferation had ended infantry war forever in the old sense. Aimless fire by flabbily trained (and often undisciplined and physically unfit) troops was gradually succeeded by new emphasis on good shooting, individual killing talent with small arms. Perversely, however, it has again become politically popular to agree with peculiarly motivated critics of marksmanship. Emotion from misdirected anti-crime promotions and from assassination is being allowed to warp basic truths.

War between men down on the ground remains much as it was in the Pacific in 1941–45. It is not always sniping, night firefights, and patrols like Guadalcanal, but much of that island campaign is still with us. It was one of two turning points of the Pacific war (the other was the naval victory at Midway). The violent Ilu (sometimes called Tenaru) River fight on Guadalcanal was "like record day at Quantico," Marine Lieutenant Colonel Edwin A. Pollock said. It was 200-yard shooting with Springfields. "Line 'em up and squeeze 'em off," Pollock ordered. The result was the slaughter of raving mad Japanese Colonel Ichiki's overstimulated and overrated detachment which was designed to sweep the fat, slothful Yankees right off the island. The Springfield has in the main gone to that great scrap-heap in the sky, but it has only been replaced by other rifles still designed to be accurately wielded by ground troops, to kill other ground troops.

Ward Just, writing in the *Washington Post* in May 1969 must have shaken his anti-gun superiors with a tale of how to succeed against the Vietcong, because the article and its source, Army Lieutenant Colonel David Hackworth, particularly stressed use of the rifle.

Although "The marvels of modern technology have caused some to believe that exotic gear has replaced the man with the rifle," it is not true, Just pointed out—quoting Army Major General Melvin Zais, commander of the 101st Airborne Division in Vietnam.

Zais, who drew Teddy Kennedy's inexpert fire for ramrodding the assault up Hamburger Hill the same month in Vietnam, replied to the short-term-service young Massachusetts Senator for the Hamburger Hill criticism (in which even Kennedy's dovish colleagues refused to join—and for which he was blasted by members of the House of Representatives in a rare departure from protocol).

Hackworth succeeded against the elusive Vietcong with stealth, guile, man-killing rifle work and all the other techniques that Australian guerrilla expert Major Peter Badcoe urged—and which the more politically oriented generals disavowed, perhaps in eagerness to please an administration carrying on a campaign against guns and marksmanship training.

Just may be a rare convert. A few years ago he wrote an article ridiculing the marksmanship training program in Washington, D.C. high schools. He suggested the civilian marksmanship program was training District youth to be urban snipers. How then would he correlate expertness with rifles, so strongly urged by Zais and practiced by Hackworth's troops? Where after all does a nation obtain its sustained interest in the shooting-marksmanship heritage if not among its citizens, and particularly its young citizens?

Hackworth told the *Post* writer, "Machines are no substitute for brave men when it comes to fighting a resourceful, well-armed, and superbly motivated enemy."

"The war is a platoon leader's war," Just reported, "and can be boiled down to four principles"—Mao Tse-tung's. Hackworth was quoted by Just as saying:

"The most important lesson to be drawn from the war in Vietnam is that a lightly equipped, poorly supplied guerrilla army cannot be easily defeated by the world's most powerful and sophisticated army, using conventional tactics."

To defeat such guerrillas, Hackworth wrote, "You must become guerrillas. Every insurgent tactic must be copied and employed against the insurgent. . . . American forces must enter the guerrilla's lair as hunters, employing skill, stealth, enterprise, and cunning."

The part about entering as hunters must have particularly upset the *Washington Post,* preening itself on its repeated (if rather unsuccessful) campaigns against guns, shooting, hunting, and all else pertinent. There must have been some squirming in those editorial-policy sanctums, so secure from rice-paddy ambushes or intruding criminals. It might have led *Post* policy-shapers to suspect there may come a day when hiring more guards or putting two more locks on the door may not spell security. But it probably didn't. Equating anti-gun "security" with Maginot Line thinking will probably come much too late for the people who control the *Post* and other publications like it.

Yet Hackworth's experiences should be studied by mothers, fathers, and others who can read and absorb what he tells about modern war. For if modern war is likely to evolve more and more into guerrilla/counter-guerrilla activity, as it threatens to do, what Hackworth and Zais say may be the Napoleonic wisdom of our age.

Quite apart from all propaganda that the rifleman is unimportant, Zais says, "Never in the history of modern warfare has the small combat unit played a more significant role . . . and the brunt of the fighting falls squarely on the platoon.

"The outcome of the war will be determined in large part by the skill, guts and determination of the platoon leader. Not a general's war, not a colonel's, not a war of massed forces—a platoon war."

Hackworth won his spurs and right to write his manual on Vietnam in various firefight episodes that also earned him six Purple Hearts and four Silver Stars.

In one closing action in the Mekong Delta, this gifted and outspoken colonel in two days inflicted a decisive rice-paddy defeat on the Vietcong. The casualties—and body counts tell the story in Vietnam and at home—were four Americans wounded to 134 VC dead. It was a significant victory, engineered by Hackworth but using principles advanced by Zais, by Badcoe, and by virtually every other Westerner who has deeply studied success in war against Red guerrillas.

As Just said, it won't evoke any fuss in Congress. It is all too simple and it entails producing young riflemen who know how to kill, not tank drivers or artillerymen or those young immaculates in the button-pushing business.

One of the factors that helped sell Israel's brilliant military thinkers on good shooting was the success of the Israelis' only formidable foes in the Arab-Israeli war of 1947–48. Robert Henriques, a trained English officer of Jewish ancestry, mentioned this in his *100 Hours to Suez* (Viking Press, New York, 1957). The Jordanian Arab Legion was the one Arab force to fight well against Israel in 1947–48 (and its military successors did well in the June, 1967 war, too). "First, the Legionnaires were trained and led by British officers for 15 or 20 years," Henriques said. Jewish leaders had also acquired their training from the British before and during World War Two in the Near Eastern deserts. Second, Henriques wrote, "The Legionnaire was either a Bedouin (nomad) or a hill man. In either case, his upbringing from childhood tended to make him military material. He had owned his own rifle. He knew by instinct how to use ground. He had to be taught only, or mainly, how to fight collectively." Other Arabs, three wars reveal, were not out of the same mold.

What weapon is best for a militiaman in 20th century America? The writer suspects the same small arms the regular infantry uses. One prime choice is the semi-automatic assault rifle with a moderate-velocity cartridge of perhaps .30 caliber, although there are good arguments for other weapons and calibers. Certainly there is an excellent argument for a lightweight .22-cal. centerfire round, either high or moderate velocity. The .22 round, such as the 5.56mm. (.223-cal.) load for our new M16 light service rifle, allows the average soldier to carry many more rounds than any .30-cal. cartridge and rifle combination.

Full-time gadfly and part-time Marine officer and gun designer, Melvin M. Johnson, Jr., who died a few years ago, did a great deal of thinking and work on a basic ground-war rifle. His ideas were as controversial in the 1940's as now. He may have been the last man to graduate from Harvard Law School who knew anything about guns except how to write senseless legislation against them. Johnson wrote in the 1960 *Gun Digest,* in an article aptly titled "Machine Gun Mix-Ups": "In view of forthcoming fire-fight realities, air-lifted gunners, and atomic-age ground dispersal, it might be well to take a fresh sheet of paper and reconsider bullet bursts, unblundered" (he refers to aimless fully automatic fire). Among other points, Johnson (whose semi-automatic rifle was widely used in the Pacific war), wrote that upcoming basic infantry arms should include two weapons. He strongly disagreed with the 1950-era Army idea of trying to devise one utility weapon that would perform all functions from machine gun to handgun.

He recommended: 1. A *holster* weapon weighing about 3 pounds, rigged with a shoulder-fire adapter. "Extended tests personally directed indicate combat-hit effect with *semi-automatic* pistol-type weapon of four to one" when such weapons are fired from the shoulder compared to one-handed. For this weapon, Johnson urged caliber .224 at a muzzle velocity of 1,700 to 2,200 foot-seconds—a moderate-power load, certainly. 2. The basic *flat-trajectory* weapon would weigh 6 or 7 pounds and be belt-fed, pod-mounted for prone and capable of semi-automatic fire only. "As you can see," he put it, *"if someone is going to shoot at me, I hope it will be without bipod support and on full-automatic."*

He favored, for reasons of recoil, range, and logistics, a flat-trajectory caliber of .224 to .250 at a muzzle velocity of 3,000 to 3,500 feet per second. This is a .22-cal. weapon with about the pace of the M16 round. Johnson's idea was for the proposed flat-trajectory weapon to fill the role of the rifle, carbine, and light machine gun. The holster weapon would replace the handgun, and within 75 or 100 yards, the carbine and sub-machine or burp gun. This, Johnson believed, would adequately replace and logistically improve on the confusing array of small-arms weapons we have retained. It is worth mentioning that among all the more advanced free-world armies, only the French have a more bewildering collection of small arms than the United States. This kind of multiple weaponry entails much difficulty in production and battlefield supply.

In between the eventual United States verdict for the 5.56mm. high-speed .22 round hand gun and the earlier quest for a new .30-cal. rifle and shortened .30-cal. cartridge, the British came up with a rifle and load that were very interesting. The British gun, styled the EM-2, used a .28-cal. or 7mm. cartridge of moderate velocity—driving a 140-grain bullet at a muzzle velocity of around 2,300 feet per second. This is similar, except for a minor difference in caliber, to the present short .30-cal. round that is almost universal among Communist-bloc armies. Due to United States influence and experience with the British rifle and load in tests during the early 1950s, the British gun and cartridge were not adopted by the NATO forces. Britain eventually abandoned the EM-2 and adopted the FN rifle in the 7.62mm. NATO (.308) load. Some British observers still think we erred in this. The United States claimed the British load lacked a flat enough trajectory for long-range hits and did not have adequate punch at longer ranges. British Brigadier C. Aubrey Dixon, who was instrumental in development of the EM-2 and its load, vigorously dissented with the dominant American decision. The earlier military small-arms thinking of the Germans and Russians tends to agree with Dixon and the EM-2 concept.

If Guadalcanal was the United States' last big campaign with the respected old bolt-action Springfield, the bolt-action rifle still plays a useful part in some limited applications. There is no doubt a militia can use the bolt gun for supplementary and sniping purposes. The post-1965 revival of classic sniping by the Marine Corps in Vietnam has shown that enemy guerrillas can be killed for 13 cents a round. The economics of this appeal when you realize that 10,000 rounds of ammunition were required to get one wounding hit in Korea—and 50,000 rounds to kill each enemy there. In the face of this evidence, a de-emphasis on marksmanship is incredible.

Many of the skills that promote effective military sniping are traceable to citizen marksmanship, to high-level match shooting, and in particular to the annual National Matches. The Army's 1968 withdrawal of financial support for the matches saved or was supposed to have saved the government about $228,000. The economy, compared with benefits gained in high quality match shooting and all the rifle lore, instruction, and pooling of knowledge acquired at matches, is open to very strong challenge.

Assay the cost of *skilled* riflery and then recall what Ohio's gun-hating Senator Stephen Young, a frequent, querulous critic of marksmanship, said in the 1967 debate on the citizen shooting program: "Furthermore, nowadays, with our M16 rapid-firing rifle spraying bullets with great rapidity, marksmanship is not so essential as it was in World Wars I and II [the Senator had apparently forgotten Korea. But one forgets much at his age]. . . . There is little time for aiming and firing, and little firing from the shoulder by GIs handling the M16 lightweight rifle." The Senator couldn't have been more wrong if he had set out to deliberately mislead people. He may have. All the testimony from the battlefields denies everything he said.

While he chattered away, the bolt-action sniper rifle was back in business. It didn't regain the niche it held until 1940 or 1941, when our M1 Garand set the new pace for mass-issue semi-automatic military rifles. But in Korea the bolt-action Springfield was hauled out of obscurity for sniping because the average issue Garand was not up to accurate fire much beyond 600 yards and was not readily adaptable to a telescope sight (top ejection of the Garand made it necessary to mount the scope off center, a handicap to some riflemen). Marines knew the Springfield, wielded by a skilled rifleman, would kill a North Korean or Chinese soldier at 800 yards or beyond. Even though armorers later successfully tuned the Garand for fine long-range match work, accuracy purists still tended, as did Roy Dunlap of Tucson, to say, "The M1 is a machine. The bolt-action is a rifle." The fact is, most semiautomatic and lever-action rifles are not as accurate as most bolt-action rifles; the bolt guns with their one-piece stocks have stiffer propping and many are more easily fitted with scope sights.

The Marines in Vietnam went back to the bolt rifle for sniping. They started with Model 70 Winchester sporting rifles, now use Remington Model 700 sporters in 7.62mm. NATO caliber, topped with a Redfield scope varying in magnifying power from 3 to 9. The great goal for the Marines' standard sniping work is first-shot, cold-barrel accuracy, and the rifle is geared for this with a free-floating heavy barrel and match-grade ammunition. This equipment has been practical for the Marines' sniping mission. Army long-range patrol units incline to semi-automatic and fully automatic rifles for greater firepower; their mobile patrolling requires greater stress on bushwhacking and reacting to ambush a long way from static, fixed positions. The Marines tend to use snipers in two-man teams, not for long-range penetration but more for operations around camps or bases. Marine patrols, like most Army combat forces, use the M16 as the basic rifle.

In cultivating snipers for Vietnam, the Marines noticed something significant but not very astonishing about the type of troops attracted. The likeliest candidates for sniper training were men who had extensive hunting exposure. The next most likely group was from among those with match shooting experience. Of the top seven enlisted snipers in the original Third Marine Division unit, six were National Rifle Association members. As Frank McGuire pointed out in a July 1967 *American Rifleman* article, "The great majority of snipers in Vietnam have been men of much hunting experience." Thirty-four of the forty-four men in one such unit had extensive hunting backgrounds.

The Marine Corps has carried sniping to a higher proficiency than the Army. Part of this goes back to the Corps' concept that "The most important man in the Corps is the individual Marine and his rifle." More may be due now to the new Marine sniper maxim: "Fifty misses are not firepower; one hit is firepower."

The former Marine major general who won the Medal of Honor and was a ramrod of key fighting on Guadalcanal, the late Merritt A. Edson, said this about marksmanship: "It is not my intention to imply that the ability to shoot straight is the beginning and the end of national security. But it is that part of national security which affects the individual more than any other." It is certainly that part which affects the militiaman the most. Edson was a forceful, respected foe of curbs on gun ownership and a staunch believer in citizen marksmanship training, especially for young men of pre-military age. General Wallace M. Greene, Jr., recent commandant of the Marine Corps, called him "one of the greatest Marines of all time."

Congressmen and Senators paid attention when Edson spoke on such matters. Civilian shooting and a good militia require another such good advocate now, when the need is even more critical than during the Korean war. Before he left a key Civil Defense command post to become executive director of the NRA, Edson bluntly and effectively opposed the notion of registering all guns. He that argued registration of guns simply made life easier for subversives or intruders seizing such records as part of taking over a government or an area. The history of Nazi and Communist power-grabs all over Europe in the 1930's and 1940's amply supported Edson.

The great value of weapons training for militiamen, indeed all citizens, stands out when you size up the wars of "national liberation" the Communist bloc has turned to in the last dozen to fifteen years. This kind of fighting uses subversion, infiltration, old-fashioned Indian-style bushwhacking, espionage, political push-and-pull manipulation of the free world's open societies. The French paratroops and Foreign Legionnaires who were overwhelmed at Dienbienphu were not defeated there; the French nation was, and the actual defeat occurred in Paris, the culmination of a political rotting-away that had started in the French nation many years before. The paratroops and Legionnaires simply paid the bill. Troops always pay the tab for the sins of their political masters, in one way or another, and for the follies of their civilian peers and masters back home.

The Vietcong and North Vietnamese Army stress small-arms training with notable success. They train everybody within reach (presumably, anyone not trustable with arms is dead or in jail in their amiable system). In his fine article "Small Arms Of The Viet Cong" (*American Rifleman*, February 1967), Army ordnance expert Joseph E. Smith points out that VC and Hanoi regulars use 42 different types of arms, donated, purchased, or captured. These arms come from the U.S.S.R., Czechoslovakia, Red China, France, the United States, Japan, and Germany. Lieutenant Louis A. Garavaglia, in the January 1968 *Rifleman*, adds that the Czech Model 58 assault rifle is the finest shoulder weapon the Reds have recently employed, but he and other long-range patrol troops have great respect for the 58's predecessor in Red-bloc use, the sturdy AK 47 assault rifle developed by the U.S.S.R. and copied and improved all over the Communist system. The entire family of Red small arms, old and new, is rugged and reliable, sufficient for its function without undue expense or prettying-up. Submachine guns and light machine guns and assault rifles are the key small arms of the Southeast Asian guerrilla/counter-guerrilla fighting, along with the ubiquitous mortar and primitive devices like the pungi stick.

Garavaglia wrote *American Rifleman* editor Ashley Halsey, Jr., that Smith's article on VC arms was required reading for trainees in the Army's Long Range Reconnaissance Patrol units in Vietnam. He said his unit had experimented with bolt-action sniper rifles, among other arms, but had discarded these for the more mobile and high-firepower purposes of the LRRP mission. Garavaglia said snipers in long-range reconnaissance patrol work eventually settled on a modified version of the Army's much-mis-understood M14 7.62mm. rifle. The unit also tried the regular M14, the M16 and various Red-bloc assault weapons, particularly versions of the AK. Garavaglia's unit operated in the varying terrain of South Vietnam's Central Highlands, in country where shots might occur anywhere from point-blank out to 700 or 800 meters. The modified M14s his unit's snipers used had straight-line stocks fitted, selectors for full or semi-automatic fire, and 2.2-power scope sights and bipods (one can almost see Mel Johnson in the shades exulting at that!). Scopes were rusted in tight to keep them from being bumped out of alignment. The modified M14 with scope was accurate for sniping up to 700 meters, Garavaglia said. Men equipped with the modification of the M14 carried nine magazines apiece, loading each with only 18 rounds instead of the capacity 20 rounds, presumably to keep them functioning a little more smoothly; both match and duplex (two-bullet) ammunition was used, the preference depending on the range.

The lighter M16 drives its .223-cal., 55-grain bullet at the afore-mentioned muzzle speed of 3,200 feet per second, compared to the M14's .30-cal. 150-grain bullet at muzzle velocities ranging between 2,700 and 2,500 feet per second (7.62mm. NATO loadings vary according to intended purpose). For the farther ranges, the M14 7.62mm. NATO load is clearly superior. For stand-up fire-fights in the bush or jungle, the M16 has advantages. Garavaglia said the M16, while not as accurate as the M14, begets more good hits in combat conditions. It is capable of sustained hits on 6″ x 6″ targets offhand at 200 meters. But it does demand regular cleaning and can easily be overlubricated. In these respects, the M16 is a more delicate weapon than United States forces have employed in quite some time.

The United States' duplex 7.62mm. load is interesting. Developed in 1964, it involves two bullets, each 80 grains, in a regular 7.62 cartridge case. The front bullet leaves the M14 rifle at a muzzle velocity of 2,800 f.p.s.; the rear bullet is rated at 2,600 f.p.s. muzzle velocity. Reasonable accuracy is obtained at most combat ranges; hits are increased by use of this load. It is not considered up to serious long-range accuracy.

Garavaglia said per-man combat loads of ammunition easily favored the M16 5.56mm. round. While personnel equipped with sniper-modified M14s carried 162 rounds, others using the standard M14 hauled along only 90 rounds of the 7.62 ammunition. Men carrying M16s could take along a minimum of 198 rounds; some carried up to 306. Garavaglia said the great virtue to the Russo-Chinese AK rifle is its ability to keep firing with even old or corroded ammunition. Here is the reason why troops and militiamen require thorough grounding with the small arms of probable opponents, and why the VC and Hanoi train their people with a variety of arms. Most guerrilla and counter-guerrilla actions in recent wars have been conducted with the captured arms of enemy forces, and this has even led to the formal adoption of some enemy calibers by regular military establishments. The British did it with German 9mm. parabellum load and the Colt-Browning 9mm. The influence of captured weapons has great weight, obviously, with ordance thinkers. The Russo-Chinese 7.62mm. cartridge for assault rifles, lighter and lower in velocity than our NATO 7.62, is an excellent cartridge for light semi-automatic and fully automatic rifles and fits in nicely with Red-bloc tactical notions. The Red 7.62mm. load is shorter than our version and drives a 122-grain bullet at about 2,350 to 2,400 feet per second muzzle velocity. There are variations in this load too for different purposes. The basic cartridge is known as the M43 and is derived from theories popularized by the Germans in World War Two.

The Red-bloc armies have used two of their own submachine gun and pistol cartridges, the old 7.62mm. pistol and burp gun load (almost identical to the German 7.63mm. Mauser pistol cartridge), and a newer 9mm. load which in power is between the German 9mm. Parabellum load and the Colt-Browning 9mm. Short or .380 semi-automatic pistol round. This new U.S.S.R. 9mm. load is used in the Makarov and Stechkin pistols. It employs 94-grain bullets at 1,000 to 1,200 feet per second muzzle velocity. Older Soviet burp guns and Tokarev pistols use the 7.62mm. pistol round. This is a fast-traveling load, driving an 86-grain bullet at 1,350 to 1,500 feet per second. The Stechkin pistol uses a detachable shoulder stock which also serves as a holster. This, again, is somewhat along the line of Mel Johnson's suggestions.

Since small-arms skills are the common denominator of militia war, how well United States troops have performed recently is vital and should be reviewed. The consensus is that while our troops' average with small arms now is a bit more deft than in Korea, they have a long way to go to be downright efficient. A United States line officer in Vietnam, Captain Michael E. Ekman, wrote in *Infantry* magazine that United States marksmanship in this area was "deplorable"—even though he commanded highly touted paratroops of the 173rd Airborne Brigade. Ekman said: "Poor fire discipline, failure to zero weapons periodically, and *insufficient time on ranges* firing familiarization and reaction courses" were headaches. The net effect: "We failed to kill far too many enemy soldiers during our fleeting contacts."

Ekman limited fully automatic fire to two men per squad in his company. Other men were allowed to fire their M16s semi-automatic only. They were required to *aim*, not spray the landscape (is Senator Young in the audience?); much more time was spent on ranges and, during lulls, on field practice firing. This, mind, occurred in the field with supposedly fully trained elite troops!

In some circles of the Senate, all that would probably be needless expenditure. One sprays VC wholesale, just as one sprays tenements full of women and children (while the sniper, so-called, gets away because no one can hit that 6″x6″ spot at 200 yards offhand).

A standard 1968-style Vietnam wire report told of about 90 well dug in United States infantrymen killing around 100 North Vietnamese troops who assaulted them head-on, massively, time after time until finally wiped out. Under standard head-on assault conditions, well-entrenched American troops should have killed two or three times that number of enemies. One suspects United States infantrymen in this firefight and many others like it showed only mediocre marksmanship, however brave or otherwise skilled they may be.

With the regular United States military, there is a cleavage of opinion on training new men with rifles. The Army has abandoned the old way in favor of what used to be called "Trainfire"— a presumed short cut to moderate proficiency, using silhouette and pop-up targets rather than bull's-eyes at unknown ranges. The Army has also evolved a stopgap marksmanship training supplement, for special application in Vietnam, called "Quick Kill." This uses air rifles and BBs and is taught as an adjunct to Trainfire (which now has a more imposing name that will be ignored here). Quick Kill is meant to give new troops a cheap, fast method of handling rapid-firing light weapons in jungle conditions. How well it has clicked may be revealed by testimony like Ekman's. Australian experts on jungle fighting, who have pioneered and perhaps kept a certain lead in this fierce way of war, at last report are staying with the old idea of aimed fire from rifle-type weapons. For submachine guns, the Quick Kill concept has been with us a long time. Quick Kill would be of no great value in such terrain as Korea, or indeed anywhere that close-growth, short-range shooting conditions are not common. Examples of terrain not suited for it include most of Europe, desert, and mountain systems outside the humid tropics.

The Marine Corps prefers the older, standard ways of rifle training. Their basic training still utilizes bull's-eye targets from set positions at known ranges. They offer more advanced and sophisticated combat-shooting situations in a later stage of training (advanced). But in "boot" training, shooting is taught pretty much as it has been for generations. It is slower. It is also more thorough. The advanced segment of training is much more difficult and demanding than Trainfire and Quick Kill.

The Marines' relative success in Korean fighting taught the Army to emulate them with a premium on rifle skill. Until recently the Army held fast to this new approach. The new Army method is apparently faster (although the Marines say they can turn out competent riflemen in three weeks). If time is not critical, the Marine process, with its slower, surer two phases, is probably superior. If time is vital, Trainfire and perhaps Quick Kill probably produce minimum skill adequate for militia purposes.

The Army attitude poses an interesting hypothesis: If Trainfire and—more important—Quick Kill are indeed to be the gun-fighting techniques worth teaching in the next decade or generation, then maybe skeet and trapshooting will have more practical value than rifle shooting as we now know it. At present, however, there isn't too much support for this. Even in the jungles and paddies, aimed fire has its great virtues, as Ekman's and Garavaglia's reports show. Certainly the Israeli-Arab war and numerous other brushfire wars of recent date argue that skilled, trained, aimed marksmanship continues to be at a premium in combat, along with bodily and mental fitness.

In Korea, the 27th (Wolfhound) Infantry Regiment proved to be a tough, mean, Red-killing outfit at a time when there were serious questions about the fitness of many United States units. Reporters asked its commanding officer, Colonel Mike Michaelis, why. He answered bluntly: He taught his men, he said, to be killers first and specialists or something else second. He said too: "We put too much stress on information and education and not enough stress on rifle marksmanship and scouting and patrolling and the organization of a defense position. These kids of mine have all the guts in the world and I can count on them to fight. But when they started out, they couldn't shoot. . . . They had not had enough training in plain old-fashioned musketry. They had spent a lot of time listening to lectures . . . and not enough time crawling on their bellies with live ammunition singing over them. They had been told to drive safely, to buy war bonds, to give to the Red Cross, to write home to mother—when somebody ought to have been telling them how to clear a gun when it jams."

But when United States troops did learn to shoot Reds, it was with shattering results, the way Americans have shot from the colonial wars right through to Burma and the Pacific. An unidentified officer who commanded the 2nd Battalion, 23rd Infantry, Second Division for eight months in Korea wrote: "A large percentage of dead enemy were killed by rifle fire. From 40 to 50 percent of those killed by rifle fire (presumably the officer refers here to his sector) were shot in the head or high up on the chest, demonstrating that United States riflemen had killed them as they raised up from their foxholes or from behind cover."

A specific example: "Reference is made to the siege of Chipyong-Ni in February 1951 when six Chinese divisions surrounded the 23rd Regimental Combat Team and attempted to annihilate it. In a savage three-day battle the 23rd RCT repulsed all assaults. . . . During this siege on the night of Feb. 13–14, 1951, a Chinese regiment (approximately 2,000 men) made an all-night assault on two hills held by two platoons of Company G . . . (total strength, 96). The hills were finally taken by the Chinese at dawn after 90 of the 96 defenders were either killed or wounded. A counterattack by the 2nd Battalion recaptured the two hills on the afternoon of Feb. 14. On one of the hills, 523 dead Chinese bodies were counted. About 60 percent of them had been killed with rifle fire and a great majority of the 60 percent had been shot through the head or upper chest. This illustrates the superior marksmanship of these infantry riflemen who were shooting at the attacking Chinese under starlight (no moon was visible on this night), and the occasional illuminating light of flares.

"Because of reduced strength, each rifle company only operated from 3 to 4 sniper rifles. These were issued to expert riflemen or men who had demonstrated their shooting ability. I personally know of one U.S. sniper who in a seven-day period killed 17 North Korean soldiers at ranges from 400 to 1,000 yards."

Somebody taught those troops to shoot, obviously. But the standard of rifle skill was seldom that high in Korea in 1950–53. A veteran retired career Reserve officer, Lieutenant Colonel Frank Muñoz, told the writer: "Kids who had been exposed to rifles or other guns before coming into service made better shots because they did not freeze their first contact with the enemy." Muñoz, who was involved in a long line of King-of-the-Hill skirmishes and fire-fights up and down Korea, is a firm believer in citizen marksmanship. He helped organize junior shooting clubs around bases where he served after returning from Korea.

Muñoz won the Silver Star for heroism leading his company in the Ch'ongch'on River sector in late 1950. Reading his record in Korea, you wonder how stingy the services can be with their decorations. Many others have been awarded more for less (a certain Navy lieutenant commander for his one air combat mission, as a spectator, over a Japanese base in the Southwest Pacific, for example). But there was a common characteristic to the Korean fighting, especially in 1950: A great many World War Two junior officers and noncommissioned officers had to do the fighting—the shooting, indeed—for a lot of lesser grades because the lower ranks had never been trained to fight. Anyone harboring grudges against officers from other wars might be referred to Korea, 1950, for rebuttal.

It was in the Chipyong-Ni fight, too (where the 23rd RCT distinguished itself for stacking up Chinese), that United States artillerymen cowered in tents and refused to fight with small arms—Chinese swarming at them and every man's services desperately in demand. Their officers fought, but the men in the artillery unit would not; they hadn't been taught to use rifles, they said.

As T. R. Fehrenbach wrote, they had been well trained to occupy Japan. But the public and the public's political servants did not think training for war was necessary. They were as unready to wage war as an American army has ever been—and if you study the War of 1812 and all our cowardices and ineptness and failures *then*, that is saying something. A very large number of captains, lieutenants and sergeants with prior (1941–45) battle time earned more than they will ever get credit for in the first few months of the Korean fighting. Even two-star General William Dean was last observed before his capture using a .45 pistol on North Koreans around Taejon. This and other courageous behavior earned him the Congressional Medal of Honor.

Sociologically unsound? Of course.

The ineptitude of most American troops with small arms during the summer of 1950 in Korea was etchingly spelled out in T. R. Fehrenbach's brilliant *This Kind of War—Korea: A Study In Unpreparedness* (Macmillan, 1963).

"Their newly issued rifles were not zeroed. . . . None of them was equipped, trained, or mentally prepared for combat. . . . Discipline had galled them, and their Congressmen had seen to it that it did not become too onerous. They were fat," Fehrenbach wrote in a caustic but apt indictment of the Congress, the administration, and the people who sent such useless men into an Asian war.

The United States Army had been in no such state of disrepair since it disgraced itself trying to capture Canada in the War of 1812.

As many a platoon or company leader knew—and told Fehrenbach, who was there too—most of the men could not shoot. They came from a nation with only about a million citizens who really shoot well. Contrary to that unpleasant summer's press, the Americans and their South Korean allies were thrust back by outnumbered North Korean troops, who all but overran the peninsula before the United States recovered and dug in and stopped them. It was not a chapter of military history for us to revel in.

"In July 1950 (during the peak of the American panic and retreat to the Pusan defensive perimeter), one news commentator rather plaintively remarked that warfare had not changed so much after all. For some reason, ground troops still seemed to be necessary, in spite of the atom bomb," Fehrenbach wrote. "And oddly and unfortunately, to this gentleman, man still seemed to be an important ingredient in battle. Troops were getting killed, in pain and fury and dust and filth. What happened to the widely heralded pushbutton warfare where skilled, immaculate technicians who had never suffered the ignominy of basic training blew each other to Kingdom Come like gentlemen?"

Fehrenbach added: "Americans in 1950 rediscovered something that since Hiroshima they had forgotten: You may fly over a land forever; you may bomb it, atomize it, pulverize it, and wipe it clean of life—but if you desire to defend it, protect it and keep it for civilization, you must do this on the ground, the way Roman legions did, by putting your young men into the mud."

Fehrenbach felt sure a good many Americans have forgotten that in this world there are still tigers. This is why, when United States forces were ordered to defend South Korea in the summer of 1950, "Most of the small arms had been reported combat-unserviceable. Rifle barrels were worn smooth. . . . There were no longer any spare barrels for machine guns." This was the postwar heritage of an acquiescent society. Yet—"Acquiescence society may not have if it wants an army worth a damn. By the very nature of its mission, the military must maintain a hard and illiberal view of life and the world. . . . Soldiers are rarely fit to rule, but they must be fit to fight."

Most of that fighting will be with small arms. The highly tuned training of American Special Forces troops—Green Berets—is an example, too. In addition to demolitions, personal combat, parachuting, diving, and medical treatment, "We were fascinated at the vast number of weapons with which we were required to be familiar," Robin Moore said in his *The Green Berets.* He did a stint with the Berets in preparing the book. He said whatever the weapon, Special Forces men had to learn to fire and field-strip it blindfolded as an essential skill. Ironically, these skills are taught at the John F. Kennedy Special Warfare Center, named after the President whose brother is making the nation's most significant contribution to degrading gun ownership and reasonable shooting skills among citizens.

It's some kind of commentary on the supposed pragmatism of our society, too, that the most basic skill in war, killing enemies with personal weapons, is today called "special warfare." It's a good yardstick for the gap between reality and some of our political as well as military thinking.

Marksmanship expert Paul Cardinal, writing in the *American Rifleman* in the early 1950's after initial reports of inept shooting filtered back from Korea, rounded up comments like these from combat-experienced officers: "The average rifleman is not well trained and will not fire in combat. . . . He's afraid to fire because he'll draw fire. . . . Good shooting is the exception. . . . The company depends too much on supporting weapons and forgets the firepower it has in its own hands."

It's remarkable how this parallels what Chinese intelligence reports said about United States troops a few months later. The Chinese reported: "Cut off from the rear, they abandon all their heavy weapons. . . . Their infantrymen are weak, afraid to die, and have no courage to attack or defend. They depend always on their planes, tanks, and artillery. . . . They specialize in day fighting. They are not familiar with night fighting or hand-to-hand combat."

Iron Curtain observers and couriers carried this message back to all the capitals of the Communist empire, which was then still cohesive. This evaluation played its part in formulation of Moscow-Peking policy for years to unfold.

Cardinal's comments also parallel Fehrenbach's book, which is fundamentally a capsuling of United States military history with a platoon sergeant's and company officer's reporting on Korea tied in. Fehrenbach's detail on King-of-the-Hill firefights through Korea reads like Frederic Remington's portraits of the old Indian-fighting Army, except that in the 1870's and 1880's we knew how to win such wars.

Cardinal showed how marksmanship and pride in it had been discredited. "The 'bolo' [duffer] and the expert rifleman walk side by side, with no special recognition for the latter," Cardinal said. He concluded the real fault was not with Army personnel or instructors, but with a post-1945 philosophy that "questioned everything but mass fire." Fehrenbach said the 1950 Army might have been ready to fight World War Three in full-house terms but was not prepared for the war Korea's political limits required. Cardinal pleaded for more hours spent on marksmanship in basic training, plus the simple old Yankee huckster art of *reselling* shooting (in which he reads like the Little Report one brushfire war later). He argued for results such as the Marines were getting—entailing much more time spent on the rifle range than the Army would put up with in 1950.

Visiting Marine Corps bases in 1951, Cardinal found "Range technique is perfect. . . . There is a professionalism in the operations that is almost unbelievable, even for a military outfit." And: "Every Marine recruit is trained primarily as a rifleman. Afterward he may become a specialist, but he remains a rifleman." The commanding officer of the Weapons Battalion training recruits at Parris Island at that time was Colonel George H. Hayes, a Pacific combat veteran who said emphatically: "Good marksmanship is necessary for combat fighting. There is no substitute for it."

Marines retreating from the political cul-de-sac of the Yalu River when China entered the war in late 1950 did so hauling out their wounded, their big guns, and their vehicles. They used their personal weapons. Many Army units did not do any of these things. This must have made a strong impression on the Army when critiques were evaluated afterward. By 1953, Cardinal revisited and reevaluated Army marksmanship training. He wrote about it with élan and told how it had been upgraded (the *American Rifleman*, February 1953): "I am happy to report that a year

and a half after I loosed a critical barrage at the Army's marksmanship training program, the Army is doing about everything humanly possible to improve its shooting. . . . It has revived rifle
competition. It has sought to instil in its men the pride of accom-
plishment. And, most important, it is building up a corps of competent rifle instructors."

Training instructors paid off in peacetime, too. The Army,
which for years had lagged behind the Marines in winning rifle
and pistol championships, soon started dominating such competitions. The Air Force, under leadership like General Curtis
LeMay's, followed the pattern. The general who was initially instrumental in upgrading Army marksmanship was Major General
Robert N. Young, who made good use of his own and others'
experiences in Korea. He offered a cutting raid-in-force on the
anti-marksmanship "experts": "Before World War II, too much
emphasis (in training) was placed on firing at what you can see.
After the war, we went to the theory of just shooting the hell out
of everything. . . . The troops need training in trigger squeezing
and aiming. They have to learn to shoot with judgment."

A career soldier, Staff Sergeant David E. Willis, United States
Army, wrote home from Vietnam (in a letter published in the
American Rifleman for March 1966): "There are currently many
young men facing death over here who would be better off today if
they had had a better understanding of weapons in years past. But
mores being what they are in some families, these young men
weren't encouraged to use firearms. . . . Yet some people want to
take away our right to bear arms. They also want to draft into the
armed forces young men who have no prior experience with firearms of any type. These same people are the ones who carry on
every time a soldier—who six to eight months before had never
had a weapon in his hands—gets killed for lack of proper training. . . . You don't issue a man a rifle and eight weeks later tell
him that he is a marksman and that he is trained to kill. It just
isn't done. To be a marksman takes many hours of dedicated
thought and training."

Willis, an ardent believer in NRA marksmanship programs, said earlier: "Over here a rifle and a pistol are a part of a person; not just an item of issue. . . . The .45 automatic I carry was purchased through the NRA, and I am proud of it. The M14 that has been issued to me is a part of me as well. Many of the young men serving over here have for the first time . . . become thoroughly familiar with rifles, and now have a desire to use them in activities at home."

One of the all-time successful United States guerrilla forces was the 5307th Provisional Regiment, also known as Merrill's Marauders, in Burma and China during World War Two. Their biographer, Charlton Ogburn, Jr. (*Marauders,* New York: Harper & Brothers, 1956–59), listed about the same training fundamentals as you'd find in a Marine's lexicon or in Michaelis' eloquent summing-up. Marauder officers evolved a training approach stressing pop-up target shooting (conventional firing was discarded, but not conventional firing *discipline,* probably)—based on Pacific combat prior to moving into Burma, plus scouting and patrolling, roadblocks, use of boobytraps, airlifts, compass and map work, and a special effort to evacuate wounded men. The Marauders were probably mishandled from above, by United States theater commander General Joseph Stilwell, Sr. But they made a mighty, if not always heeded, contribution to United States military thinking. One veteran officer, Major Samuel Vaughan Wilson, told Ogburn: "In the next *world war* . . . we are going to have to rely on Galahad (code word for Marauder)-type forces—small, free-ranging units. . . . The massing of armies is out in an era of atomic weapons."

American experience in Korea and Vietnam, even without use of nuclear weapons, has produced nothing to refute the major's prediction. The success of the Marauders, until they were ground down by overuse, may have made them the most successful of all larger-scale United States guerrilla forces. The unit contained "idealists and murderers . . . some [had] the wildness of the hunting male or the nomadic instinct . . . some . . . a cause." Ogburn said. It is a breed of male for which we still find great need, sociologists and politicians notwithstanding.

Officers in the high-class guerrilla regiment included Franklin Orth, now executive vice president of the NRA; rifle champion and hunting writer John B. George, who wrote about his experiences in *Shots Fired In Anger* and several advanced military thinkers like Wilson. There were few political jockeys in the 5307th. Orth became a high official in the Department of the Army but remained essentially a shooter and military man. The top political eminence to serve in and with the Asian theater was Dean Rusk. Unlike his persistent critics, he heard bullets zing in the paddies. The more thoughtful of his critics should find this disturbing.

Out of the average Russian (or Red-bloc) infantry division, approximately 75 percent of the personnel are or can readily become front-line fighting men; out of a United States division, the front-line effective proportion cannot go beyond 50 percent without radical shifts and exertions. Russia has a considerably larger pool of manpower to draw divisions from, as well. The arithmetic here should not be tortuous; far too many American troops are tied down to the supply or other rear-echelon chores—hauling up cigarettes, ice cream, or movie stars. Far too few American troops are hard-bellied riflemen who could stop the truck and get out and do a rifleman's job.

It wasn't always so. In the Civil War, American troops on both sides were soldiers—riflemen—first, as with Michaelis' 27th Infantry Regiment. Even a cook or baker or clerk knew the rudiments of a soldier's job, and he was expected to be able to go do that job on demand. The rear-line soldier of 1861–65 who might be building a bridge, teamstering, or striking for some general could put down the axe, the whip, or the shinebox and go use a rifled musket.

Rifle marksmanship played a significant role in the ability of an outnumbered South to resist Northern invasion and suppression. The remarkable nature of the South's resistance is at least partly explained in writing like that of Edwin B. Coddington (*The Gettysburg Campaign*, New York: Charles Scribner's Sons). Coddington aptly deflates the popular Hollywood-fiction concept of the Southern army as one of fluid-flowing cavalry, surrounded by shuffling black retainers toting baggage, and illiterate, barefooted infantry of nondescript vagueness. The fact was, sharpshooting by the Southern foot soldier was a major factor in the South's surprising success in the first two years of war, notably in the East—the crucial theater of war.

Too much misinformed writing celebrates Southern cavalry and too little attention is paid by the Tinpan School of "historians" to the quietly efficient marksmanship of the infantry in Robert E. Lee's Army of Northern Virginia. Overconfidence in his superb infantry apparently forced Lee into the one great miscalculation of his command career, the disastrous frontal assault at Gettysburg. Meantime the Southern cavalry was wandering aimlessly around the combat area, missing most of the action and failing in its primary function—keeping the Confederate command informed of Northern movements and tactics.

Coddington shows—as do other historians not primarily wrapped up with presenting something sociologically pristine— that marksmanship was a Southern monopoly in most of the major as well as minor clashes that made up the Gettysburg campaign. At Gettysburg, however, for one of the first times in the Eastern theater, the South met Yankee infantry equally adept with the .58-cal. rifled muskets that infantrymen on both sides generally used. These were troops from what was then "The West"—Michigan, Minnesota, Wisconsin, and other frontier areas where proficiency with guns was still virtuous and in fact downright necessary. The Westerners were more skilled in long-range shooting, while Lee's infantry excelled at bushfighting—a sort of quail-hunt skirmishing that put its premium on quick work in cover. But both shot more expertly by far than the masses of city-recruited New Englanders or New Yorkers. It was interesting, too, that in the main Western theater of war, where the North's troops were widely drawn from farms and frontier settlements, Union affairs went better almost from the outset than was the case in the East. It can be debated that this was due to a generalship advantage for the Union—Lincoln's generals in the West did not have to cope with Lee or Stonewall Jackson, and the one outstanding Southern General in the theater, Albert Sidney Johnston, was killed rather early in the war. But the fact remains that, as even a sociological historian like Henry Steele Commager pointed out, in the West the Union's boys from ranches, farms, and frontier were a match for Southerners from similar environments. In the East, granted like numbers, the Southern forces were usually victorious and regarded their enemies with a certain contempt. Even in the 1860's, there was a getaway gap in fitness for war between country-reared and city-reared Americans.

Coddington, who appears to have done as objective a job as anyone can do on something as monstrous and senseless as a civil war (for sheer inability to be objective, try any Western European or American on the Spanish Civil War), was no Southern sycophant. But he recognized an allotted tribute for the South's superior craft with weapons. Marksmanship explains to a large degree why and how an outnumbered agrarian-based South could defy the Union for four bitter and costly years.

Nor is the rifleman obsolete now. It is our tactical employment of riflemen that is obsolete. After each new employment, it is a new game—each engagement involving the use of riflemen simply retires all the old judgments and principles and replaces them, or should replace them, with a new set of future possibilities. Nonetheless, most generals go right on planning meticulously for the last time, while politicians ascend to Never-Never Land and plan for Utopia. History shows that sociology doesn't prevent war; sometimes sociology defers or delays war. But often such deferments cost the peaceful, law-abiding, and humane peoples much more—by giving their would-be oppressors extra time to prepare. For example, a hardheaded appraisal of the free world's chances might argue that the preventive-war generals may have been just right in 1945. And in 1947–48, when President Truman punished service professionals who backed such views.

By 1953, the U.S.S.R. was in a far better position to harm us, or at the very least to neutralize us. And neutralizing the free world is a major victory for a probing, flaw-seeking aggressor without scruples. It becomes simply a prelude to some final, greater aggression.

The kindly people who seek to defer Armageddon may be doing their people no kindness at all. This may have been the great flaw in Robert McNamara, who for a time was almost everybody's all-star Secretary of Defense. McNamara forgot or more probably never believed that a citizen, republican army should be built from the man up, not from the machine down. For all his brilliance, he built armies the way he built cars. He assembled a crew of civilian experts to assist him, mainly men who had never shot at other men nor been fired at; they didn't comprehend the basic tool, the rifle. They produced generally decent hardware for the public's money, but they missed altogether the basic idea—a good small-arms system. If you have to defend the country (Lyndon Johnson was wont to say "sustain the republic") with young men who no longer grow up playing Cowboys and Indians, then you must teach them to play Cowboys and Indians. Because that is the name of the game right now in war. In our technological serenity, anyone with an IQ of 90 or more can push a button (and often avoid the draft). A far smaller percentage can shoot well.

(There is a list of militia weapons, suitable calibers, and other detailed data in Appendix B.)

✳

How to Do It, and How Not

✳✳✳✳✳

"Every man must be trained to fight as an infantryman first."—General John R. Hodge, Chief of Army
ground forces during the Korean War

"A DEFINITE CORRELATION EXISTS BETWEEN MILITARY MARKSMAN-
ship and the activities of your gun clubs." That was recent Army
Chief of Staff General Harold K. Johnson addressing the 1966
annual meetings of the National Rifle Association. He was basing
his statement on the top fact in the 1966 Arthur D. Little Report
on the Army's NRA-related citizen marksmanship program. The
General just as well could have spoken from the many facts of
recent history of the realities of modern war. He could have
recited from the facts of recent life as demonstrated in that most
thoroughly armed state of our time, Israel. Or he could have been
citing evidence from the accumulated history and lore of vigorous
and independent nations like Sweden, Norway, Switzerland, or
Finland. Or from the prodigious wartime accomplishments of our
fellow members of the English-speaking world—Canada, Australia,
and New Zealand.

All of these nations, to one degree or another, can illustrate how
shooting—hunting as well as marksmanship in some, or predomi-
nantly one of the two in other countries—plays a striking part in
planning for national defense.

Sweden, Switzerland, and Israel in particular have excellent militia programs. The armed citizen has been a bulwark of Swiss independence through generations of hostility between France, Germany, Italy, and, formerly, Austria. Sweden has a highly sophisticated militia-reserve program. Norway, which suffered agonies under five years of Nazi rule in World War Two, has a less formal but perhaps just as effective program geared to guerrilla war.

Israel is the ultimate democratic garrison state, for excellent reason. It exists in a 24-hour-a-day, 365-days-a-year atmosphere of hate unequaled since the Communist, Nazi, and Japanese vilifications of the 1940's. The Israeli has learned to live—and revel in—a state which is the antithesis of all that many Jews were reared to believe in. Israel is a fully armed nation in which troops take their Uzi burp guns home with them on leave, in which paramilitary weapons and fitness training are mandatory for adolescents, in which a quarter-million skilled troops can be summoned in an incredibly short time. Women serve willingly alongside or just behind their men. Marksmanship with all weapons is firmly stamped on all this. Americans of Jewish extraction who worry about teaching our troops gun skills haven't done their homework.

Oddly, the Israelis have seized in good part upon experiences which were once more characteristic of life in the United States. Israel's method is the kind of demanding but rewarding experience General Johnson might have cited to the NRA if the evening's program had provided the time. Mass marksmanship was an American contribution to the world, built upon the need for citizens to learn to shoot to defend the nation, their families, and themselves. Yet nowhere, paradoxically, is this still-valid tradition more disparaged and more endangered than in the United States. The sophistication that comes with urbanization, unchecked crime, the fear of assassination, and other factors has led us to this (while the USSR expands its marksmanship training for teenagers).

Soviet bloc nations, while urging the West to crucify its preparedness adherents (notably the National Rifle Association), were in 1967–68 converting their own youth and sports groups more and more to fitness and weapons training. This was especially notable in press reports from the USSR, East Germany, and China. After the Russian occupation of the Czech state in 1968, Yugoslavia discovered its Red-bloc frontiers weak or unready. It sacked a cast of Russophile generals and oriented its armed forces to a "people's war" not wholly unlike the strikingly successful guerrilla war it waged against Germany in 1941–45.

The New York Times News Service commented from Belgrade that the partisan-style all-people's war, emphasizing training and arming of everybody capable of fighting, was unpopular with professional soldiers. It usually is, regardless of the country where the idea is broached. President Tito, who personally achieved notoriety and eventually succeeded to command of the Yugoslav state through his guerrilla leadership, was not deterred by carping from the career soldiers. He had been a witness to the failure of Yugoslavia's career army against Germany in the spring of 1941.

In the USSR, East Germany and the other more historically militant parts of the Soviet empire, propaganda against arms training for American civilians was attendant to upping the stress on such training for young Communists—and not on a voluntary or incentive basis as the program was rather feebly conducted in the United States. The entire prestige and pressure of the Soviet-style police state was brought into play. The USSR said it intensified marksmanship training for civilians "to meet present-day needs." *The New York Times* on May 20, 1966, reported a military training society had been organized—presumably the *Times* should say reorganized, since a strong sports-shooting society had long existed in Russia—to provide rifle training for millions of youngsters. About the same time, the USSR undertook to upgrade marksmanship in Cuba; at the Pan-American Games in Canada in 1967, one of the top surprises was the potency of Cuban shooters, no doubt in large degree due to the Soviet coaching assistance.

Meantime, *Pravda* attacked the NRA's civilian shooting program by saying it was amusement for "murderers . . . robbers."

In East Germany, perhaps the key satellite state in all those under Russian rule, *Volksarmee* Major General Guenther Teller demanded and won stiffer pre-draft military training for youngsters "to recognize the necessity of military service as part of the class struggle," according to Hubert J. Erb's Associated Press story from Berlin on September 29, 1968. Youth groups in the Soviet German state comprised both sexes, ages 16–18; subjects ranged from military vehicle driving through marksmanship to parachute jumping.

By comparison, the NRA program of rifle and shotgun marksmanship schooling and coaching—and some competition—appears tame and unsophisticated. One cannot avoid speculating at what the anti-gun reaction would be if the NRA or Wildlife Federation started offering courses in tank-driving, parachuting or other paramilitary subjects—something that is done with no fanfare and as an absolute matter of course in nearly a dozen nations east of the 1945 German border.

The drive behind the East German pre-induction training is to have the Red youth's "moral, physical and mental capacities . . . so concentrated that when a youth enters the military, he already has accomplished basic military skills." Among these, the most basic is shooting.

While it continued under assault here, General Johnson upheld the civilian marksmanship program. "The Army is not unselfish about this" (the impact of the Little Report), he said, "for we realize there are on the order of 215,000 potential military riflemen in your rifle clubs." Of even greater value, however, is the contribution these skilled marksmen can make—as they have made before—as coaches, instructors, and leaders in training other people in time of national peril. While the NRA Director of Civilian Marksmanship program is geared in part to produce riflemen, it is more important in providing experts to train young men and others. If every expert shot Johnson mentioned trained 10 people, it could provide a military reserve of over two million persons with rifle ability. This function of the marksmanship program is too often ignored by both foes and friends of the Army and the DCM.

Johnson said the Little Report showed "the dramatic influence the clubs have had upon the quality of Army marksmanship training." War in Vietnam, like war in the Pacific jungles in 1941–45 and Korea 1950–53, still requires closing with the enemy to get the job done. No sociology, no wishful thinking has indicated that this can be avoided now, any more than it was avoidable at Tours or Hastings or Berestechko or Gallipoli.

"There can be no question that a man who has been a shooter before he enters the Army is probably going to make a better military rifleman than his less-experienced associates," Johnson added.

The Little Report pointed out a few things that are so obvious they shouldn't need repetition (yet most Americans have never heard them). A young man exposed to civilian rifle club training prior to induction tends to make a better soldier. He is likelier to become a leader or instructor in service. He will probably serve both his country and himself better. In very great likelihood, he has a better chance for surviving combat. The great message of the Little Report is its accent on saving young men's lives. It is actually a pretty clear endorsement of humanitarianism. Yet its arguments are usually rejected by humanitarians, who shortsightedly see only that guns are dangerous (true only if mishandled), and familiarity with them somehow fosters a warlike spirit (which is not necessarily true). Churchill described Britain's people as warlike but not military. Yet the British Home Office has virtually disarmed the public. Somehow they remained warlike a generation or so even without guns, at least until recent developments cast some doubt on many of the old British qualities.

This chapter will deal with how free peoples cope or fail to cope with demands or need for a skillfully shooting citizen reserve or militia. Examples of how to do the job correctly will include Israel, Switzerland, Norway, Sweden, and to a lesser extent the Down Under Countries. Outstanding examples of how to do it *wrong* will be England, Japan, and Italy.

Italy was never really in World War Two, and however valiantly Italians may have striven in the 1914–18 war, they set a modern standard for ridiculously poor soldiering in the sequel. In *Alamein and the Desert War* (Times Newspapers Ltd. and Derek Jewell, 1967), one source wrote: ". . . Men . . . were. . . decisive. The Italians tried to transform this alien land [the desert theater of war] in their image, instead of learning to live with it. They built marble monuments, they had the luxury of fine sheets, grandiose uniforms, good food and drink, ice cream; even mobile brothels. It was preposterous; a recipe for defeat." This does not alter the fact that Italians are as fine people as anyone, it is hardly necessary to add. In *Rommel, The Desert Fox* (New York: Harper & Brothers, 1950), British Brigadier Desmond Young commented: "Rommel was right to see that it is such qualities (lively intelligence, gaiety, good hearts) which constitute civilization—*though a rougher soldiery may still be needed to defend it.*" Matters have not changed much since Young's remark.

No nations have ever produced better regular soldiers than Britain and Japan. British infantry has set the standard for stubborn and unflinching courage since Saxon times. Even with an undue measure of miserable generalship (and a few amazing exceptions from King Henry V through Wellington), the British infantryman has been a paragon of the profession, admired by friend and foe. The same is true of the Japanese. Almost all Japanese soldiers deserved medals, as John Masters wrote in his *Road Past Mandalay* (New York: Harper and Brothers). Perhaps it is due to this high valor and attendant discipline plus the sea-power concept that Britain has usually done its best to avoid training an effective militia force in modern times. Japan, an autocratic state until 1945 and since then increasingly anarchistic, feared to allow its ordinary citizens to have arms and even in today's democratic posture fears it. It totally bans handguns but has the world's fastest-rising gangsterism. But with China across the Sea of Japan tuning up a militia of 200 million, Japan may have to reconsider its post-1945 pacifism.

Britain, meantime, has a crime rate rising twice as fast as ours, per capita. Britain's gun laws are even stricter than Japan's, over-all.

One great reason United States Marines and Army troops defeated Japanese in the Pacific war was a higher average skill with firearms. Americans sent to the Pacific in 1941–45 were quite a way downhill from our old eminence as a nation of riflemen, but they were still better with rifles, man for man, than their Japanese enemies. This was significant against an army which was fanatically brave and intensely fit. But the Japanese were inept with small arms below the crew-served level. Their "snipers" were about as expert as the hoodlum gunmen who shot from rooftops and windows in our ghetto riots. Usually these Japanese snipers were simply ordinary riflemen (judged by United States standards) tied to trees and firing judiciously from camouflage at close range. A United States sniper in the full professional sense of the term is capable of killing at 800 to 1,000 yards with a scope-sighted bolt-action rifle.

One of the interesting sidelights on the real skill of Japanese snipers is that a high percentage were flushed and killed with burst fire from short-range fully automatic or semi-automatic weapons. Real sniping would have been conducted from ranges putting a premium on bolt-action rifles with telescope sights—several hundred yards. Such distances require killing by rifles or full machine guns. Their standard "sniper" was a bushwhacker, and while he killed all too many Americans, it was not particularly skilled long-range shooting in most cases. In many cases Japanese snipers operated at shotgun ranges.

The British Army, for all its superb regulars, drew in reserve from a population long disarmed when it went into World War Two. The average Tommy arriving at British depots in World

War One was unfamiliar with rifles; by 1939, he was woefully ignorant of them. If time and geography should again allow, this can be corrected by massive organization, planned training, and emphasis. The next war is unlikely to grant such a luxury, and in particular this is unlikely for the United States—the real concern of this writing.

Just why Britain has in modern times so drastically curbed wide gun ownership is hard to understand. The English are not a people prone to violence with weapons, any more than are Scandinavians. Until a few years ago crime was a minor problem in the United Kingdom. In pre-firearm days it was a staple royal policy to encourage archery among the lower classes. Advanced skill with the longbow (learned, curiously, from the Welsh, who must have ever after regretted it) was the key to English victory, time and again, in battles with the bigger, massed land forces of Continental Europe. At Crécy, Poitiers, and Agincourt against French chivalry and Genoese crossbowmen; nearer home against stubborn, sword-wielding Scots, and all over Western Europe, the British established an awesome reputation for cold bravery and showers of aimed arrows. Englishmen in the late Middle Ages grew to manhood with the longbow the way our frontier youth matriculated with the rifle and sixgun.

But when firearms followed the bow and steel arms as standard infantry weapons, England moved gradually toward disarming its common citizens. By the 1850's, when war with France suddenly threatened, it became necessary to organize an entire system of rifle clubs for home defense. Over the centuries, though, young Englishmen with a yen for adventure had to take to the sea; the small regular army was almost a closed shop, sharply limited by parliamentary budgets, commanded by younger sons of the nobility or gentry and manned by some of the realm's most scrofulous people. But most of them could be converted into excellent troops by harsh discipline and pride—and were.

In the last 60-odd years, the British government has squeezed through more and more gun-control legislation that has disarmed nearly everyone, a few privileged landowners and gun-club members excepted. Tight restrictions on rifles and tighter ones on handguns have recently been extended to cover shotguns too, although Home Office people admitted sporting guns played almost no part in crime. The Home Secretary of the mid-1960's somehow thought it best to cover shotguns anyhow. A docile nation accepted this unhesitatingly, aside from a few outraged hunters.

The fact that most British gun laws date back and are attributable mainly to the Irish "troubles" of the early 1900's has escaped almost everyone. There are few Irish troubles now, at least not many of a shooting kind. The South of Ireland is independent. Even the once-zealous Irish Republican Army (a political terrorist organization) is now disowned by its own government. It has as a rule stopped shooting people (it never hit many anyhow) and contents itself with the occasional gratifying violence of blowing up some empty customs house or post office.

The great between-wars theorist of British military thinking, who retired as Field Marshal Lord A. P. Wavell, told a staff college group at Camberley that the qualities ideal for the best infantryman would be "part poacher, part cat-burglar, part gunman." While this must have set the Home Office back on its heels, it is as apt a recitation of good foot-soldier qualities as the Anglo-Saxon tongue has yet produced. Note Wavell's emphasis on two qualities relating to shooting—poacher and gunman. Two out of his three infantryman "virtues" were shooting skills.

It is a definition, too, well worth the consideration of those who study or plan war in this latter part of the 20th century. Because whatever it is called—guerrilla or brushfire or post-nuclear war—it tends more and more to be fire-fighting between small, dispersed, and fluid units which must exercise great *controlled* firepower and individual skills in the field. Poaching, cat-burglary, gunmanship. The same qualities, modified by primitive weapons, stood out at Thermopylae.

To the far-seeing, this pattern emerged in our resistance to the Japanese overwhelming of the Philippines in 1941–42. The most successful United States guerrilla fighter there, Wendell Fertig, was a called-up National Guard officer whom destiny and his own particular qualities put on the spot. He and some other fugitive officers and men, regulars and reserves, rallied and formed what evolved into a capable resistance on Mindanao. Other officers and men, even surviving the first shock of the invasion and conquest, quit. Some officers, most with Japanese bayonets at their spines, got on the radio and ordered all United States elements in the islands to stop fighting. Fertig's band of Americans and Filipinos included a good many types that the more delicate of our commentators would call anti-social. They had, however, pride; they were full-grown men capable of standing up on their hind legs, and they exacted a toll of Japanese in ambushes and sniping that even our Washington–New York–Hollywood dilettante axis welcomed, at least at that time.

Fertig told his biographer, John Keats (*They Fought Alone*, Philadelphia and New York: J. B. Lippincott Co., 1963): "The stories fell into pattern. They [Fertig's guerrillas] were men like Kenneth Bayley, who two years ago had been an 18-year-old boy living on a farm near Plainview, Texas. Bayley illustrated a general rule: It was chiefly the city-bred Americans who had surrendered, perhaps in the belief that if they kept together someone would have to look after them; while the country boys escaped to the country, where they felt sure they could look after themselves. There was another rule, too: The young Southern and Western farm boys thought more highly of personal liberty, and of the word *patriotism*, than the more sophisticated personnel from the Northeastern American cities."

The country-boy contempt for repression and enemies is apparently a declining trait. The trademark of urban youth is conformity, even in its drive to profess nonconformity. The refusal to yield to the Japanese because they were "slant-eyed yellow bastards" might qualify as racism on some campuses in 1968 or 1970. But people who rail against such "racism" never knew, or chose to forget, the bestiality of Japanese occupation and guard forces toward Caucasians—not just male military personnel but civilians of all ages and sexes, including nuns, women with children, priests, and physicians. No one cares to remember now what Japanese guards did to American, British, and Dutch prisoners in dozens of genuine horror camps within the perimeter of the Greater East Asia Co-Prosperity Sphere. We are still regaled at length, 25 years afterward, with Nazi mass murder. But most of the barbarities committed against Americans in the Second World War were done by Japanese.

And in a primitive way, Fertig's unreconstructed freedom fighters must have sensed this. The Bataan Death March was known, even if only by island grapevine. In their small numbers, they and other bands became guerrilla fighters the same way the Viet Cong have done, though Fertig's men had at least part of the populace with them, and they lived off the land and their enemies.

The American Revolution, after all, was won with only about a third of the colonies' people actively supporting independence.

Another case-lesson evolved out of the Japanese advance in Burma. As in Malaya, conventional British arrangements disintegrated. A good many native Indian troops put up a poor fight; many succumbed to anti-white Japanese propaganda and helped found the Indian Nationalist Army, which the British dubbed the Traitor Army. Burmese generally supported the invading fellow Orientals, or at least the down-country Burmese did. (The hill people became excellent guerrilla-fighting elements for the Allied forces, mainly because they had been discriminated against by the "city" people from Mandalay and Rangoon.) All this and his experiences in Palestine (policing Jewish-Arab uproars in the 1930's) and North Africa (expelling Italians from Ethiopia) influenced British guerrilla thinker Orde Wingate a great deal. When the brilliant but erratic Wingate became a major general and pet novelty for Winston Churchill, he went to work in earnest. His Chindit guerrilla columns—British and imperial troops operating behind the main Japanese front and hacking lethally away at their communications and logistics—helped halt the Japanese before they were able to consolidate their Burmese conquest.

Not many Americans know even now about the Burma campaigns, where the Chindits, Merrill's Marauders (a United States guerrilla outfit), and other, more conventional Allied groups gradually rolled back the Japanese after much fierce and debilitating combat in some of the world's most unpleasant conditions. The great credit doubtless goes to Field Marshal William Slim's entire Fourteenth Army. But Chindit and Marauder operations played a key role. If Wingate did in fact overrate the guerrilla mission (he wanted to turn the entire Fourteenth Army into guerrilla columns), he made a strong contribution to victory and to planning for the future. He felt guerrilla war could gain total victory; most other strategists said its role was limited, as our own Revolutionary War had proved. Wingate's death in a plane crash ended the potential argument. One hardly envies Slim, a moderate man but resilient officer, the job of coordinating matters with such bizarre characters as Wingate and "Limey"-hating United States General Joseph Stilwell, Sr.; whatever their skills, they were irascible, intensely egotistic men. Stilwell had great talent for training and husbanding his Chinese forces, but he was beyond his depth in the political responsibilities of the job. He worked the Marauders virtually to death trying to "burn up the Limeys," but refused to commit his Chinese until he had a 5–1 or 6–1 numerical advantage over the good Japanese troops in his theater. He accused the Chindits under Wingate's successor of chickening out, with great injustice in most of the charge. Wingate, who had tried to kill himself in Africa because he felt his feat of restoring Ethiopia to independence was not properly appreciated, had a messiah complex. Although not Jewish, he had become mystically committed to leading Palestine's repatriated Jews to form the state of Israel. It was his intention to get this done as soon as his World War Two assignments abated. As it turned out, the Jewish state made it without him—it has developed military leaders probably as brilliant if not as irritable as Wingate.

In the 1930's Wingate trained Jewish "police" for Britain and predicted and noted the Jews' military success. Most British officers, seeing only the Bedouin nomad's qualities, didn't think much of the chances of the European Jews if and when Jew and Arab were left alone to settle their quarrel. Wingate found his young Jewish trainees exceptionally adept. His only complaint, a minor one, was that they talked too much. He left us this thought. Its accuracy is being proven to a very high degree. It will probably disturb urban America if and when urban America gets around to considering it: "It is time to realize that most modern war is guerrilla in character." And what Wingate practiced in Burma was, as Ogburn observed, "irregular warfare of the kind known in America as Indian-fighting." We may have forgotten how to do it. Others have not.

Wingate was a ruthless man. So, in a coiled-spring way, are the military leaders of Israel. It is remarkable how their execution of war sometimes resembles that of the German Wehrmacht. However uncomfortable the comparison may be to the survivors of Nazi mass killing, the parallel exists. There is more of Heinz Guderian and Erwin Rommel (primarily German soldiers and patriots, not Nazi politicians) in Israel's 1956 Suez and 1967 June War successes than there is of Montgomery and his British Eighth Army officers. Yet it was in the desert army that General Moshe Dayan and his colleagues learned their trade. The Jews took their courses in war with Britain but studied post-graduately on Rommel's texts, updated.

The military success—and thus the survival—of Israel is built on foundations which would repel all those scholarly or mercantile Jews whose few grandchildren survived Hitler's mass death and Russian pogroms. The survivors formed a state in which prestige in service and patriotism are the highest motivations. Remembering the price of non-resistance to oppression, they have taken a positive stance astride what they feel is their land. They are not just groping for survival in some scared way. Historically they may be right or they may be wrong, but they assert their right to exist with restrained armed force. Unleashed three times (at this writing) in 20 years, their forces have repeatedly humiliated the Arabs who tried to tear into Israel from all directions.

Jac Weller, a writer on military history and small-arms war, said in the February 1968 *American Rifleman* that paramilitary training for adolescents is a main prop of the Israeli system. Israel has an excellent military reserve, perhaps the world's best. It has first-class weapons for most applications. Certainly its small arms are first-rate. The Israeli system emphasizes—and results show—skilled marksmanship with all weapons. Israelis fight well at night, something United States troops have not always done the last few generations. Israel's troops are physically durable and mentally prepared, as Robert Henriques' Suez visit and Weller's most recent tour indicate.

A sizable part of Israel lives in fortified villages, on or near the hostile Arab frontiers (although some of this was changed by the June War victory and subsequent extending of boundaries). The Weller article reads like a description of some Southwestern United States frontier outpost of the 1880's, transported into our time. "Every home in these exposed villages is stocked with arms, ammunition, and reserves of food and other essentials." Middle-aged men and boys go on patrols and fight. Girls as well as boys receive small-arms training in paramilitary groups. In their 30-month national-service stint, all Israelis learn more about small arms, especially the Uzi submachine gun (developed by an Israeli army officer) and one or another of the various rifles, plus how to handle heavier weapons. Israel doesn't accept failure to qualify with weapons; rejectees are put back through the courses until there is satisfactory completion. The rifle training program is related to the United States Army's Trainfire idea; this concept was devised by an Idaho civilian rifleman, Howard Sarvis, and adopted by the Department of the Army under the Eisenhower administration. Critics of civilian marksmanship kindly note. (Canada also uses a form of Trainfire.)

The basic Israeli rifle is the Belgian Fabrique Nationale, a very successful weapon. Most English-speaking countries have adopted it although the FN failed American tests that led to our adoption of our own M14 rifle. Like virtually all English-speaking armies, Israel uses the 7.62mm. NATO cartridge in its FN. Its Uzi burp gun employs the 9mm. Parabellum or Luger round, which is nearly the universal pistol and submachine gun cartridge of our time. There are still some bolt-action Mauser and other manually operated rifles around, but these are being phased out of regular troop issue. Israel now uses handguns in 9mm. or .38 caliber. It copied the American Smith & Wesson revolver and adapted it to the rimless 9mm. round in the same way the United States adapted revolvers to fire the .45 semi-automatic pistol load in 1917–18. Israel also uses 9mm. semi-automatic pistols. Its machine gun, Weller reported, is of the FN type preferred by Canada. Since we are, in this book, primarily concerned with weapons relating to individual marksmen and militia, heavier ordnance—heavy machine guns, recoilless rifles, bazookas, and so forth, not commonly associated with individual marksmanship—will not be considered.

In the fortified villages' militia formations, war-surplus guns are the standard. There are old British Lee-Enfield .303 rifles, British 9mm. Sten submachine guns, .303-cal. Bren light-automatic rifles, .455 and .380 British service revolvers. German light machine guns and Mauser rifles in 7.92mm. caliber are also used. The Israeli Defense Force is probably the most thoroughly trained army in the world, thanks mainly to its reserve system. It offers a distinct contrast to the reserves of most nations which, as Weller said, tend to be sedentary, poorly organized, and sometimes exist chiefly on paper.

Weller has studied, visited, and written about the armies of most of the free world. With the exception of a very few peers such as S. L. A. Marshall, Weller is probably the most authoritative writing critic around. On small arms, he may be our most astute critic.

Switzerland has had a small arms-emphasizing militia program for hundreds of years. The quality of its weapons training and weapons is excellent. The nation has 650,000 shooters and gun owners, which according to Frank McGuire's December 1966 *Rifleman* article equals 11 percent of the population. It is probable that only the United States, Canada, and perhaps Israel have as high an incidence of gun ownership.

The Swiss militia is fully armed, with arms kept at home. Issue weapons include submachine guns, automatic rifles, bolt-action carbines (for older reservists), and pistols. Ammunition is issued to all reserve troops to be kept stored at home. Through gun clubs, citizens are encouraged to own and shoot guns and militiamen are urged to buy extra ammunition—the price is kept low—and to practice with their issue weapons. Yet Switzerland has a low crime rate. Most violence there is committed by foreigners, like Arab Nationalists and French extremists during the Algerian war. Both were jousting for new arms from the Swiss and caused Swiss police trouble. They were arrested and jailed with majestic impartiality, however. Switzerland has three ethnic groups, German, French, and Italian. They get along well, govern themselves at the local level in most instances. Swiss gun policy is based on (a) familiarity with weapons as a duty and heritage, (b) respect for law, and (c) severe penalties for violations—not on the curtailment of personal freedom for the law-abiding. One kind or another of military obligation claims most Swiss males aged 20 to 50.

Handguns in Switzerland are licensed but licensing is reasonable. There is no red tape in the purchase of rifles or shotguns. When service models are changed, the obsolescent model is made available to the public. This is like the former DCM policy in the United States which has caused so many irrational alarms and which has been curbed by the political arm of the Defense Department for purely political reasons that might translate into cheap panic.

Neither Australia nor New Zealand has good militia programs, but both have recently instituted forms of national service. Gun clubs may be tied to citizen marksmanship programs in most but not all areas. Both nations were jarred by Indonesian super-hero posturing during the Sukarno regime. Sukarno, much like Egypt's Nasser, had boundless gall and a big population (100 million), but fortunately for everyone else, a pathetic army (like Nasser). But the population of Australia, 12 million, and New Zealand, 2.7 million, would be severely menaced if some Sukarno- or Nasser-like figure again acceded to command in Jakarta. Australia is supposed to have upwards of 30,000 troops, New Zealand about one-fifth of that number. The fighting men of both Down Under nations won proud spurs in the two world wars and various free-world brushfire efforts since. Both have made significant contributions in men and blood to the swampy business of combatting Asian Communism. Both have developed advanced training and theory on guerrilla war. The late (Australian) Major Peter Badcoe's admonition to Americans on Vietnam is cited elsewhere in this book.

Badcoe and his colleagues have the credentials to advise anyone on the subject of developing jungle-war techniques. Some Aussies have participated in half a dozen bush wars since 1940. Both Anzac nations expect to fight in jungle-type habitat. Australian troops fought one of the less publicized and filthiest campaigns in World War Two in New Guinea. It was in a habitat where United States Army forces incurred a worrisome rate of psychological and physical breakdowns. More than one well-starred United States general was sent hustling up from Australia to find out what the hell had gone wrong. But the answer wasn't in New Guinea. It was somewhere back along the line between a guns-are-bad childhood training and flabby military training. In many cases the United States Army did not train its men for the Pacific war the way Marines did.

Australian small arms include the FN semi-automatic rifle and 9mm. burp gun, most of the latter home-designed and manufactured. Marksmanship and the nuts and bolts techniques of ground war, especially jungle war, are at high premium. A drawback is a welter of sometimes confusing gun laws that could work a severe hardship on sparsely populated Australia if invaded by one of the Asian population masses. The *lebensraum* (living space) idea is captivating to several Asian governments; most are not at all opposed to conquest if it can be gotten away with. An armed citizenry would be a distinct asset in the exposed position Australia holds in the Pacific.

The same is true for New Zealand. But New Zealand has less urbanization and a high incidence of hunters, a military advantage. There is a problem of overpopulation by deer. Hunting is directly encouraged. Handgun ownership is almost nil except for officials, though revolvers with barrels longer than 12 inches are allowed. New Zealand's military small arms are about like Australia's, and its strategic and tactical ideas follow the same pattern. Marksmanship, not unaimed fire at unseen objects, is a key to rifle training, Weller notes in the *Rifleman* for September 1966. Capability with personal weapons and patrolling are the main goals for infantry.

Norway is a nation which to a strong degree has absorbed what it learned from German occupation in 1940–45. It lived five years under a police-state regime. Today the Norwegian home guard is split into small, fluid units intended to fight dispersed as guerrilla forces in event of foreign invasion or nuclear attack. Few centralized files are kept on this. It would be difficult now for an invader to identify and corral potential resistance fighters as the Germans did in 1940. The Nazis in 1940 rapidly overran a poorly armed nation, then used central gun-registration files to disarm citizens who could otherwise have fought back by dispersing into remote areas and conducting guerrilla operations. The Allies expended great effort to rearm that part of Norway's population which could operate as an underground. There was a certain reward— attrition on German forces. This also paid off in Yugoslavia,

France, and most other countries Germany had invaded. People who scoff now at the concept of an armed population resisting aggression or tyranny need only look at recent history.

After the war, Norwegians wished to keep guns and did so, frustrating the predictable social-service desires of some policemen to round up all guns. Scandinavian writer Nils Kvale reported in the *American Rifleman* for July 1966 that gun control measures were defied as long as they were severe. Laws were loosened to meet public demand, and Norway is now in a position to take its toll of any massive invasion in as realistic a way as a small nation can. Its home guard and related programs are probably not as streamlined as neighboring Sweden's (the two nations have the precarious mutual bad fortune to be near the Soviet Union). Norway's program is that of a less industrialized nation.

Sweden has a well-armed militia program. It has gone deeply and widely underground in providing for facilities to keep the nation alive in event of nuclear war. It might thus become one of the few technologically advanced nations to survive such a war. There is wide interest in target shooting and hunting among its citizenry. A few years ago, Sweden, with its seven million people, had a gun club enrollment of 300,000. The reloading of ammunition, not widely followed in most of Europe, is encouraged in Sweden. The Swedish service cartridge, the 6.5 x 55mm. was changed from Berdan to Boxer-type priming so that it could be more easily reloaded by civilian and military marksmen. The Swedish home guard has modern weapons, at least compared to most other militia organizations. Periodic militia maneuvers are held.

Sweden is aware that it almost fell prey to both German and Allied seizure during the Second World War. Norway was grabbed by Germany in April 1940, just ahead of a British try at the same thing. Both nations sought to deny the other the advantages of Norway's strategic position on their flanks. Sweden's traffic in iron ore with Nazi Germany was a goad to the British government. Britain lacked the force to ram through the Baltic and stop the traffic with naval forces. But the British government, in mounting its expedition to seize certain parts of the Norwegian coast, originally instructed its commanders to proceed over into the Swedish iron-ore fields at Gullivare and ore-shipping area around Lulea and deny them to German use. This would have been a violation of both Norwegian and Swedish neutrality. The Germans beat the British to Norway and had no reason to imperil Sweden as long as Swedish ore was forthcoming.

Kvale, a ballistician as well as firearms expert, pretty well sums up the feelings of many Scandinavians who recall Norway's peril. He called it a "doubtful good" to have all citizens' guns registered. The Nazi experience taught a lesson many peaceful Scandinavians have not disregarded, at least not as thoroughly as most other Western nations have. Finland was invaded and stripped of some of its territory by the Soviet Union in 1939–40, and Denmark was overwhelmed by Germany in a few hours at the same time Norway was subdued.

Canada, according to Weller's June 1964 *Rifleman* treatment, may have the free world's most mobile military forces. More recently it has moved toward unifying its forces into one central service. The new Canadian government intends to get most Canadian overseas forces back home, partly for reasons of economy and partly to concentrate the defensive effort in Canada's own back yard. The premise is that if and when Canada fights it will be over the Arctic or at least in the Far North. Canada has a smallish but usually good reserve behind its forces. Canadians fought very well in Europe in World Wars One and Two, and in Korea. A lot of Canadians still use small arms, especially shoulder weapons (handguns are kept and used under license). The basic Canadian military small arms are the FN 7.62mm. rifle and the 9mm. burp gun. A few handguns of 9mm. caliber are issued to the military. This is about the same situation as that prevailing in Australia and New Zealand.

Canadian small-arms training stresses personal skills with a version of our Trainfire, using silhouette targets. Canadians have not bothered with developing guerrilla-war capacity but operate on what Weller calls a "prepare-for-the-worst" approach. This means war in or near Canadian territory. Post-nuclear devastation has preoccupied much Canadian thinking. Much of the country is flat and lends itself to mobile war. If the Canadians haven't prepared for guerrilla war, there is still the World War Two lesson of General Yamashita's Japanese troops in Malaya. Well-trained and resolute troops can adapt and fight well anywhere. Yamashita's troops did so well that for years afterward British sources insisted they had been specially trained for jungle war. Yamashita's biographer says not.

Canada gets "a high percentage of recruits who shoot rifles well before they join the army," Weller wrote. "Officers and men . . . are fine physically and mentally . . . superbly trained and well-equipped for the type of war they are most likely to fight." If gun ownership remains popular and unhampered by excessive regulations, Canada will have a large number of potential guerrilla fighters to augment regular forces. Its population, now 20 million, has always provided a high number of qualified riflemen. American imperial aspirations in 1812–15 were thwarted many times by outnumbered but sharpshooting Canadian militiamen, stiffened by a few British regulars. The same kind of troops left their mark on Germans in both World Wars.

In surveying the Indian Army in the June 1969 *Rifleman*, Weller reported a distinct emphasis on riflemanship. "Every recruit learns every detail of the new Indian service rifle"— the FN. He is also thoroughly grounded in the old British Short Magazine Lee-Enfield bolt-action rifle. "An Indian infantryman is truly a rifleman in more than just name," Weller observed with some surprise.

This Indian Army, although saddled with a politico-religious maze that renders a large part of the nation hostile to or unavailable for military duty, managed to fight China to an approximate standstill in 1962 and "definitely beat the Pakistanis in 1965,"

Weller remarks. Perhaps his evaluation of India's success against China is optimistic, but it would be fair to say that India fought China under incredible disadvantages and managed to survive with its military and national integrity.

The Indian Army training and tactical mentality is set against that favorite ploy of the anti-gun confreres, wild spraying with fully automatic fire. "They (the Indian Army leaders) know all about the capability of the United States M14 and M16 and the Communist AK47 to fire bursts, but they do not want this type of firepower in their army," Weller said.

The Indian Army has borrowed some United States "trainfire" schooling but also insists on the old hold-and-squeeze instruction which helped British regulars mow Germans down in 1914—and for which, under most circumstances, no better substitute method has yet been devised. "The NCOs who conduct this instruction give careful individual attention to each man" and "they know how to shoot and how to teach others."

Weller rather succinctly said, "Riflemen do not fire wildly." Moreover, "A rifle company can carry all it needs to live and fight for 10 days. If they do get in a jam, they rely on themselves to get out of it. They have not become accustomed to massive artillery and tactical air support at their level."

The Indian Army, despite unfavorable conditions both politically (in a pacifist-ridden country) and geographically (it must fight anywhere from sea-level tropic humidity to almost 20,000 feet along the Chinese border), is the fourth largest in the world and inherits much of the richness of the British Army tradition (Weller remarked that "Indian officers resemble more closely than I thought possible those of the British Army"), and they seem to have made efforts to retain the more valuable military concepts the British left behind. Their sincere application of small arms and disdain for sophisticated tactical ways-out are worthy of study.

None of the ideas sketched in this chapter are necessarily just right for the United States. A huge nation cannot realistically maintain in peace the all-out preparedness Israel does around the clock. But it can do much better than it does, for what are I hope by now rather clear reasons of self-interest. And this self-interest can be tempered with honest altruism, for if the United States were to disappear, almost all of the still politically free world would go with it, in months, days, or hours.

As Chapter 2 and other parts of this book show, Israel maintains its own deterrent against ganged-up Arab ambitions. But Israel's deterrent against the Arabs' great friend the Soviet Union is the United States. Thus it is very difficult to reconcile the understandable pro-Israel stance of many Americans, Jewish and others, with their illogical fear of a broadened and more effective American defense plan, one providing for a responsible militia and nuclear protection and other devices that would help insure survival of this country and its friends. Perhaps the dual standard exists because Israel's appeal to Americans is both emotional and logical, while thus far too many Americans have thought of their own national survival in no terms at all. Right now our entire national attitude reads like something out of late Gibbon—*very* late Gibbon.

If the Czechs in the summer of 1968 had chosen to resist the U.S.S.R.'s invasion, what might have happened? Certainly Russia could not have used nuclear weapons in virtually its own and its allies' front yard. Enormous Russian superiority in conventional weapons and manpower would have cleared or reduced the cities, but resistance could have continued in the countryside—especially in the mountains. Would world opinion, especially that of neighbors or sympathizers in West Germany or Yugoslavia, have rallied to the Czechs? It might. And if the Czech people had been armed, rather than ruthlessly disarmed in the classic style of all totalitarian states, resistance could have developed.

How many satellite Red-bloc troops might have been perverted by this concept of a small nation trying to free itself? Would the East German or Hungarian or Polish armies—all susceptible to

Western ties and ideas—have stayed staunch? Would the Russian troops themselves have been infected?

This, after all, was an example of a state—somewhat free—trying to squirm out of the grasp of a monolithic totalitarian giant. It was a movement led largely by the young, intellectuals, and laboring people. These were the textbook apostles of Communism—trying to get rid of it.

Would a rifle-armed Czech nation have managed to stay alive until help formed? Perhaps. Disarmed as the Czechs were, we'll never know. It is true that history never repeats itself in precise detail—the Czechs of 1968 were not the Hungarian rebels of 1956. But another great opportunity, like 1956, has gone forever.

Nothing shows the failures of a militia rushing to war with poor or no small-arms training better than the Spanish Civil War (1936–39). As Hugh Thomas's *The Spanish Civil War* (New York and Evanston: Harper & Row) showed, one of the Republicans' great problems was the sudden arming of thousands of inexpert irregulars. Almost from the outset, the rebels—who went on to win and form a right-wing state under General Francisco Franco—counted on marksmanship as one of their assets. They were outnumbered throughout the war and on almost every front. But the sharpshooting Foreign Legionnaires, Moorish regulars, Navarrese militiamen, and young Falangists who, along with the formidable Civil Guard, comprised the hard core of Franco's armies consistently outperformed their Loyalist foes with rifles. Rifle fire almost unquestionably helped avert capture of the Nationalist Alcazar in Toledo—"alarmingly good shots" within the historic old fortress prolonged the resistance into an epic one. It made a singular contribution to the Nationalist propaganda at a crucial time in the war's early, unfolding stage. The garrison was mixed—Falangists (members of the dominant right-wing party), regular troops, cadets, Civil Guard. All, or most, evidently shot well.

The Loyalists helped create their own dilemma. At the beginning of hostilities in July 1936 Loyalist (Republican) militiamen demanded to be armed. While Franco and his Italo-German allies and auxiliaries airlifted dedicated pro-Nationalist troops across from Spanish Morocco, the Loyalist government in Madrid caviled at arming the masses of trade-union militia of all philosophies on the political left. Such militia, on which the Republic almost immediately came to depend for its existence—in spite of massive Soviet aid—was miserably untrained. When it was too late—with the enemy growing in strength moment by moment—confused, futile efforts were initiated to train the militiamen. Arms were passed out. As Thomas implies, if the arms had been passed out even one day earlier, there was a chance the Nationalists might have been forestalled—headed off before their widespread rising gained momentum. A one-day delay may well have spelled the eventual doom of the besieged Spanish Republic (there has been interminable arguing about the two causes, Nationalist and Republican; the concern here is that the procrastination and lack of training involving militia forces were probably extremely costly to the Republic whatever its good or bad points before the Reds took complete control).

The proletarian Loyalist militia—in some ways these troops would not be unlike urban masses abruptly raised to defend the United States—was so inept with weapons that newspaper correspondents in or near Madrid were besought to help train them with small arms. This was done to a limited extent. (One wonders what would happen to a militia forced to depend for small-arms schooling on newspaper or TV reporters of the 1960–1970 breed; those of the Spanish Civil War era had served in sterner schools and were perhaps somewhat more elemental and less neutralist —albeit all on one side—than the sincere, bespectacled, academic gentlemen who grace our fourth estate today.)

The Loyalists as an army never did learn to shoot well. Probably some of the International Brigades were exceptions to this, although even most of those were Europeans from big cities—some with World War One or revolutionary experience (Thomas says few of the Americans fighting for the Republic had prior military exposure) or both. The typical Loyalist militia has "no opportunities for rifle practice and no rifles for such training" (almost all rifles were drastically needed up front, not in replacement depots). This shortcoming helped lead to defeat on all fronts in the summer and fall of 1936 when so much was in the balance. "Bad marksmanship [on the part of the Loyalists] continued to be the rule." It was a fatal flaw.

✳

Chapter 6

Hunting

✳ ✳ ✳ ✳ ✳

"Most game cannot be stockpiled, and a majority of each high-turnover species won't live a year whether hunted or not."—Grits Gresham, veteran conservationist

THE MAINSTAY OF MOST OF THE UNITED STATES WILDLIFE MANagement and research programs is firearms hunting by the general public. Revenues from it produce the wildlife management, research experimentation, and restocking that provide enjoyment for all users—not just hunters' but naturalists' interests and observations, research in ecology and habitat, zoological and biographical studies, and just plain nature watching.

If firearms hunting were seriously crippled, there would have to be drastic—and the word is not an exaggeration—revisions in the wildlife management planning and operations of all 50 states as well as within the management programs of the Departments of Interior and Agriculture.

The lack of popular response to archery hunting has shown that hunting in forms other than by firearm simply does not attract the interest and participation that are mandatory for successful wildlife management.

Non-hunting naturalists talk a good game. But they do not produce the funds to keep programs moving. The relative failure of the federal government's special $7 annual recreational-facilities visitor fee is one indication. Another is the failure of most fund-gathering campaigns to back wildlife management, aside from a few localized efforts to buy small acreages for refuges. But conservationists are discovering that most refuges are unproductive and not serving desired purposes. Many states are reopening refuges to limited general use, including hunting.

Robert Ruark, whose writings on African hunting, World War Two, and his hunting-fishing Carolina seacoast boyhood won worldwide acclaim, had sparse charity for the non-hunting outdoors breed—with particular disdain for the non-hunting camera fan in Africa:

"You can hunt or you can take pictures, but you cannot hunt *and* take pictures . . . . The camera bugs are always fretting about the light and trying to maneuver closer so that the animal will be squared off just so for the lens framing. They like to stir up the animals and always they want to get a little bit closer and wind up by spooking the whole neighborhood . . . . Then they always brag about how they are so stinking humane, they wouldn't think of killing one of the lovely beasties that God made so beautiful, and they don't see how a hunter can be so horrid as to shoot something when all they want to do is imprison its beauty on film. This is of course a lot of crap," Ruark concluded in his *Horn of the Hunter* (Fawcett World Library, 1952–53).

"Every time some brave camera hunter drags you into the living room after dinner for two tedious hours of blinking at his amateur Africa film, you can reflect that the rhino which charges directly at you from the screen did not stop charging after the shutter stopped. You cannot say to a rhino: 'Knock off, bud, your picture's took and you don't have to charge any more.' Some poor, harassed professional, standing affrightedly flat-footed while the camera hound runs, has to shoot the poor old faro as he comes barreling on, whether he's any good or not as a trophy."

Ruark emphasizes: "This applies to any dangerous game that gets itself annoyed into charging for the selfish benefit of the camera. The self-admittedly humane Martin Johnsons killed more game than rinderpest in getting their pictures, and the animals were slaughtered after deliberate incitement to nervousness and a final charge. Some black boys got killed, too . . . ."

Harry Selby, Ruark's white hunter in the story cited here, "spat and curled his lip" about camera "hunters": One group "went out without a professional and they deliberately gut-shot a lion, wounding him just enough to make him sick and nasty. . . . Going to make an epic, and didn't mind deliberately wounding the animal to do it," the hunter said. "Some natives chanced by . . . (and) found the two camera blokes ripped into ribbons and dead as mutton. Lion was dead a bit farther on, but his mouth was bloody and his claws were full of—things," Selby epitaphed with some gusto. "I'm never going on another one of those Hollywood picture safaris, where they want you to rile up the elephants for day after day, and finally you have to shoot some old cow that gets nervous, splits off from the herd, and chases the cameraman."

Selby, who at last report was still in business in now native-ruled East Africa, fairly well summarized the view of the hunter in the same exchange with Ruark: "I can understand killing something you want so badly that you are willing to go to weeks of trouble and great expense to collect it, so that you will have it and enjoy it and remember it all your life."

Ruark agreed in a more expansive and expressive way. "The hunter's horn sounds early for some. . . . For some unfortunates, prisoned by city sidewalks and sentenced to a cement jungle more horrifying than anything to be found in Tanganyika, the horn of the hunter never winds at all. But deep in the guts of most men is buried the involuntary response to the hunter's horn, a prickle of the nape hairs, an acceleration of the pulse, an atavistic memory of his fathers, who killed first with stone, and then with club and then with spear, and then with bow, and then with gun, and finally with formulae. How meek the man is of no importance; somewhere in the pigeon chest of the clerk is still the vestigial remnant of the hunter's heart; somewhere in his nostrils the half-forgotten smell of blood."

The description may upset some of our latterday civilized men who profess to find great sin in taking game with weapons—but who find all kind of excuses for human-to-human violence provided it is committed upon the comfortable by the allegedly underprivileged (and preferably done in gang assaults with knives, chains, tire tools, bats, or the like). But it is also quite true, and it will go so far toward explaining why a National Wildlife Federation report discovered that only six percent of the American public actually prefers living in a large city.

The game and fish (conservation) agencies of the 50 states have vigorously opposed most federal and the more restrictive state firearms-control proposals. They feel these are unfair, unwise, and fail to produce the desired results. Certainly evidence cited in other parts of this book amply covers that field.

There is no particular shortage of most species of wildlife in the United States today. Most species that are hunted are either hunted under controls that assure wisely maintained populations or are in populations so large that firearms hunting has only a minor effect on numbers. This last is generally true of upland game—small game with a high population turnover and reproduction rate. In some parts of the United States, big game is as well off. In others, certain species can be hunted only under some degree of control.

Overpopulation, wildlife conservationists have discovered in the last 40 years, can be a much more lethal enemy of wildlife than hunting. A second and extremely dangerous factor is habitat destruction. The constant, gradual encroachment of urban America on wild lands and on farm lands—all game cover in one way or another—is a bigger menace than hunting.

It has been established by surveys in virtually every state that habitat destruction and excessive populations of wildlife are to some extent controllable. Much can be done with overpopulation; the main tool is hunting. Weather, food conditions, disease, and predation decree that a certain percentage of any species will not survive; consequently, the use of sport hunting to harvest the approximate percentage which these conditions will not kill provides controls, recreational hunting for a large segment of the population, and revenues for future programs.

Not nearly as much control is possible on habitat destruction. People cannot be managed in the way wildlife is. Hunting as an aid to deterring wildlife overpopulation helps reduce habitat loss by keeping ranges in better shape. But in this respect hunting is not as efficient a tool as it is with overpopulation itself. This has led to the great problem facing hunters in the next generation or two: *space* to hunt in. There are more people, more hunters, more persons interested in a growing diversification of outdoor interests. Thus, while there is more game than ever before in our history, there are also more problems connected with regulating the conditions under which it is to be hunted.

The depressed or ruined areas of the United States—some parts of Appalachia, certain sections of the Great Plains states, the more isolated parts of the Deep South and Far North—probably offer better hunting with fewer trespass, danger, or other "people" problems than in 1920 or 1930. But in much of the United States, notably fast-growth states like California, Arizona, Florida, and Texas, hunting poses essentially human problems. Land values are up, more people are buying land, many Western states comprise primarily publicly administered lands which are not for sale. In the East, more city dwellers are purchasing rural land as retreats. Swamps and marshes—ideal waterfowl and related habitat—are being drained for housing or agricultural development. The sum of all this is that diverse pressures mount and grow more competitive daily on both private and public lands. All this entails deep thought, careful planning, and reasonable attitudes from all of the users of wildlife and public lands.

Aside from license revenues, the chief source of funds for wildlife management consists of Pittman-Robertson Federal Aid in Wildlife Restoration Act funds. Pittman-Robertson provides an 11 percent excise tax on sporting firearms and ammunition, which is refunded to the states in ratio to the number of hunting license buyers. This is a valuable aid to many states and of some consequence at least for almost all. Figures from these sources and other state information indicate that there are between 17 and 20 million hunters in the United States, many of them not countable because they are minors or other classes of persons entitled to hunt without licenses. Thus about one American in every ten hunts to some extent. Providing space to hunt is accentuated when it's considered that this is a radical rise in numbers since World War Two and it will undoubtedly grow bigger; the President's Outdoor Recreation Resources Review Commission of the early 1960's found that many more citizens would hunt if they had a better opportunity—quicker travel time or better communications or transportation.

Some sources, not too well tuned in to reality, think hunting is becoming a sport of the past. But trends and statistics don't bear this out. Dr. Ira N. Gabrielson, President of the Wildlife Management Institute, has pointed out that hunting of some species— deer, notably—is on the rise because deer herds are increasing. So are most other big game herds. Gabrielson's chief deputy, C. R. Gutermuth, has written that space, not game, will provide the chief difficulty for hunting in the future. "If the future for shotgunner (declining habitat for small game) appears spotty, that of the big-game hunter and rifleman was never brighter," Gabrielson wrote in a May 1960 *American Rifleman* article.

Gutermuth (also in the *Rifleman*) said, "What might be called the modern phase of American hunting began in 1933, when Aldo Leopold published his book *Game Management*, and brought into existence an entirely new approach toward wildlife management." Leopold argued—and most trained conservationists have agreed— that if environment or habitat is not suitable, stocking or husbanding wildlife is useless. "The way to increase wild creatures is to expand the habitat," Gutermuth quoted Leopold, who is now widely regarded as the architect of *modern* United States game conservation.

Leopold's then-radical theories fairly well erased the old protec-

tionist concept that all one had to do to rebuild wildlife populations was to curtail hunting or slow it down—usually taking only
males of each species.

Experiments in many states have proven Leopold right, although there is still opposition. In states where there has been
unusual resistance to Leopold's theories big game herds have
failed to progress in the way they have in other states. In other
words, states which accept the more flexible standards of modern
management seem to be those with the healthiest and best-distributed herds and flocks.

Most critics of hunting share two characteristics: they try to say
they represent all non-hunting outdoor people, which is open to
vigorous challenge, and they are regarded as uninformed and uneducated Johnny-come-latelys by conservationists who have been
studying and dealing with the problem for a generation or so.
There are almost no critics of Leopold's theories within the leadership or ranks of technically educated wildlife managers, scientists, and the like. Hunters and their technical colleagues within
the conservation departments have been fighting for intelligent
management practices for two or three generations (some, like the
Boone and Crockett Club, for much longer than that). Almost all
of the critics of modern wildlife management—those who condemn
hunting—are individuals with no formal training in conservation.
They are much more likely to be literary people (Joseph Wood
Krutch) or entertainers (Dick Cavett) or pure sentimentalists
(Cleveland Amory). These people fail to realize the basic management fact that surpluses of wildlife on any habitat will die off
or otherwise disappear due to combinations of natural factors,
hunted or not; what the hunter does is harvest the surplus which
the range could not carry over into another season or year. Each
range has a certain carrying capacity; this varies with many factors,
but at each time of the year there is a capacity beyond which
populations do not go—for long. The hunter in effect achieves his
return for his investment in wholesale support of wildlife programs by helping remove the surplus. Anyone who looked at the

economies of some states or regions of the United States might discern certain parallels concerning *human* populations, as a matter of fact.

Modern conservation departments virtually make sure, by following policies developed from and since Leopold's pioneer treatment, that excessive harvesting will not result. "We are not in business to put ourselves out of business," conservation leaders say when asked about hunt quotas, bag limits, seasons' lengths, and other flexible elements. And most are correct, because state conservation employees today to an increasing extent must be graduates of four- or five-year courses in wildlife management or other related courses. The era of somebody's political henchman or the party chairman's cousin getting a game warden job is very nearly ended everywhere. Today's game wardens, field biologists, and research personnel know far more about their subject than their critics.

Hunters and conservation agencies have not halted at just maintaining or increasing inherited populations. They've reached out for exotic species and in some cases have succeeded in introducing these. The pheasant is the outstanding example, although there are very many others. In some states, a sizable percentage of the huntable wildlife has been introduced from some other area or even other country. Restocking thinned-out or nearly extinct native populations has been significant, too.

Most of the game populations which did become extinct in the 1800's we now know were not simply shot out. There were other factors. Certainly sport hunting was not significant. Market hunting was. So was the wholesale attrition of habitat. The buffalo all but disappeared from the Great Plains because of market hunting *plus* the introduction of the range cattle industry. Beef competed for grazing with buffalo. Ranchers, understandably from their viewpoint, were interested in producing more beef; ranchers had friends in Washington who heeded their complaints. The Indians were the buffalo's only friends, and the War Department had decreed the only way to corral and control hostile, mobile plains tribes was to remove their commissary—the buffalo. The War Department gave full support to the extermination of the buffalo. In a Congress obsessed by economy, it was a far cheaper solution than hiring more troops to chase and punish rambunctious Indians.

When the Texas legislature discussed institution of controls over buffalo hunting, the War Department almost erupted, and it had its way to a great degree. Between farming, ranching, market-hunting on an unprecedented scale, and the benevolent instigation of the War Department, nothing could have saved the buffalo. Sport hunting, while even it required some controls, had a relatively small effect. It never had a chance. This was and remains the classic example of factors ganging up to expedite a species' destruction. Perversely, only the Army really benefited. The cattleman to a great extent had to yield his arbitrary but illegal hold on the public domain to the farmer. A generation later, nature blew most of the farmers somewhere else. Much of the Plains today is reverting to grassland, although it will never return to the fine original tough grass that marked it for thousands of years. The few buffalo surviving are in state parks or small private herds. There is some very limited public hunting of them in a few states. The only way buffalo could ever stage a massive comeback would be for the white man and his domestic stock to disappear from the Plains, to leaving them as free and open as before he reached them. While this appeals to Red Power extremists, it is improbable.

Gutermuth well described the modern hunter as a paradox. "He comes from no particular walk of life. . . . The next hunter you meet in a field may be a bank president or a day laborer, a shop clerk or corporation executive. He feels that he has a proprietary interest in the game he hunts, and a moral responsibility for its perpetuation. . . . He considers himself a shareholder in a state game agency." The average American hunter now is "honest, law-abiding, and concerned over the future of his favorite sport, and whenever he can be shown a clear need, he is willing to make sacrifices to assure its continuation," Gutermuth added.

Unlike the game in many parts of Europe, American game belongs to the public; in the United States, the ownership of game is vested in the commonwealth. This has always been so and is perhaps the main reason why hunting is so widely popular here; in much of Europe, it is limited to the privileged few. In most of free Europe, hunting is regulated by landowners, who use both hired help and shooting friends to control herds and flocks. In the Communist nations, there is some public hunting but the more desirable shooting is restricted to party dignitaries. Gun ownership is politically connected in the Red world. A good Communist may own rifles and other arms. A non-Party type has a hard time even keeping a shotgun. In Britain, hunting tends to be socioeconomically based; the better your class connections, the easier to hunt or own guns, or both.

In Communist China the trend seems to be for the people to hunt each other.

No state has more complex population-recreation problems than California. Plenty of other states have more game; a few have more area. But no other has as many people; while the population of California has grown 210 percent the past 20 years, its land area obviously has remained static. California, unlike many states, has subscribed to the message of the President's Outdoor Recreation Resources Review Commission Report—putting a premium on much more diverse recreational spending and planning, including great stress and care for the "simple pleasures," such as walking, car-cruising, and picnicking. Many conservationists say the ORRRC Report is in error (descriptions range from "mistaken" or "poorly balanced" to "ridiculous"). But even with its acceptance of the report's thrust, California continues to plan and provide for hunting and fishing as the two staple outdoor recreations. The California Fish and Wildlife Plan Board, which always plans for the long-haul, made this clear in a 1966 report.

Members of the planning board were Dr. A. Starker Leopold, Professor of Zoology at the University of California at Berkeley— Aldo Leopold's son; Thomas L. Kimball, Executive Director of the National Wildlife Federation, Washington, D.C.; Dr. M. B. Schaefer, Director, Institute of Marine Resources, University of California, La Jolla; Richard H. Stroud, Executive Vice President, Sport Fishing Institute, Washington, D.C.; and Carl W. Buchheister, President, National Audubon Society, New York City.

The presence of an Audubon Society leader of long standing on the five-man board is interesting. Cleveland Amory and other critics of hunting have sought to make Americans believe that the society and most other non-hunting conservation bodies violently dislike or disagree with sport hunting. Buchheister's and other Audubon leaders' frequently stated positions don't support Amory. The fact is, the majority of Audubon thinking supports public sport hunting. There are areas of disagreement, but then there are also areas of disagreement within the organizations of shooting sportsmen—notably on waterfowl hunting—where opinions, research data, and other factors vary greatly.

The California board's plan vigorously endorsed continued sport hunting. The report focused on California in 1980 and beyond, with a state population of 28 million foreseen by 1980 (40 percent more people than now live in all of Canada). The plan said the goal was to "provide for varied types of fishing, hunting, and other enjoyment of the fish and wildlife resources." It also said hunting safety "demands certain amounts of space." This summed up exactly what hunting has to reckon with.

As the California Wildlife Board of Consultants said, such former criteria as bag limits and seasons no longer mean much. The wildlife is there, and post-1930 studies have shown conclusively that in most cases hunting does not deplete game numbers beyond a certain harmless or controllable point. In state after state, game that was once wholly removed from hunting has safely been reintroduced to hunting; game that was huntable only under controls has become huntable under general conditions, with most or all of the once-tight controls removed. This has worked so well, so widely, and so often that those who are familiar with it do not question it. The only challenges come from the sentimental and technically uneducated critics of hunting—people who may be very advanced or grounded in their own fields (Krutch, Amory, for example) but who know literally nothing about scientific wildlife management.]

Deer in Indiana and about three dozen other states; wild turkeys in Arizona and many other states; various species of upland game birds all over the West; antelope in half a dozen states, elk in most of the mountain West—these species offer examples of how intelligent wildlife management has brought hunting in the United States since 1900 to a point where most hunting is much better than when Puritans and Cavaliers tumbled retching and bewildered off the boats on the Atlantic seaboard. The adaptation of elk from a plains to a mountain animal in the West has been a striking feature. So has the enormous return of deer populations in Midwestern states where deer were once almost extinct. The author has hunted in or visited and written about the hunting in about one-third of the states, as well as Canada and Mexico. Even within his lifetime, improvements in game management in many of these states have been enormous.

Gabrielson wrote in the *Rifleman*, "The [deer] kill has been rising steadily for many years, and we still do not seem to have reached the peak. In most states, the deer population is still increasing." The same is true, he said, for most other big game. Antelope, elk, and wild sheep are generally expanding (in some areas of the author's knowledge, elk are literally crowding deer off high-country habitat). While some small-game shooting may be down—bobwhite quail (most Western quail species are not as much affected by habitat destruction as bobwhites have been) and pheasant are typical—it is not due to excessive taking by gunners but to changes in agriculture that have drastically affected bird habitat. Most of these changes as they affect upland game involve the new so-called "clean farming," in which game cover is erased to provide greater productiveness.

"The future for the quail or pheasant hunter, particularly those living in states where the conservation departments have been

slow in preserving open areas for their shooters, is less bright,"
Gabrielson summed up.

An even greater problem is the shrinking habitat and nagging
droughts that have seriously reduced waterfowl populations in the
last decade. This is harder to deal with. A few years of cover-res-
toration emphasis in soil conservation planning—like the Soil
Bank plan in part—might help restore upland game habitat to an
appreciable extent. But dealing with declining waterfowl is a
much more complex problem. And it is an international one—
ducks and geese generally migrate from Canada to Mexico in the
autumn, back north in the spring. Treaties with the two neighboring countries have eased but not solved all international-level
problems. The efforts of Ducks Unlimited and other major and
minor conservation groups have done much to acquire wetlands
for waterfowl breeding and nesting and to reclaim and preserve
more habitat.

But the predominant modern agriculture pattern of large, intensively cultivated single-crop farming has hurt small-game management quite seriously in the farming states (though not so much
in the ranching belt). The bobwhite quail, pheasant, and cotton-
tail rabbit—the usual "big three" of modern United States small-
game hunting—require a diversity of cover which is absent from
many specialized farms today. They throve best when the United
States was fundamentally a nation of small family farms with subsistence agriculture uppermost (curiously, so did the nation—as
Thomas Jefferson predicted it would). Offsetting the "clean farming" trend now are programs to recapture some habitat, like DU's
and similar efforts by the National Wildlife Federation. The National Rifle Association has opened up a program of hunting clubs
to assist in obtaining more lands to hunt—thus broadening its club
approach into two areas of interest where it was once mainly concerned with target-shooting groups.

Leased-land hunting, in which farmers or ranchers turn over
parts of their acreage at certain times to private parties who pay
for the privilege, is becoming increasingly important. So are game

farms or preserves, where operators sell hunting by membership, by the day, by the bag, or otherwise. These arrangements are primarily of importance in the Eastern states, the South, Texas, and California. In the mountain West, most hunting lands are part of the public domain and are managed by the federal government to provide for hunting along with other uses—grazing, lumbering, mining, and recreations.

In Texas, the Parks and Wildlife Department has to a great extent allowed—by necessity, not choice—the growth of a dual game-management plan which allows some landowners to help manage wildlife in return for leasing hunting rights to those interested in it. Most big Texas ranches are exclusively in private ownership. There is nothing in Texas like the typical Mountain West ranch in which the stockman owns only a small acreage but has leased or permit-approved grazing rights on a much bigger expanse of public land—usually National Forest or Bureau of Land Management land.

The Texas approach is vehemently criticized in the public lands states of the Mountain West. But its critics live in states where 40, 50, or 75 percent of all lands may be in federal ownership, with recreational access open to everyone for any reasonable purpose. They don't have Texas' problems. Permits or leases allowing cattlemen, sheepmen, miners, and lumber interests to use *federal* lands for some specific use do not as a rule convey the right to do anything else on such lands—certainly not the right to block access by the public.

Most huntable land between the Atlantic Coast and the eastern slopes of the Rocky Mountains is in private ownership—including the Plains states. Thus hunters, concentrated to a growing degree in big cities or megalopoleis, fan out in all directions seeking lands to hunt on. In most cases they should and do obtain permission to enter private lands and conduct themselves impeccably with respect to private property. Unfortunately a minor percentage fails to conduct itself well. It is at such individuals that most states are aiming their firearms-safety, hunter-education, and training programs, on the theory that only education can avoid a continuing reduction in private lands available to hunters. Otherwise, there would be what amounts to a landowners' rebellion; this has already appeared in some areas, and in the Eastern two-thirds of the United States it could lead to catastrophic harm to hunting and wildlife management, science, and administration.

In the public lands states of the West, most land is administered by one or another of the federal landholding agencies. The major ones are the United States Forest Service, under the Department of Agriculture, and the United States Bureau of Land Management, under the Department of the Interior. These agencies devote at least a sizable part of their land use to recreational hunting (the trend is growing in the BLM and is long-established with the Forest Service). Interior's National Parks and Monuments Service, for reasons of its own (some of them obscure and rather pathetically out of tune with the time), allows very little recreational hunting on its lands. Interior's Fish and Wildlife Service operates refuges and other programs in usually good cooperation with the various state game agencies, however—somewhat offsetting the old protectionist, hunting-is-naughty ideology of the Parks Service.

The Parks Service permits other recreational activities, but even in its growing accumulation of remote and unvisited areas does not permit sport hunting except under unusual conditions. And then reluctantly. Most other federal agencies with small holdings—the Defense Department, for example—cooperate with wildlife-management authorities and planners when they can, without damaging their own missions.

Indian tribal lands are not public lands in the full sense, even though many people mistakenly consider them so. One way to describe the status of Indian lands is that they're privately owned but often administered in some trust form—they often belong to the Indians on a tribal basis and are so operated. State game agencies normally cannot make hunting regulations for Indian lands except with the cooperation and consent of tribal officials or councils. This has raised curious constitutional and legal points, since on all non-Indian lands the public at large is considered to own wildlife—not just some specific landowning element. Cases reflecting this conflict between basic land law and special land-use and ownership laws and policies on Indian property are beginning to reach the courts in the West.

The various Western states hold lands of differing size, but in the West state land administration is seldom as efficient or as fair as either state land management in some Eastern states or federal land management generally. Pennsylvania, New York, and some other Eastern states have efficient and usually equitable state forests and parks systems (Pennsylvania's state forest system is a kind of a classic on how states can acquire public lands for diverse uses). In the West, the federal government has done most of the good land management that has been achieved. State land administration in the West frequently is lax, enforcement of basic rules is very flexible or nonexistent, and stock-raising interests can sometimes simply exercise their own authority in casual defiance of state land regulations. Overstocking state lands and denial of public access for hunting or other uses are very common practices. Police agencies fail to enforce regulations because in many areas it is locally expedient to fail. Ranchers and others using state lands can sometimes get away with practices that would cost them their grazing rights if tried on Forest or BLM lands.

The best hunting for most Western species is on Forest lands. The quality of BLM and state lands is usually poorer, although some of this offers excellent small-game hunting. There is some excellent hunting on private lands, as in the East, but in the West the hunter behavior problem is a little confused by the fact that the landholder is a lessee or permittee himself—not the owner. Relations are often poor between sportsmen and lessees or permittees on grazing, mining, or timber lands because of littering, uncared-for fires, damage to livestock or improvements, and gates left open so that stock gets into the wrong pastures. But also quite often the relationship is the landholder's fault. He is no more the owner of public lands than the recreational visitor. Many land-holders on public lands are prone to illegally deny public access by locking gates, fencing off roads, putting up illegal no-trespass signs, and otherwise bluffing away recreational users who have every right to be there. The more conscientious public administrators—the Forest Service, particularly—strive hard to correct such violations. But much of the enforcement is divided between unwilling county officials and overworked game rangers. Most Western states have found punitive practices don't work as well on either hunters or landholders as does education; overall, this approach seems to work fairly well. Statistics kept by the state game agencies and the National Rifle Association show a marked decline in hunter mistakes and accidents after firearms-safety and hunter-education courses have had time to take effect.

The probable outcome of this long-range emphasis on education is that in many or maybe all states, sooner or later, hunters will be required to satisfactorily complete firearms-safety, hunter-education training. This is now mandatory for certain age groups in many states—or for first-time hunters. It is a growing practice. It is a modified version of the rigorous, complex hunter-licensing system practiced in West Germany. Indications are that it is the best approach yet devised to insure fewer foolish or harmful hunters and more restrained, intelligent hunters. The German approach, in its Teutonic rigidity, goes too far for American tastes, but more strenuous hunting and licensing standards in the United States might be desirable.

How well training courses have succeeded in reducing accidents is demonstrated by figures from participating states. Most states provide, and some require, one kind or another of training, however minimal. The basic format is about the same. No statistical evidence is available on the reduction of vandalism caused by education, but most conservation officers say there is a considerable improvement over 1950 or 1945. According to the *American Rifleman* for June 1966, New York's hunter-casualty list declined appreciably, based on a comparison of 12-year spans, after the course was instituted, even while license sales soared. New Jersey cut its toll in half, again with a rise in the number of hunters. New York, for example, registered a 30 percent increase in hunters during the same time that there was a 35 percent drop in fatalities. Thirty-nine states and two Canadian provinces had joined the program by the end of 1966. The top results have been among young hunters—in the 12 to 18 year old category—at whom such training is primarily aimed. This is the age group where most casualties occurred prior to initiation of the training.

California, with a rise in licensed hunters between 1954 and 1964, reported a drop of 37 hunter accidents; Missouri, with a gain of 100,000 hunters in the same period, had a rise of just 5 hunter accidents, and Oregon, up by 30,000 licensed hunters, reported a decline of 13 accidents on the same comparison of years. One of the most hunting-oriented Eastern states, Pennsylvania, had a drop from 531 to 359 mishaps while hunter numbers remained around a million. Utah went from 71 accidents in 1959 down to 27 in 1963, even while the number of hunters grew by about 25,000. California, Oregon, and Utah require the program for certain groups, while in Missouri and Pennsylvania it is voluntary. The NRA cites results from most other states comparable to those shown here. British Columbia, the province in Canada which probably depends more on hunting revenues than any other, is considering initiating a form of the training.

Instruction by conservation officers, leaders in gun clubs, Scout leaders, 4H officials, policemen, servicemen, and others is vital to the course. Most instruction has been and probably will remain voluntary, without compensation except for expense outlays. Many conservation officers teach training courses, too, on their own time, after regular job hours. The bulk of the instructors tend to be those most active in sportsmen's organizations, and indeed in many states the program would simply stop without them. As it is, more competent instructors are always in demand. However, the program is considered effective and progressive by those exposed to it, and almost all thinking sportsmen find it a worthwhile alternative to unwise gun legislation—usually aimed at criminals but invariably harassing only honest citizens.

✗ Hunters and the NRA were instrumental in devising the fire-arms safety programs. These have evolved into various mixtures of gun safety in the field, knowledge of the game codes involved, first aid, survival in the field, some reasonable exposure to basic shooting skill, and the like.

Opposition to this training has come mainly from a few extremely individualistic sportsmen who feel that while it may be a good idea, requiring it is a form of government coercion or interference with private rights. It does sometimes briefly tend to lower the number of hunters, at least in certain age groups, until people adjust to the requirements. Most conservationists would be hesitant to endorse full-scale mandatory firearms-safety hunter-education training for everybody because of this. But the long-range effects might be considerably more beneficial. More good, safe, responsible hunters would be turned out—and the hazardous and incompetent hunters would be kept home until they showed capability and common sense.

✍ Put in simplest terms, sportsmen generally have done everybody a lot of good, in spite of the sad or idiotic behavior of a few. They have in many cases devised their own programs to improve wild-life for all purposes. The wetlands acquisition approach is accompanied by efforts to return more land to upland or big-game cover —benefiting everyone, including landholders and naturalists who loathe hunting and wouldn't be caught with so much as an alpen-stock in their weaponless custody.

But as non-hunting Purdue University Professor Howard Michaud said, "Only the constant, vocal, insistent pressures of hunters for places to hunt, and of fishermen for places to fish, have preserved the forests and primitive areas that have enabled nature to maintain an adequate, life-giving water table over much of the United States."

✗ *Guns Magazine* editors wrote: "Take away the forests, the primitive areas, the game habitat that result from hunter demands and are provided by hunter money—and you destroy that most basic resource of all, our underground water. Without that water, there can be no life—no wildlife, no human life."

Nor would there be wildlife management in anything like present terms. Anti-hunting naturalists who now decry a supposed shortage of wildlife would have to get out of their station wagons and go look for it on foot.

Interior Secretary Stewart L. Udall, writing in *The World of Guns*, paid high tribute to shooting sportsmen contributions to wildlife restoration through the 11 percent Pittman-Robertson tax. He said that far from selfishly trying to stop enactment of the tax (on guns and shells), representatives of the sporting arms and ammunition industry joined sportsmen as its chief supporters. "It is undoubtedly one of the most important pieces of conservation legislation that this or any other country in the world has ever known," Udall said.

In the mid-1960's when sportsmen were offered the opportunity to help remove the tax, they overwhelmingly urged its retention.

Pittman-Robertson funds have gone for habitat restoration, rebuilding large-game populations (deer, antelope, turkey, others) and transplanting exotic species experimentally to new ranges. Research, the development of new technologies to improve wildlife programs, range acquisition, establishment of refuges, the sale of waterfowl stamps—these are among many P-R projects which would not exist, or would exist in abbreviated or desiccated form, without the tax revenues on guns and shells.

The problem of improving and enlarging big-game populations and a declining or static small-game situation poses a real paradox in an urban society. The high-powered rifle is the standard weapon for hunting big game—deer, elk, bear, antelope, and so forth. Yet the high-powered rifle is also the farthest-reaching weapon, and thus is the most dangerous in or near a built-up area—not just a city or town and environs, but also in certain kinds of intensively cultivated farmlands; dairy belts like those in Wisconsin and New York are examples. More and more, hunting in such areas is being diverted from the use of big-bore rifles toward shotguns, usually with rifled slugs (to extend accuracy to a certain extent without reaching the danger range of high-powers) or buckshot.

Hatcher's Notebook, a small-arms work written by the late Major General Julian S. Hatcher, former chief of Army Ordnance, and the Sporting Arms and Ammunition Manufacturers Institute show that the maximum lethal range of the more modern high-powered rifle calibers can be 2.75 miles or even more than that in a few instances. The maximum lethal reach of the rifled slug fired from a shotgun is under a mile—usually well under it. The maximum lethal reach of buckshot is less than 600 yards. The problem is, the *accurate* range of the rifled slug on big game is usually under 100 yards, and for buckshot the accurate coverage is about half of that. Hunting with shotguns in built-up areas is thus an attempt to compromise between efficiency and safety. The high-powered rifle is usually perfectly safe—when used by competent persons—out in the more typical or rural hunting countryside with a small density of population and less intensive agriculture. There the accuracy range of the big-bore rifle—up to 400 or 500 yards for hunting purposes (or 1,000 yards or more for target shooting by really skilled riflemen)—can be utilized.

The rest of the quandary is that while the shotgun is obviously safer in semi-urban or suburban areas, the game for which it is really most efficient—birds, rabbits, and so forth—is, as Gabrielson said, either largely static or declining due to changes that have nothing to do with hunting. Thus, we have more big game for high-powered rifle hunting, but a tendency toward urban population sprawl and other safety problems that restrict some of the area in which a high-powered rifle may be used. The shotgun can be used in closer quarters, but the game on which it is ideally used is a little less plentiful than it used to be—in some areas, anyhow.

It is possible the large-caliber handgun—usually a revolver but sometimes a semi-automatic pistol or single-shot pistol—may grad-

John Browning—one of America's great gun inventors.

The Browning 9mm. automatic pistol in a highly engraved form. *(both courtesy of the Browning Arms Company)*

**9mm
Renaissance**

Samuel Colt, inventor of the revolver.

The Colt .45 automatic, sidearm of the United States Army since pre-World War I days.
(both courtesy of Colt Industries)

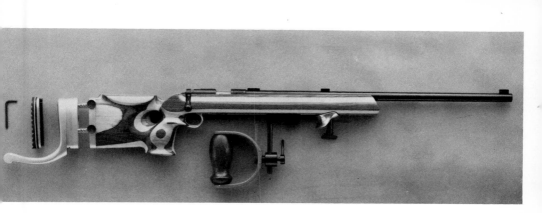

Model 52 International Match Rifle by Winchester.
(courtesy of Winchester-Western)

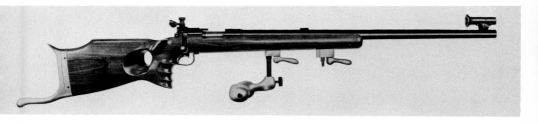

Remington International Match Rifle.

Cutaway of a modern rifle cartridge.
(both courtesy of Remington Arms Corporation)

Winchester competition air rifle.

(both courtesy of Winchester-Western)

Winchester competition air pistol.

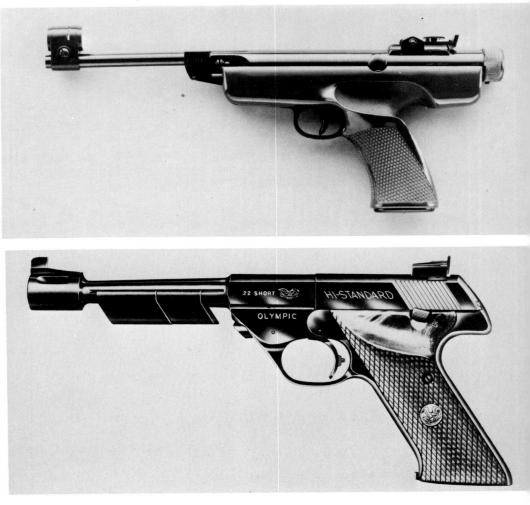

.22 automatic competition pistol.
(courtesy of Hi-Standard)

Teddy Roosevelt was an avid hunter and gun collector. He is shown here with his Winchester rifle.

A modern Winchester hunting rifle.
(both courtesy of Winchester-Western)

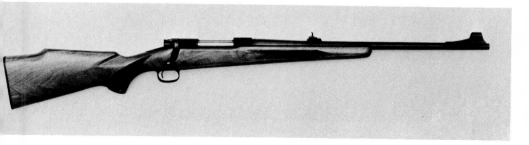

A father teaches his son the basics of shooting and handling a rifle.

A careful hunter never carries a loaded rifle while climbing a fence or similar obstruction.
(both courtesy of the National Rifle Association)

The rifle should not be loaded until the shooter is ready to begin hunting.
(courtesy of the National Rifle Association)

The fundamentals of shooting are often best taught with air rifles.
(courtesy of Winchester-Western)

A civilian and a law-enforcement officer shoot a .45 pistol match at the National Matches at Camp Perry, Ohio.
(courtesy of the National Rifle Association)

A soldier and civilian match their shooting ability with M14 military
rifles at Camp Perry.

Young shooters learn the basics of rifle marksmanship at the National
Matches.
(both courtesy of the National Rifle Association)

Two veterans of International target matches practice with telescope mounted free-rifles (so called because they are almost free of restrictions).

Free-rifle target shooters on the firing line.
(both courtesy of the National Rifle Association)

New York Port Authority Patrolman trains with his pistol.
(courtesy of the National Rifle Association)

Marine sniper on the lookout for soldiers of the North Vietnamese
Army near Khe Sanh.
(courtesy United States Marine Corps)

"VC, 1,000 meters" confirms the spotter of a Marine sniper team as his partner squeezes the trigger. In the age of weapons that fire 6,000 rounds a minute, the individual marksman can still take a deadly toll of the enemy at incredibly long range.
(courtesy United States Marine Corps)

The PMI, or preliminary marksmanship instructor, explains the importance of a steady hand and good breath control to a Marine recruit. *(courtesy United States Marine Corps)*

United States Army Chief of Staff General Harold K. Johnson test
fires the controversial M16.
(courtesy Army News Features)

A new sniper platoon lines up on the firing line for a day of practice
shooting.
(courtesy United States Marine Corps)

The first week of a Marine recruit's rifle training is spent in dry firing.

An instructor checks rifles to make sure there are no obstructions in the barrel.
(both courtesy United States Marine Corps)

ually be more widely used in big-game hunting in marginal belts where the 2.75-mile or 2.5-mile danger reach of the high-powered rifle is undesirable, but where the human population sprawl has not reached the point where only shotguns should be allowed.

The maximum danger range of the most powerful handgun cartridges is about 1.3 to 1.4 miles. Thus the big-bore hunting handgun lies nearly halfway between the typical modern big-caliber hunting rifle and the shotgun with buckshot. And the big revolver is only a little more far-reaching than the shotgun with rifled slug. It is also considerably more accurate than any shotgun if used by a trained, skilled shot—probably accurate to at least twice the range of the shotgun with rifled slug.

If municipal and state authorities in the big Northeastern States and West Coast jurisdictions (in particular but not exclusively), where handgun controls are severe or discouraging to their use, can be led or forced to cooperate, large-bore handguns can be helpful in providing humane, effective hunting as a compromise between shotgun and high-powered rifle use. Advances in handgun ammunition and metallurgy in the last 15 years have enormously improved the effectiveness of both. The modern magnum revolver loadings are in many instances more accurate and efficient game-takers than most of the rifle calibers in use around 1900.

The chief danger to hunting, aside from the thrust of unwise gun legislation and habitat destruction in the path or swathe of urban sprawl, is a mountingly serious number of raids on the available hunting domain by the National Parks Service. This is the only big federal recreational land agency which doesn't like or generally provide for hunting. The NPS is using the probably excessive emphasis on "simple pleasures" in the Recreation Resources Review Report to justify taking as much land as possible away from other agencies—Forest, BLM, state—and including it in ever more grandiose parks systems.

Other United States agencies, most state game departments, sportsmen, and others are fighting to stop some of these land grabs. Among those which have been blocked (at least for the time

being), or reduced in scope are efforts to take over the Cabeza
Prieta Game Range in Southwestern Arizona and to seize almost
all of the National Forest lands in North-Central Washington.
Both areas, now open for various widely approved multiple uses,
would pass into National Park status if Parks had its way. The
North Cascades Park plan, successful in part, will eliminate hunting and other uses in a wide belt of high country—an area that
drew a high degree of hunting participation from Seattle and the
rest of Washington State's urban complex. The final compromise
on the Cascades was a victory for Parks and galling for sportsmen.
The Cabeza Prieta seizure would mean, for all practical purposes,
an end to a game range set aside almost 30 years ago to help
rebuild the desert bighorn wild sheep, rarest of the four basic
types of wild sheep in North America. The Cabeza Prieta experiment has worked so well that limited hunting has been reinsti-
tuted in the area. But no wild sheep herd will stay long around
park-type areas which people visit in large numbers. Unlike deer
and some other wildlife, bighorn sheep are not compatible with
people. One informed conservationist said that opening the
Cabeza Prieta Game Range to the general public would be a
new form of Alliance for Progress program, since it would simply
result in chasing all the sheep across the adjacent border into Mexico where they would feed a few people for a short time. The
park plan would also further menace an already endangered
species, the Sonoran antelope.

There are other cases of Park Service power plays. The feeling is
inescapable that the language and methods used in the ORRRC
Report stimulated the Parks Service to get all it could while the
mood and momentum of the report were still fresh, and lest the
leadership of Interior might undergo some change in basic philosophy. The chairman of the commission, Laurence Rockefeller, has
himself become very controversial in the area of land administration—he has plenty of enemies as well as supporters over his
maneuvering for more park lands in Wyoming. His commission's

report certainly has not been widely accepted, although it has been followed in some states.

There is an interesting relationship between hunting and bullfighting, and individuals who condemn hunting with firearms yet approve of and vigorously support the old Hispanic-American sport. There may be something warped in the thinking of those who regard bullfighting as a high art form but who are queasy around guns. Nogales, Juarez, and many other Mexican border cities periodically draw large crowds of American aficionados—writers, artists, other people who tend to be in the humanistic mold that disapproves of guns and hunting. These people form sub-cults that worship a sport involving the goading of a bull to furious death amid all kinds of ritual and panoply. Yet many of these people regard hunting with a quick, efficient firearm—hunting of an essentially surplus animal or bird under the rules followed in the United States—as cruel or grim. Somehow slow, agonizing gore spellbinds these people. But quick, humane taking of excess animal or bird life with bullet or shot disgusts them. The vegetarian who knows how unsavory some killing of domestic meat is may be entitled to criticize both killers and eaters of meat with piety (although he probably has his own quirks and foibles that would make them feel superior). But the individual who eats his meat out of a butcher shop or supermarket is in one degree or another part of the same process that causes some to be fascinated by bullfights and others by hunting; he cannot consistently condemn either group.

Certainly no other kind of recreation can even come near providing the funds sport-hunting with firearms does. Even if cross bows were legalized (they are banned for most hunting in most states) to supplement participation in, and revenues from, long bow archery hunting, there would be nothing like the turnout of people and investment involved in gun hunting. Nor would there be adequate wildlife management control. And, if some psychologists are right that firearms hunting is a restrained outlet for old, deep human urges, it could be (and the writer suspects is) a suitable release for a lot of people who might otherwise do considerable damage to society. There is a pretty good line of thought that many urban violences among ghetto residents and the more affluent—all of whom spend most of their lives in crowded, pent-up conditions—might be avoided by giving them a better opportunity to work off all those tensions and emotions. Certainly hunting is a basic way to do it. It is at least as worth trying as turning our city parks into basic training camps for thugs and perverts.

Veteran conservation authority and writer Grits Gresham summed up the more orthodox case for hunting in the September 1965 issue of *Western Ourdoors Magazine*: "Death by gunshot— even a poor shot—is merciful by comparison" to death by other ways in the wild. Most people who dislike or are vaguely disturbed by hunting never see the winter-kill statistics, don't have any notion how much wildlife starves to death or dies from disease or predation, don't know how habitat conditions vary between seasons and aberrations of climate. They don't realize most wildlife lives and dies without being influenced—except beneficially, from license revenues—by hunting. "In capsule form," Gresham wrote, "here's why it doesn't hurt, and frequently helps, to kill a substantial part of a game population each year:

"1. Most game cannot be stockpiled, and a majority of each high-turnover species won't live a year whether hunted or not.

"2. Hunter harvest comes largely from game which would be harvested by nature anyway.

"3. Game habitat has a definite carrying capacity, and not shooting the animals on it won't make it carry more. To the contrary, allowing a habitat to exceed its carrying capacity of big game will invariably result in decreasing the carrying capacity through range destruction or deterioration.

"4. Mortality from all causes—disease, predation, accidents, and hunting—is greatest in a dense game population, and losses from all of these causes become progressively less as a portion of the population is removed by hunting.

"5. Reproduction is more successful in a game population which is below the carrying capacity of the range—less where the number of breeders exceeds the available habitat."

For the year 1964, hunters paid out about $72 million to state game agencies. This can be considered representative for almost any year in the last eight or ten. Gresham adds that hunters have paid out more than $220 million for state wildlife improvements through Pittman-Robertson excise revenues, contributed more than $80 million in duck-stamp funds since 1934, and another $12 to $14 million through Ducks Unlimited. Hunting provides another $50 million each year for developing private lands for wildlife. The basic contribution to the national economy overall—buying guns, shells, reloading equipment, clothes, hunting accessories like telescope sights and binoculars and calls and much other gear, boats, gasoline, accommodations—is estimated in astronomical amounts. The figure runs well into hundreds of millions of dollars annually, whichever source you care to credit. This is why the measured criticism of the Recreation Resources Review Report by such an outstanding conservationist as Stroud—a fishing expert and member of the California panel—is important.

"Much misdirected stress has been placed on the so-called 'simple pleasures' of driving, walking, picnicking, and sightseeing as making up the central thrust of outdoor recreation," Stroud said. "This has led to the seriously mistaken notion to newly attracted generalists that driving and walking for pleasure, picnicking, sightseeing, etc., have suddenly displaced fishing and hunting as the principal outdoors pursuits by Americans."

Stroud said, using the ORRRC's own figures, about 17 percent of all American adults hunt regularly. He adds, "Close examination of recreation data, indeed, makes it increasingly clear that the substantial (if not the principal) thrust of several 'recreation activities'—particularly the relatively passive picnicking, driving and walking for pleasure—are ancillary to more dominant traditional outdoor interests. If so, it would be a major blunder to de-emphasize the role of fishing and hunting in outdoor recreation.

"The new generalists in conservation—more concerned with simple pleasures than hunting or fishing—seem to believe that the naive magic of providing X number of picnic tables and litter barrels, etc. will solve the myriad problems that have so long confounded resource specialists!"

The ORRRC Report said there is evidence that hunting will be increasingly popular in virtually all regions of the United States. Even in urbanized areas like the Northeast and Great Lakes, the prospect is good. The only state where the future appeared threatened was California, with its swelling population, arid range difficulties, and fan-out or urban sprawl. But California, with its Wildlife Plan, appears to have gone a good distance toward planning to cope with those headaches. The rest of the country, in varying degree, is in decent shape. The outlook is good if common sense is the guide. If emotion or panic takes charge, the entire wildlife conservation movement in the United States can be shot down—and not by hunters!

✳

Chapter 7

Sport Target Shooting

✳ ✳ ✳ ✳ ✳

"The names of our top shooters—Wright, Thompson, Anderson, and so on—are household words in a lot of the world, like Wilt Chamberlain and Carl Yastrzemski here."—Roy Dunlap, international shooting authority

WHOLLY APART FROM ITS MILITARY USEFULNESS, TARGET SHOOTING in the United States has important applications.

Over the world, competitive shooting may be the most widely popular sport. There is a set of statistics arguing that more people shoot rifles, shotguns, and handguns at various inanimate targets than participate in any other sport. This may be true. Certainly it *would* be true without any challenge if the more repressive and authoritarian governments of the world would let up on their gun laws. Unfettered by various restrictive laws, shooting would easily outdistance any other worldwide sport—even soccer.

Both free and tyrannical governments levy great deterrents on the ownership and use of guns, even those which are obviously or primarily intended for target shooting. This is commented on at great length elsewhere in this book. Suffice it to say here that such regulations don't make sense in free nations—and accomplish almost nothing except harassment of honest people. In China, the U.S.S.R., and similar states there is strong reason for denying guns to people with the wrong political inclinations. Hitler did the same thing. It contributes to the longevity of oppression and all the calculated inhumanity that goes with such forms of government.

But even in oppressed or harassed societies, a few people, at least, are usually allowed to own guns. Most nations are now showing growing interest in international-type target shooting. The Olympics (every four years) and the in-between world matches of the International Shooting Union (ISU) are big sports events in much of the world. They are generating so much new interest that many governments are *lessening* restrictions on owning and using guns and on accumulating ammunition, in order to satisfy the new popularity of shooting.

One indication is that DWM, a German firm that manufactures, sells, and exports great quantities of sporting ammunition, recently switched the priming method in its cartridges in order to make the cartridge cases easier to reload. The reloading of cartridges is long-established in the United States and to a lesser extent in Canada and a few other places. But it never amounted to much in Europe until just a few years ago. Sweden changed from Berdan to Boxer-style priming some years ago to facilitate reloading of its 6.5 x 55mm. service cartridge for military and civilian shooters. Swedish ammunition is now widely offered for export with easily replaced priming. The decision by DWM to follow suit clearly indicates that the shrewd German cartridge makers have decided the future is bright for selling ammunition that is cheap and easy to reload.

Reloading cartridges enormously increases the amount of shooting the average person can do—the amount of practice he gets—because it is cheaper than buying new cartridges intact. Also it often makes for more accurate-shooting ammunition.

Roy Dunlap, an American shooter and gunsmith who has earned wide eminence custom producing high-quality rifles for international shooting as well as for United States shooting, thinks it is all a little ironic. "Most foreign countries are loosening up on their people about guns," he said (not the Red-bloc nations, however, as a group). "Yet here in the United States and a few other nations, the trend is the other way. There are people in this country who want to do away with or seriously constrict shooting."

Aside from the military and semi-military role of target shooting—life-preservation—and its defensive role in a crime-stricken society, it has enormous world propaganda value.

"The names of our top shooters—Wright, Thompson, Anderson, and so on—are household words in a lot of the world, like Wilt Chamberlain or Carl Yastrzemski here," Dunlap says. People in Europe follow shooting avidly. So in a new and embryonic way do sports fans in Africa, Latin America, and Asia. The ISU recently decided to allow less complicated and less expensive .22-cal. rifles in its small-bore competitions; a similar move is being readied on big-bore rifles. The reason? So that the less well-bank-rolled or less technically matured nations or both can afford to provide practice and competition match rifles. They want to get involved in international shooting. They objected to a price ceiling that allowed the more advanced nations to buy or build rifles beyond the range of poorer countries. The new or forthcoming ISU rules will mean many more nations can participate in ISU and Olympic matches.

In a vanished era the United States used to do quite well in international competitions. During the prewar and postwar decades it slipped. The Scandinavian nations, always inclined toward high interest and great skill in shooting, tended to monopolize the ISU and Olympic medal-winning. The United States stayed aloof, preferring to focus on track and field, swimming, and other sports, until in the early 1950's when the Soviet Union came into the world sports arena with great determination to win all medals— realizing the ideological and propaganda values if Communists wore all those heroic spangles and ribbons.

The U.S.S.R. genuinely shook the sports world, including shooting; in a few years, the old Scandinavian throttlehold on top shooting awards was jeopardized and the United States looked positively ridiculous. Those in charge of American shooting, both civilian and military, set to work to correct this. Largely due to a close relationship between civilian shooting (through the NRA) and the armed forces—which had the facilities and personnel to dedicate fulltime—the United States forged back during the 1950's and by 1964 dominated shooting contests at the Tokyo Olympics.

In 1966, the Americans all but monopolized the ISU Matches at Wiesbaden. Our application, techniques, and personnel counted, including superb women shooters like Margaret Thompson and a few others. How long the United States can maintain this supremacy in a culture where a certain vocal element of the political and media leadership is hostile to or suspicious of shooting is something only time will tell. Certainly championship shooters are not likely to be produced in a society where there is increasing preaching against guns.

Yet in early 1968 there was an excellent chance that our shooting team would be one of the few United States entries with first-rate, world-championship possibilities unmarred by internal racial turmoil, anti-this or pro-that super-political considerations, and all the other implausible folderol that has been somehow linked to sports. The majority of top United States shooters happen to be white, but neither they nor those who are Negro have been infected by college campus Black Power movements. Most Negro and white shooters have matured past the campus activist antics stage.

A striking number of top United States rifle shooters, and some pistol and shotgun competitors, learned the skill in high school or college programs connected with the Defense Department and the NRA, the so-called DCM program. Later many of these young people went into service and sharpened their skills to such an extent that we now have, as Dunlap said, the best and deepest shooting talent of any nation. The role of these shooters, developing through NRA-DCM junior clubs and scholastic competition is significant. Most of the "name" rifle shooters we have were so developed. To a lesser extent, this is true of pistol shooters.

One of the points the Little Report brought out was that gun clubs are essentially a middle-class and lower-middle-class activity in the United States. Through the DCM program, new shooters—juniors and adult beginners—are able to learn to shoot with low-price, government-supplied arms and ammunition (all of which is declared in excess of need and would be destroyed by the services if not issued to clubs). Later most of the more interested shooters buy their own equipment. The role of the gun club with NRA-Defense affiliation is that of a starter for newcomers and a polishing-up agent for mature shooters. A lot of young people would not get interested in shooting if it were not for DCM clubs and their inexpensive guns and ammunition. Reloading of shells is also a big factor.

In 1968, the Defense Department followed up 1967 cuts in the DCM program by reducing it to bare subsistence levels. Defense Secretary McNamara told the Senate Appropriations Committee that the curtailment of the program was "a temporary reduction brought about by the desire to hold fiscal year 1969 expenditures to the lowest possible level."

But veteran Arizona Senator Carl Hayden, a former marksman with a keen interest in the program, told the author: "In all frankness, I must say that the present atmosphere does not augur well for the renewal of the program as we have known it."

The program in 1968 was limited to .22-cal. rifle shooting for junior clubs. Senior clubs which do not have junior affiliates were no longer to receive excess government arms and ammunition; indeed, only match-grade rifles .30-cal. and .22-cal.—and very limited supplies of ammunition—were available to even the most qualified clubs.

Foes of the program who uphold excessive English gun laws, for example, never mention that even in Britain rifle clubs draw guns and ammunition from excess military stocks.

Hayden's allusion to "the present atmosphere" can logically be interpreted to mean that the continuation in office of present policymakers or their political heirs spells a fadeout for the marksmanship program. Thus, so long as people who think like

McNamara, Clark Clifford, and Ramsey Clark hold office, fewer and fewer young Americans will have a chance to become adept with firearms before being drafted into service.

The same reductions wiped out the DCM pistol program. This won't have a drastic immediate effect. But unless pistol-club support is restored in a year or two, competitive handgun shooting in the United States with calibers larger than .22 rimfire will probably decrease rather gradually over the next several years.

The shotgun-oriented clubs—trap and skeet—have no government support. But they seldom need it. Trap and skeet have evolved differently in the United States. They are "country-club" sports that draw more affluent people—economically in the same brackets as those who join country clubs to play golf. Trap and skeet cost more to shoot, round for round, in most instances. There is more socializing attendant to trap and skeet. This may tend to change, however, if emphasis on international shooting continues to grow. Because, while through the military the United States has evolved a fairly broad base (not yet nearly broad enough, though) from which to select rifle and pistol team stars, military interest in skeet and trap has not been as great, except perhaps in the Air Force where it is closely tied to gunnery drills. There has been a stronger trend toward producing top trap and skeet teams in the various forces the last few years, however. Also, in some shotgun sports the awards system is worked out so that amateurs win cash prizes and professionals get only hardware— trophies. This is just about the reverse of most other sports. In rifle and pistol, there are few cash prizes; top prizes are new guns, big trophies, and silverware. Lesser awards are usually medals, plaques, or small trophies. Yet somehow rifle and pistol tend to have more participating competitors, due in part to the DCM assistance and perhaps also in part to the historic heritage Americans have with the rifle and pistol. However, people *own* more shotguns than rifles or pistols.

Politics, aberrant sociology, and what not aside, there is a space problem confronting rifle clubs. Until population started expanding into suburbs, there were in the United States, a fair number of rifle ranges with firing points for 1,000 yards. Many ranges had 600-yard arrangements. Today there are relatively few 1,000-yard layouts, and 600-yard ranges are disappearing all too rapidly. People who dislike or worry about target shooting probably watch this with glee, but it has serious connotations. There have been some solutions worked out, led by the engineering development of fully baffled safety ranges. These are very successful, even in downtown, highly urbanized areas, if they are properly constructed. The difficulty is, such ranges are extremely unhandy and costly to build for long-range, high-powered rifle shooting. They can be built pretty readily for 100-yard shooting and shorter distances. Typically, these safety ranges provide for rifle shooting at up to 100 yards and for 25- and 50-yard pistol shooting. Baffling is constructed so that with proper range supervision, a chance wild shot is virtually impossible.

But the future for long-range, high-powered rifle shooting is not too good unless and until some other solutions are reached. Skeet and trap layouts don't require great safety buffer zones and can be put almost anywhere that the price of land permits, from a practical standpoint.

High-power ranges have been forced farther out into rural areas, quite understandably, as suburbs were created around many cities and towns. Many today are located 25 to 50 miles away from downtown metropolitan centers. This does not make for the desirably wide participation such shooting requires to prosper, either for the clubs' sakes or for that of the national stake in international competition. Even in the West where big cities are widely scattered, range removal has become a thorny affair. Long-view planning is the solution. Ranges with good backstops to thoroughly control high-power rifle bullet dispersion are the best solution now—and range construction to eliminate all menace; if and when suburbs follow ranges out into the bushes, they can be compatible if bullet strike, range control and other provisions are planned with safety in mind. That still leaves the nuisance of noise, but this too can be overcome with long-range planning and common sense. The downtown or suburban safety range for small-bore rifle shooting, pistol shooting, trap and/or skeet shooting has plenty of future. So have shortened ranges for big-bore shooting. The NRA, the military, and others have started making moves in that direction with reduced-scale targets, new courses and the like.

Air-rifle and air-pistol shooting are very advanced in Europe. But they tend to predominate in those sections of Europe with long, dreary winters. Not too much of the United States has Black Forest-type winters. And outdoors, shooting with even super-accurate air weapons is a rather short-range and perhaps tame sport. In a nation with a very diverse climate (much of it conducive to being outdoors), with a long tradition of *public* hunting (unlike Europe), and with a national zest for something big and loud, it may be that air-gun shooting will not become as popular as in Europe. It has certain limited training value. However, one United States producer of air guns, Daisy Manufacturing Company, is introducing firearms advancements such as one form of the new caseless cartridge and a rifle to fire it. The caseless cartridge and the gun for it are probably the world's next great new stage in firearms development. But for the reloading target shooter or hunter, they now have no strong value since there is no empty case to reload. Everything is burned up in propelling the bullet.

Another outlet shooters and planners might consider is the indoor range. There have been ups and downs in indoor (usually called "gallery") shooting in the United States. It is stronger in those states with inclement winters. Usually gallery ranges are safe or practical only for .22-cal. (small-bore) shooting. Some are set up to provide for limited larger-caliber handgun shooting. Anything that teaches safe and competent shooting is worthwhile, but it might be useful for those thinking about new indoor ranges to consider making a provision for all-caliber standard handgun competition. Many police ranges are built in basements and are entirely safe for any caliber handgun policemen normally would carry—.38 Special, .357 Magnum, .45 semi-automatic pistol. This is worth consideration for shooters who plan to ask city leaders to include a safety range in a new convention center, multi-use arena building, or recreation building.

Controlled target shooting is perhaps the safest form of such activity that humans can indulge in. It is considerably safer than hunting because it attracts or trains skilled, competent, careful participants who know much more about guns than the average once-or-twice-a-year hunter (but experienced hunters who are also competitive target shooters are probably our most valuable shooters). It is actually far safer than driving, taking a bath, or eating breakfast, statistics indicate. It makes an extraordinary contribution to gun knowledge, to safety training, and to recreation—and as indicated, it is a sport of international prestige far beyond what most Americans realize (you seldom see Camp Perry or the ISU shooting matches on television). Most of those who criticize it have never seen a registered or approved NRA pistol or rifle match or a registered trap or skeet shoot. It is as far from ridiculous Hollywood and television leather-slapping, counter-spy snub-nose antics, and cops-and-hoods melodrama as you can imagine. And then some. No one winces more deeply than the skilled target shooter when he sees some movie or television detective snap a revolver shut with a flick of the wrist (this can speedily ruin the gun's fine tuning). No one shudders more than a shooter who sees movie types idly punching or pointing guns at each other, or World War Two "combat veterans" handling firearms like kindergarten inmates. People who behave like movie-television gun toters would last about 30 seconds on most, if not all, approved rifle, pistol, and shotgun ranges. They would be evicted, one way or another, with or without ceremony. Because such fools get people killed. Trained target shooters do not.

★

Crime, Police and Guns

★ ★ ★ ★ ★

"The only good laws that curb crime are those which make the price of wrongdoing so high it's prohibitive."—John M. Schooley, experienced Treasury agent and police official.

A SEARCHING LOOK AT THE FBI's *Crime In The United States—Uniform Crime Reports* for any recent year erases the argument that crime rates are low where laws make guns tough to come by.

In fact, there is a tendency in the opposite direction. But the Justice Department, headed during the last decade by Ramsey Clark, Nicholas De B. Katzenbach, and Robert Kennedy, has used very carefully culled statistics trying to create the impression that crime drops in direct ratio to the severity of gun-control statutes. The probable truth is just the opposite.

That this entire argument has not been effectively challenged tells a lot about how the public at large fatuously accepts whatever bureaucracy feeds it—whatever bureaucracy's motives may be or however honest the message.

The outstanding example of this hucksterism on high deals with the Phoenix homicide rate for the last few years. Clark and Katzenbach in turn proclaimed that Phoenix in 1963 had a horrendous homicide rate in comparison to New York. The moral, of course, was that Phoenix and Arizona have lax gun-access laws, while New

York City and State exult in the strictness of the Sullivan Law, that peculiar institution of the disarmers which grants the police literal life-or-death power over ordinary citizens.

What Clark, Katzenbach, and the others do not mention is that in 1964 and 1965 Phoenix had a *lower* homicide rate than Sullivan-insulated New York City.

This same sort of highly selective statistic slanting has been the rule, not the exception, from the Justice Department's top leadership and from some, but far from all, police heads across the country.

Similarly, Quinn Tamm, executive director of the International Chiefs of Police and a much-sought tocsin ringer for gun haters, tries hard to convey the impression that all or nearly all police officers are in a fret to help enact strict control legislation. Tamm, when asked about the National Police Officers Association and other groups who disagree with *his* presentation of the International Chiefs, will argue that NPOA is not up to the standard of his organization.

The basic difference between the IACP's leading personnel and the National Police Officers is that the chiefs tend today to be primarily administrative, deskbound, and sociologically inclined individuals while the NPOA's membership is drawn more from on-the-beat, practical-exposure policemen. Tamm even hinted, in 1967 Senate testimony, that the NPOA might be of somewhat questionable repute. But his pique may be traceable to the NPOA's outright refusal to sanction stiff gun-control measures and many other IACP goals.

Tamm, a former FBI agent, might consider himself in line for a return to that body at some high level if there were changes in Washington politics. He certainly has not severed lines of communication with political elements who subscribe to the apology-for-criminals approach to curing crime.

The treasurer (1967) of Tamm's organization, Tucson (now Miami, Florida) Police Chief Bernard Garmire, showed that Tamm has a long way to go to insure wide agreement with his own stand even inside the IACP. Garmire told a Tucson civic group he doubted registration and like controls would materially affect the crime rate. The fact is, a good many chiefs of considerable stature do not agree with the IACP. Los Angeles Chief Thomas Reddin was one. The Chief of Milwaukee's police is another. Many state and police area organizations have solidly voted *NO* to registration. Others have tactfully eased away from public agreement with some of the politics of their civilian chiefs. But interestingly, when the American Bar Foundation polled chiefs across the United States on the efficacy of registration laws, most said they did not feel they were particularly workable.

The one gun-related measure most chiefs and officers *do* accept is a tentative shutdown on gun sales during civil disorders. Beyond this, police views diverge as widely as do everyone else's.

The experience of New York with the tight control on handgun sales built into its Sullivan Law is convincing to many officers who disavow repressive controls. Despite all the contrived statistics, in the year 1965—not at all untypical—there were 127 metropolitan areas with *lower* homicide rates than New York City. The New York City rate was 6.1 per 100,000. Among those with the same or lower rates—yet cities with easier access to handguns—were: Cincinnati, 4.2; Denver, 4.1; Des Moines, 2.6; El Paso, 2.5; Harrisburg, 4.9; Indianapolis, 5.2; Los Angeles, 6.1; Milwaukee, 2.3; Minneapolis-St. Paul, 2.1; Oklahoma City, 5.7; Phoenix, 5.2; Pittsburgh, 3.5; Portland (Ore.), 3.0; Salt Lake City, 1.2; San Francisco-Oakland, 4.3; San Diego, 3.4; Seattle, 2.7; and Wichita, 3.5.

Cities which, like New York, have restrictive legislation included Boston, with a 2.8 homicide rate, Philadelphia with a 5.5 rate, and Buffalo, New York, 2.3.

Major Southern and Texas cities averaged higher in homicides than most cities with strict controls. But cities in the Middle West and West tended to have less homicide per capita than New York. Anyone familiar with American history is well aware that the South, white and black, has always been an area with a higher

incidence of resorting to personal violence than is the case elsewhere. The Bowie knife was a distinctly Southern evolution in
social cutlery that antedated the Colt revolver; among devoted
hell-raisers, it was considered worth more than the average pistol,
too, because it would keep going long after the pre-Colt single-shot
handguns of the early 1800's were out of business. Knife fighting
was an advanced art in the South well before Colonel Colt developed his revolving pistol. The dueling code lasted longer in the
South than elsewhere too (so, interestingly, did good manners,
which may or may not be relevant).

The regional yardstick holds as true with states as with cities. In
1965, New York State's per-capita homicide rate was higher than
that of 29 other states, all of them with less red tape and tom-
foolery involved in getting a handgun. These were: Colorado,
Connecticut, Hawaii, Idaho, Indiana, Iowa, Kansas, Maine, Massachusetts, Michigan, Minnesota, Montana, Nebraska, New
Hampshire, North Dakota, New Jersey, Ohio, Oklahoma, Oregon,
Pennsylvania, Rhode Island, South Dakota, Utah, Vermont,
Washington, West Virginia, Wisconsin, and Wyoming.

New York didn't improve with time or flurries over "badly
needed" legislation. In 1966, New York's homicide rate of 6.1 was
higher than 131 other major United States cities. And as E. B.
Mann wrote in the September 1968 *Shooting Industry*, London
has about 35 to 40 homicides a year—while New York had 654 in
1966. Yet London and New York City have gun laws of approximately equal severity—and London is repeatedly upheld as an
example of how stiff "gun-control" laws succeed.

"The London–New York figures merely prove what scientific
crime studies have told us: That the presence of the gun does not
cause crime, nor does the absence of the gun prevent it," Mann
remarked. He added that comparing gun homicides between New
York and London is "like comparing the number of people killed
by poisoned darts in England with the number killed by poisoned
darts in certain African countries."

If New York has many times as many murders as London with

similar gun laws, where is the answer? It rather clearly isn't in the firearms codes, one must conclude.

The comparison is full of interesting points. Three of the states with homicide rates lower than New York's are those popularly associated with rural violence and the auto banditry—Bonnie and Clyde—of the 1930's: Indiana, Oklahoma, and West Virginia. West Virginia, also interestingly, had more Congressional Medal of Honor winners than any other state in World War Two. It is accurate to say that all three of these states contributed well beyond their share of highwaymen and auto bandits during the turbulent 1930's. But, television and film scripts notwithstanding, rural gunmanship mainly ended with the end of the Depression as World War Two unfolded. Today in all three "badman" states it is easier to get a pistol or revolver than in New York. It is also markedly easier to *stay alive* in those three states, and to defend one's home if it is intruded upon. Correlation between guns and crime? The more proper correlation may be that in states where guns are widely owned, criminals are more careful. Or conversely, that in states where citizen-victims are disarmed by law, crime is a little safer.

Vermont, with 1965's lowest homicide rate—0.5 per 100,000—is Eastern but rural. The states with low rates tend to be Midwestern, New England, or Western and to contain dominant or strong English or Scandinavian racial strains. Ethnically or historically their residents tend to be less violence-prone than people in states with big Celtic, Negro, or South European concentrations. The South has two racial stocks a little more likely than most to commit violence—Negroes and Scotch-Irish (Scottish with a small adulteration, mainly from a stopover in the North of Ireland). The big cities of the Northest have large Sicilian populations with old-country traditions of personal vendetta that have slowly but not yet completely passed. The rural Scot, the city Sicilian, and the Negro in the city have made a strong contribution to homicide rates for many years. Much of this is lessening and the rest will disappear as the country becomes more homogeneous. As racial and national strains are more assimilated, crime may persist—but it will probably be caused by other groups for other reasons.

In most of the Midwest and West, you can buy a handgun, rifle, or shotgun with freedom. Crime rates reflect no great peril in this, certainly not as much personal danger as exists in most big Northeastern cities. A good many practical police leaders acknowledge this and resist the cheap, easy, and sometimes lurid way out that New York, Philadelphia, and some other cities adopt.

Harlon B. Carter, for many years head of the United States Immigration Border Patrol, is a vigorous and persistent foe of repressive laws that result in depriving citizens of sporting or defensive arms. He headed the National Rifle Association for two years. He had the rather complicated responsibility of opposing his own chiefs'—the Justice Department's—official stance for tighter controls. Carter repeatedly cudgeled the idea of strict controls and in particular the concept of licensing gun ownership as embodied in the Sullivan Law and similar, registration-of-all-guns laws in New Jersey (enacted 1966), Philadelphia (1965), Illinois (effective mid-1968), and Chicago (early 1968). That Carter went on opposing such legislation while the top people in Justice were bleating for more controls is a good yardstick of just how popular Ramsey Clark's views were with many federal police officers.

The Border Patrol, which Carter headed, is probably the United States' most pistol-proficient police agency. Its 1,500 officers usually produce the nation's top police pistol team and quite often also the top individual police marksmen. This is done in competition against large metropolitan police forces—New York, Los Angeles, Chicago—and state and federal agencies.

John M. Schooley, a 25-year veteran of Treasury Department enforcement work before retiring, also helped the Denver police as interim manager while corruption scandals there were being cleared up. He has contempt and bluntness for some of the federal officials who seek passage of strict controls. Like Carter, he was a president of the NRA. His particular argument is that few of the police officers and penologists who advocate disarming the citizenry ever faced an armed criminal or experienced gunfire.

A prime target is James V. Bennett, retired chief of the United States Bureau of Prisons. "Bennett was never an enforcement man. He faced his criminals only in the penitentiary where they were on their good behavior," Schooley says. He also said most policemen who belong to shooting groups "have faced gunfire at one time or another. I have myself—Bennett is the chief mollycoddler, one of the first to apologize for criminals."

Like Carter, Schooley is a firm advocate of stricter penalties for the misuse of firearms. He does not believe in making it harder for law-abiding citizens to get or use guns. He pretty well speaks for a great many officers when he says, "I'd urge legislation to punish the misuse of firearms. . . . There are plenty of state arms laws. The only good ones [laws], that curb crime, are those which make the price of wrongdoing so high that it's prohibitive."

The former Washington, D.C. police chief, Robert Murray, courted the ire of political supervisors when he strongly opposed a Sullivan Act for Washington. He said he felt it would be "a disaster." This took some courage; the United States Attorney for the District of Columbia, David Acheson, was pushing hard for the ordinance, as were some members of the commission governing the district. Acheson, while he failed to get the ordinance passed, was promoted to a key federal enforcement post. Murray retired not long afterward.

Pennsylvania State University economist Alan S. Krug's study on guns in crime turned up some facts that would astonish the anti-gun people—if they weren't so busy manipulating half facts. Krug said that serious crimes involving firearms in the United States constituted about 0.0035 of the total—with rifles and shotguns accounting for only a particle of even that small percentage.

This deviates quite a lot from lurid claims by Dodd and others that the nation is on a violent rampage. The fact is, there are 125 million firearms owned by 40 to 50 million persons according to

Krug (the author of this book is inclined to think Krug may be a trifle low on the ownership tally). Yet guns, including outlawed "gangster" weapons, toy guns, and homemade guns, were involved in only 3.4 percent of the 3.2 million serious crimes in the U.S. during 1966. Krug pointed out that criminals easily substituted other weapons for guns acquired in commercial channels—they use whatever they can get, however they can get it. Homemade zip guns were used in more murders, robberies, and assaults than were rifles and shotguns in New York State in 1966. Homemade zip guns are illegal—as are all unlicensed handguns in New York. Rifles and shotguns are legal for unlicensed ownership in New York at this writing (although the Rockefeller administration, having studiously ignored fact and reason, is trying hard to change this). Thus we have the specter of illegal guns being used in more of certain kinds of serious crimes more frequently than guns that could be bought over the counter without red tape.

Krug wasted no academic sympathy on the anti-gun pleaders: "Many of those who espouse firearms legislation as a means of reducing crime rates are doing the public a disservice by leading people to believe that such legislation will successfully solve the crime problem. Or for that matter, even a significant part of it." He added: "The facts dictate that it will not. Misleading the public in this way tends to reduce the public's justifiable concern over our alarming crime rates. It delays positive action aimed at the real causes of crime. These, as many studies have shown, are socio-economic in nature."

Krug's research agreed with this author's in suggesting that there is no positive correlation between the availability of guns and crime rates. Indeed, Krug added, "There appears to be a negative correlation." In other words, there tends to be less crime where the average citizen has a gun—or has a chance to own one without police interference. This is the one hard, consistent fact that keeps turning up as big Eastern cities—degunned or exercising bureaucracy and arbitrary controls over guns—are compared to Midwestern ones.

Krug argues strongly that scientific findings, not emotion, should guide the framers of gun laws. "As long as the issue remains a moral one, the public will continue to be unduly influenced by the propaganda and false statistics disseminated by the anti-gun faction." He said the cost of total firearms-licensing in the United States would be between one and two billion dollars. The cost would be about $10 a gun or $25 a person. The cost of administering New York City's new all-guns licensing law was reckoned at somewhat the same figure per capita.

The evidence that homicide with firearms in the United States is spiraling is not substantiated. In 1930, the national homicide rate with firearms was 5.7 per 100,000; in 1965, it was 2.9. Just for the record, during the period 1950–65 when the overall number of permits in New York City was being sharply reduced, the homicide rate rose there from 3.7 to 6.1.

Concerning crimes in general, the sociological factors recede before economic ones, judging by the FBI's *Uniform Crime Reports*. Gun laws again seem to have little relevancy. The FBI carried crime statistics on 183 major metropolitan areas for 1965. The majority of these cities were much safer than New York. Crime rates higher than New York's 1,981.6 per 100,000 occurred in just 32 cities. Most were resort cities or spas—Tampa, San Antonio, Phoenix, Miami, Honolulu, Las Vegas, Los Angeles, Ft. Lauderdale, Atlantic City. Also included in the list with higher crime rates than New York were such generally nonhealthy climes as Gary, Chicago, Detroit, Flint, Louisville, Newark, and Washington. But the upshot was that among 183 cities grouped as metropolitan centers, 150 were plagued with less crime than the city where police have made it almost impossible for the average homeowner to acquire a handgun—and where Commissioner Howard Leary and Mayor John Lindsay made it equally difficult to own a rifle or shotgun.

Statewise, New York's rate of 1,608.2 crimes per 100,000 in 1965 is exceeded only by Nevada, Maryland, Michigan, Florida, Hawaii, Illinois, Alaska, Arizona and California. Again the overall incidence of crimes appears to peak in vacation states—Nevada, Florida, Hawaii, Arizona, and California.

Woodson D. Scott, an NRA official, longtime New York attorney, active shooting sportsman, and dedicated foe of Sullivanism, told Congress this about the New York law: "We look in vain for evidence that any general registration law would assist in the prevention and detection of crimes of violence." He rapped the New York police for charging $20 for a handgun permit, plus more than $2 for photos, and $10 for annual renewal. The fees stay in the police pension fund whether the permit application is okayed or not. Scott said application forms are scarce in most city police stations, applicants are discouraged by stories that their chances of approval are slight; complex and embarrassing vouching processes are involved, and applicants may be delayed as long as 18 months. (In Philadelphia, moreover, under the new all-guns registration law, one man after waiting two years to have a permit to carry a handgun approved, was forced to resort to getting a court order.) Under Sullivan, Scott said, licensing "is a matter of administrative discretion. . . . not reviewable by the courts except where it can be established that the action of the police commissioner is arbitrary, unreasonable, and capricious, a charge that is difficult if not impossible to prove."

Most of the time, when the police are too abusive of the vast power the law confers, the only recourse a citizen has is an expensive suit reaching the state court of appeals. The cost of this is prohibitive for most citizens. One New York attorney—himself rejected for a handgun permit on what he said was a whim of the police—estimated it would cost a good many thousand dollars to appeal a Sullivan Law "finding" by the police to the state appeals court. To take such a case to federal courts would get easily into five figures, he said.

Not everybody supinely yields to police abusiveness. One New York City area college student, wishing to take up handgun shooting after several years as a rifle shooter in a number of different (and approved) gun clubs, was rejected for a handgun permit because his father had been arrested (not convicted) for book-making some years ago. Perhaps to the astonishment of Commissioner Leary, the state appeals court overturned the police decision and ordered a permit issued to the young man. Not many shooters are as persistent or as fortunate.

Some people after having been denied permits time and again, even after being robbed or assaulted, have gotten handguns illegally, used them in self-defense—and then been booked on more serious charges than those who robbed or assaulted them. This is so commonplace as not to be worthy of unusual mention in New York City. The police have gradually constricted the number of handgun permits despite an accelerated rise in crimes committed on ordinary citizens. People in New York City accepted the fact that their parks and streets are unsafe a good part of the time. How the police and political hierarchy can honestly or logically defend such conditions is not evident to research. Yet police and politicians keep pressing for more gun-control legislation.

Outside the New York metropolitan area, judges of county courts issue Sullivan permits, rather than the police. It is usually easier for a legitimate sporting shooter or concerned home-owner or businessman to get a handgun permit in "upstate" New York than in the city proper or immediate vicinity. A prosecuting attorney in a Western state, who migrated West after growing up in New York, said his research on the Sullivan Law even in relatively moderate upstate jurisdictions convinced him the law was "administered capriciously. . . and is clearly a failure and an harassment of honest citizens." The young prosecutor, Lars Pedersen, had been chosen to debate *for* such legislation before a Chamber of Commerce forum. The more deeply he probed the law, the more reluctant he became to defend it. He got on the rostrum and simply refused to do so and explained why. The law is indefensible, he said, because it has no standards or criteria.

Chiefs of police in many major cities as well as in suburbs near crime-ridden metropolises have sponsored or assisted with "clinics" at which potential crime victims are taught self-defense—usually including firearms proficiency. The list of larger cities where this has occurred includes New Orleans, Tampa, Phoenix, Kansas City, Oklahoma City, and San Diego. Others schedule such schooling from time to time. The suburbs of most major cities have increasingly been stricken by crime that is more mobile than a decade ago, and suburban police officers have offered similar training. A great misfortune is that some people have seen anti-Negro undertones or some other kind of racism in the desire of citizens to defend themselves. But this is seldom the case. The constants have been that crime is on the rise, that it is stretching out more to once-secure suburbs, that homeowners are worried about this—more about violence to their persons than holdups or burglaries—and that Negroes, for various reasons too deep to go into here, have been committing a disproportionate share of crimes.

Most of the persons interviewed while learning to shoot at police clinics specified crime, not fear of urban riots, as the prime motive. Some—in certain areas, many—were Negroes who live in or near ghettos and are themselves the major victims of violent crime. In Kansas City and Detroit, specifically, police clinics attracted Negro citizens who said as much. This went unreported by most media, with reporters preferring to read into the classes numerous implications that were not expressed and probably not felt by most of the trainees.

William J. White, a Hempstead, New York, Negro citizen who is also an Army Reserve major and electronics specialist, told the *American Rifleman* readership that anti-gun laws hit hardest at Negroes: "It appears that the distinguished gentlemen pressing for the strongest anti-gun bills either know absolutely nothing about firearms or are using the bills as a cover for some less obvious venture. Anti-gun bills could in fact disenfranchise the Negro of his right to bear arms and to protect himself and his property."

White boiled over because the last available FBI figures showed that 54 percent of United States murder victims were Negroes. "They are much victimized also in other types of crimes." White's statements are reinforced by those of Negro residents of Harlem—

who say their streets are not safer than those in "whitey's" territory. White's complaint that "one of the thinnest arguments. . . .
in support of anti-gun bills is that Negroes used firearms extensively for sniping" is supported by the President's Commission On
Urban Disorders. The commission, which ranged far afield into
wild fancies of sociology and futuristic planning in other realms,
was realistic enough to spell this out. Sniping was overstated and
overrated many times, by newspapers, by television, by radio, and
by the police. Most of the people killed in urban riots in 1967
were the victims of police or military fire, much of its misdirected.
There is more on this in Chapter 2 and elsewhere.

Deep surveys of the role of guns in crime tend to refute the
strict control advocates. The district attorney of Los Angeles
County, Evelle Younger, discovered after studying guns used in
crimes in his area that only 7 percent of the felonies surveyed
involved guns. The same study indicated that few guns used in
felonies were acquired through legal channels. "Only a small
number were purchased in a manner to require local registration," Younger said. Most guns used in the felonies were stolen or
otherwise illegally obtained. The evidence should have shaken the
Los Angeles Times, which printed the story, but a few days later
it came out for gun registration—Younger's survey notwithstanding.

A somewhat similar but much more detailed analysis of the
same subject was made by Krug while at Pennsylvania State University (See Chapter 3). Some other studies turned up approximately the same results.

Even the riot commission, loaded with apologists for rioters,
said: "There was widespread misunderstanding and exaggeration
of what did occur [in the rioting of summer, 1967]. The most
notable example is the belief widely held across the country last
summer that riot cities were paralyzed by sniper fire. Of 23 cities
surveyed by the commission, there had been reports of sniping in
14. What is probable, although we could not secure firm evidence,
is that there was at least some sniping. What is certain is that the

amount of sniping attributed to rioters—by law enforcement officials as well as the press—was highly exaggerated."

It was, however, enough to drive some politicians to cover (Ted Kennedy was impelled to call 1967 "the summer of the sniper"), some to Congress (Governor Hughes, emotionally begging for passage of strict federal gun controls), and some to the psychoanalytic couch where they "perceived" the Army issuing "cannon" to civilian gun clubs.

The view of police officers who advocate helping citizens to help (that is, defend) themselves when police are not available was rather well stated by the police chief of Lawrence, Massachusetts —a Kennedy fief at that!—Charles F. Hart. He said: "Criminals are acquiring broadened protective rights. It is time we began thinking of law-abiding, respectable citizens and their right to added protection." Hart is for making it easier for reputable citizens to obtain a pistol permit and firearms training. Handgun permits are required in Massachusetts as in New York, Michigan, Hawaii, and other areas. Hart and others who agree with him were greatly influenced, apparently, by the success of the first major clinic for women and others, held in Orlando, Florida. It drew many more applicants than expected. The Orlando idea spread rapidly despite discouragement from some metropolitan chiefs, some civil-liberties groups, and others who felt it would spread, not help curb, violence. The philosophical antecedents of such people refused to appropriate powder and lead for the frontier militia in Pennsylvania to defend itself during the Indian wars.

A great many other peace officers agree with the Lawrence chief. In one brief period of 1968 alone, three state associations of officers voted against gun registration. They favored mandatory penalties for crimes of violence and stricter controls on the use of concealed weapons. One group went so far as to tell Tamm's school of thought: "Hereafter, those of you who feel you need a talking point for these ridiculous gun laws, please do not claim law enforcement as a whole to be on your side—we're not."

Significant expressions of disapproval of registration were

voiced by statewide associations of sheriffs and chiefs of police in Washington State and sheriffs in Texas.

Police Chief Leary, before he went to New York to help Mayor Lindsay enact city-wide licensing of all guns did the same job in Philadelphia. How well it has worked is debatable. Ephraim Gomberg, Philadelphia Crime Commission employee, who was an architect of the ordinance there, said it was a moderate success. District Attorney Arlen Specter, who tried to buck the city political machine of Mayor James Tate, considered it a flop. He told one magazine writer the ordinance attacks crime from the wrong angle. Another city official, Controller Alexander Hemphill, called it a "politician's sop for calming down the hysterical citizens who, legitimately, want to cut down crime." Hemphill also said sportsmen could have done a much better job of fighting the bill.

While Gomberg brays about the law's success, the facts-and-figures jury is still out. Statistics bearing on the law's success have been juggled this way and that. The probability is that the ordinance has had very little if any effect on crime in the city of Philadelphia. Getting it off the statute books, even though many of its former backers are now unhappy with it, is much tougher than simply saying it is a failure or debatably valuable. The ordinance lacks any easy, inexpensive appeal machinery for people who reasonably want firearms for valid purposes. It is certainly a controversial matter. How long the Philadelphia ordinance may last is not necessarily relevant to the current suit over New York City's ordinance. The New York ordinance has an appeal provision written into it—a hearing for those who feel unfairly turned down for rifle or shotgun ownership. But there is no easy appeal hearing provision in the New York City ordinance for handgun rejectees. On that, the old Sullivan Law prevails, with all of its inequities and arbitrary features. It is probably our closest approach to police statism.

In New Jersey, the statewide all-guns licensing law does have an appeal and hearing provision. How effective this really is and will be is also open to speculation. So far some shooters and others feel the Jersey law may be fairer than what Gomberg and friends wrought across the Delaware. The Illinois state law—effective in 1968—appears to have far more fairness written into it. Time, again, will show how well it works. A gun-licensing law with positive, foolproof safeguards against police arbitrariness—against abuses and arrogances such as are committed in New York City— might find wide acceptance. But it would have to have inflexible safeguards for citizens. Perhaps in states where such legislation has been passed, sportsmen and other citizens might work toward getting more positive safeguards amended into the laws.

The truth about guns and safety on the streets appears to have gyrated out of a United Press International story from Saigon in late 1968. Saigon, UPI admitted, was safer than much of the United States.

One American newsman remarked, "I'd rather leave my wife at home alone in Saigon than in Brooklyn. If someone tries to break down our door in Saigon, she has a loaded M16 to protect herself with. In the U.S., she has nothing."

Try and get a permit for a gun for your wife in New York City, sometime—or for yourself. The police, you will be told with majestic aplomb, will defend you.

"An American woman . . . can walk past a dozen bars filled with uproariously drunken soldiers without any problem," UPI said. "This all boils down to the fact that Saigon is a relatively safe city," compared to many major metropolises in the States—terrorist gunplay, rockets, and bombs in the Asian capital notwithstanding.

In Louisville, where a liquor-store owner killed a 19-year-old thug forcing his way into the man's store, the proprietor was charged with manslaughter. Isolated or unusual case? Not at all. The incident and outcome were par for the course during 1967–68 rioting. Like cases across the country became too numerous to repeat as crime soared. And as citizens were pilloried for defending their lives or property, self-defense against even the greatest outrages became socially stigmatized in a certain small but influential segment of American society.

Registration laws appear to fail. So does that pet quasi-scientific fantasy of some ballistically ignorant politicians, the firing and filing away of a sample bullet from each firearm. This allegedly would make tracing of weapons used in crimes easier. But one of the nation's foremost ballisticians, Dr. J. Howard Mathews of the University of Wisconsin, scuttled this dream in a *Rifleman* interview a few years ago. It is, he said, "utter nonsense." First, Mathews explained, lead or copper bullets oxidize, and their value for comparison diminishes after a few years. Second, there is no known method for classifying accidental bullet characteristics fired from otherwise similar weapons. Nor will this work at all, not even right away, for shot or slugs fired from smooth shotgun barrels.

The problem of trusting police chiefs with discretionary powers to license guns appears sharply when Chicago's situation is closely examined. Former Police Superintendent Orlando W. Wilson told the *Chicago Tribune*, "I have no objection to a law-abiding citizen having a gun in his house if he is in fact a law-abiding citizen." But the Illinois State Rifle Association charged Wilson's department refused to issue handgun-purchase permits for even the most proper reasons to even the most law-abiding citizens: target shooters or those genuinely in need of a handgun for protection.

During Wilson's tenure, he simply ignored that part of the Chicago handgun ordinance which reads: "It shall be the duty of the commissioner of police to grant such permit if he is satisfied the applicant is of good moral character." Wilson—asked about arming more citizens to help stop crimes—said: "No, I don't favor such a move. I think our gun laws should be made more restrictive because at a conservative estimate there are 100,000 handguns in the possession of Chicago citizens who have no business having them." Wilson implemented his beliefs by circumventing the language of the ordinance. Target shooters, frightened homeowners, others were turned down. The Chicago police simply led to additional defiance of the city ordinance; law-abiding shooters and others, probably, just went elsewhere and got what they needed. The target shooters used their weapons on ranges like the one built in Waukegan for the 1959 Pan-American Games. No one is sure on just what all the non-legitimate shooters—the *non*-concerned citizens—used their weapons. Whatever prevails with the law, however, such individuals will go right on using their equipment while only the law-abiding gun owner complies with the rules.

The Illinois State Rifle Association—which includes handgunning members—stated its case in a way that speaks for most sports shooters: "We fully support legislation designed to prohibit sale of firearms to persons who have been convicted of a crime of violence, fugitives from justice, drug addicts, mental incompetents, and other undesirables. We object, however, to legislation which places the power to determine who can or cannot purchase or possess a gun *within* the *arbitrary control of any police official or agency.*"

The association also favored stronger penalties for those who misuse guns. Such a bill was enacted by the Illinois legislature earlier. Governor Otto Kerner vetoed it. He preferred stiffer restrictions on reputable citizens.

There is loud fanfare in the metropolitan press and on the television networks when individuals misuse guns. But the far more frequent incidence of citizen use of firearms for personal or home defense or to protect other citizens is often obscured or not reported. The *American Rifleman* monthly compiles and lists many such cases. Appendix C contains a sampling from recent issues.

One of the undiscussed ironies in all the skirmishing about the Dodd-Celler approach—that dealing with the dumping of cheap, surplus military guns—is that John F. Kennedy himself originally tried to stop some of this importation, but for economic reasons. Gun-making plants in JFK's home state were hurt by the deluge of surplus European guns. Savage, in particular, was in deep trouble.

Kennedy sought to help by imposing import limits. He was defeated—not by the NRA or the "gun lobby," but by the State Department. State did not wish the Europeans supplying the surplus guns to get upset about losing income on a fairly profitable traffic.

Very few people ever mentioned this. Nor has the administration ever admitted what many Washington insiders know—that the State Department and the Johnson administration had the power to stop such imports whenever they desire. Johnson's administration preferred to keep trying to attack the NRA for opposing its legislative goals. It made much more sensational television and newspaper copy that way, however factually astray.

Nor did John Kennedy's brothers ever mention that State, not NRA, foiled his own economically motivated proposal.

In the summer of 1968, spurred by the killing of Robert Kennedy, his former power base of Massachusetts enacted a gun-owner licensing law. Governor John Volpe took off for the governors' conference with a copy of it, self-assuredly assuming (out loud) that all other states would be impelled to follow suit. Instead the governors' conference took a "to-each-his-own" standpoint that upset Volpe, Vermont Governor Philip Hoff, and a few others.

Meantime, big-city mayors were leading movements against guns. San Francisco's Mayor Joseph Alioto urged people to turn in their guns for fusing into a memorial to "the victims of assassins' guns." A few women's groups and others conducted drives to make children surrender toy guns. A few clergymen conducted highly histrionic cry-ins.

No one cried for the thousands of young men who died in various recent wars because their mothers and clergymen didn't want them exposed to guns as children—when they might have learned skills to keep them alive later, in rice paddies, on hillsides, or on beaches.

No one cried for the thousands of unarmed victims of violent crimes who were refused or discouraged when they sought guns to defend their homes.

But on the other hand, not too many people, after sober reflection, bought *all* the anti-gun messages. The reaction set in, too, in Congress. Senators and representatives who buckled under an inundation of anti-gun mail staged by the Kennedy publicity machine in late June and early July were hardening again in late July and August. The reaction from "home" in most cases was not nearly as condemnatory of guns as the initial, murder-sparked emotion. The usual smears, slogans, and jargon were evoked—vicious lobbying killed all sane gun controls, and so forth—but the simple fact was that people in general weren't sharing Ramsey Clark's fixation that guns cause most of our evils, no matter how often and plaintively he repeated the cant.

*

Chapter 9

No Racism Necessary

✳ ✳ ✳ ✳ ✳

"The results of our study indicate that the Civilian Marksmanship Program sponsored and supported by the Army . . . administered by the Director of Civilian Marksmanship contributes significantly to the development of rifle marksmanship and proficiency and confidence in the ability to use a rifle effectively in combat on the part of those who participate in the program or benefit indirectly from it. Unfortunately only a relatively small percentage of Army trainees appear to have been members of DCM-affiliated gun clubs (just over 3 percent of our sample) or received any marksmanship training prior to entering service (32 percent)."—the Arthur D. Little Report

IT IS IMPOSSIBLE FOR A REASONABLE MAN TO BE A RACIST WITH A Negro veteran of Vietnam or Korea. Because there is no gainsaying the kind of equality won in places like Vietnam or Korea. There is a more perfect democracy of merit, an egalitarianism, within the military structure, that no segment of our society here at home has been able to achieve.

Time magazine, which has difficulty recognizing marksmanship, reported all *this* quite clearly from Vietnam during 1967. It was a perversity of our time that those struggling most violently for racial justice at home—the Black Power advocates—were also anti-military, because it has been among the military that the American Negro first realized reasonable equality and it has been among the military that he has come closest to fulfilling his own role as a free citizen with strong responsibilities and unchallenged rights.

The people screaming the loudest against the Vietnamese war, however right or wrong they may have been from other standpoints, failed to recognize that the Vietnamese war is where the Negro American filed full claim—long overdue—to his proportionate share in America's future.

Instead, the anti-racial involvement got off on such dramatic but historically wobbly pleas as how the Negro was doing much more than his share of combat duty and taking more casualties than was right, and other complaints.

They are, of course, right. Negro troops are serving in higher proportion than whites, in combat and in the military generally. But there are rather obvious economic and social reasons for this. And more pertinent, racial or national minorities have so served in the United States Army during all of its wars except the great wars—the Civil War and World Wars One and Two were the *only* ones in which the full cross section of the population played its part.

Negro-Americans and Spanish- (or Mexican-) Americans are probably serving in less disproportionate numbers now than Irishmen did in the Old Army of the 1870's or 1880's. WASPs fought the Mexican War—largely WASPs from the South and West.

In the decades right after the Irish famines of the 1840's and the liberal unrest in Germany and most of Europe of 1848, Germans and Irishmen served in numbers hugely out of proportion to their number in our population. They comprised a large segment of the Regular Army which formed the nucleus of the Union forces at the start of the Civil War.

Irish and German troopers were the hard enlisted core of the post–Civil War army that fought its way across the Plains and quieted the Indian frontier. There were probably more Irishmen in the United States Army in 1870 or 1880—per capita—than there are people of *any* minority bloc today. In some units, more than

50 percent of the troops may have been of Irish descent or birth at that time.

The Irish accordingly gained a reputation as a fighting or martial race. But the truth was, they gravitated into the United States Army because it was a way up in our society, a refuge for many (whom hard discipline and good leadership molded into good troops), or a career, however socially limited. The Germans, the various nationalities from Austria-Hungary, from Russia, and elsewhere sought Army service for the same reasons.

It was no accident that the field music of our 1870 Army was largely Irish in origin, because the Army was largely Irish, at least from master sergeant down—and there were West Pointers and other commissioned officers of Irish origin as well. The Irish were not necessarily more warlike or martial. In fact, a high porportion of them were and are poets or politicians, not so much soldiers (although St. Patrick's Day oratory would lead one to believe otherwise). But the less educated, the more feckless, and the groping among them found homes, temporarily or for life (sometimes a very short life) in the United States Army.

And so it is with Negroes and those of Mexican descent in the 1960's. It is nothing new, nor anything to get unduly wrought up over. Most of the Negro career soldiers and officers acknowledge, if you read the press dispatches, that they have had better opportunities within service than they would outside it. Perhaps this is a sad commentary on a supposedly democratic society—but it is not the Army's fault. The Army, starting with the Korean fighting, has done more on the positive side of democracy than all those supposedly democratic, liberal forces which constantly berate the military as undemocratic and illiberal. All those people who caper around anti-Vietnam demonstrations (acutely on camera, most of the time) and point with scorn to the "fascist" Army and the "warmongers" of the Pentagon and the "butchers" in Saigon should police their own house first. For compared to the astringent, pragmatic egalitarianism of the military, their house needs much cleaning.

The military is not democratic in the socio-political sense. There is rigidity and some caste, and there have to be rank and distinction and discipline. No military service can have a town-meeting, first-name congeniality. But within the spare bounds of military rank and rigidity, there is democracy. A colonel in the Air Force is a colonel, black or white or in between. A good, tough sergeant in the Marines is just that, color be damned. On an Army or Air Force base a Negro master sergeant's wife and kids are just as "good" as a white master sergeant's.

Can all that high-culture white liberalism outside the military, with its great concern for humanity in the mass but its boredom with individuals, accomplish as much? They worship Martin Luther King and grovel when Stokely Carmichael berates them. Would they understand Air Force Colonel Daniel (Chappie) James, who is a colonel United States Air Force because he is a damned good combat pilot and shoots down MIGs and made colonel neither because of nor in spite of the fact that he is a Negro?

The writer shot as a member of a state pistol team at the 1965 National Matches at Camp Perry. An enlisted Marine, white, scored and changed his target. A Negro sergeant was telling him and a couple of dozen other Marines, white and other colors, when and how to do this. This same routine was repeated all up and down the line, by hundreds of white and Negro officers, sergeants, corporals, and privates, Army, Marine, and Air Force, as 2,400 competitors shot each day. There was nothing much to it, really, for those who were there. Negroes ordered whites around, whites ordered Negroes around. The real surprise was on the outside, where this did not occur often.

On how many campuses, in how many newsrooms, in what offices, on which industrial or craft jobs could that free yet disciplined equality be duplicated?

Negro troops have always been in the Army, increasingly so since emancipation. The Indian-fighting Old Army used four Negro regiments, two of cavalry and two of infantry, to help police potentially hostile territory from the Milk River to the Mexican border. Sometimes they were sent across that border, too, in dutiful and calculated violation of international convention, because hostiles took refuge in a republic which could not police itself. There were Negro troopers in the expedition which chased Pancho Villa, that earlier-day Castro. However, Negroes never fully came into their own as free men in the service until the Defense Department started to tear apart segregation in the Korean-era Army. Thereafter there was an accelerated improvement in the morale and quality of Negro American soldiers; it continues up to this date.

In NRA and other military rifle competition, too, there have long been Negro shooters of note. One was Sergeant Emmit Hawkins of the old 24th Infantry Regiment. Hawkins was the first and perhaps only shooter to score a perfect 100 x 100 in the old military skirmish match, according to the article "Days Of The Krag" by the late Colonel Townsend Whelen in the 1960 *Gun Digest*. The skirmish run was an intensely practical course—one still worth considering, incidentally, for training troops with rifles.

The Negro citizen can participate in marksmanship and hunting at home to the degree he wishes. The Little Report found small evidence—some, but not much—of racial discrimination practiced by gun clubs. There should be none, and it can be fairly well counted on that the Defense Department and Director of Civilian Marksmanship will ferret out what little there is, or will do so if frantic politicians do not succeed in dismantling the DCM altogether.

And in hunting, the writer can again testify personally how well whites and blacks get along. I lived for a time on a cotton and grain farm managed by a Negro—we rented the dead owner's home (his survivors moved into town) and dwelt exactly next to the manager and his family. We all hunted birds and wild pigs and deer and kept guns as we did vehicles or groceries or whisky. No one menaced anyone else. Kids played together, white and black, with little of the "whitey" and "nigger" animosities or backlash.

In fact, if it hadn't been for television news and daily papers, we'd not have known those tensions existed outside a few fanciful imaginations.

If young Negro citizens are to be serving their country, they deserve the same chance to learn to survive that other citizens receive. This includes pre-induction marksmanship training. Those hell bent to dismantle the marksmanship program and turn ranges into social-gospel parks should remember that. Marksmanship can play as vital a role in the training of young Negro (or other) citizens as Scouting, church, or the selected political sermons of the latest demagogue. It may even have more lasting value than these others. Because if Negroes are getting shot at for "whitey" in Vietnam, it is also being done for black people, for self-respect and pride at home, and for yellow people who do not care to be butchered or enslaved by others. If white men fought a war to eliminate slavery in the United States, they also did it, in a way, for their own self-respect and freedom.

✳

Where Are All The Brownings?

✳ ✳ ✳ ✳ ✳

"He requested me to take it apart and show the 'in-
wardness of the thing' and was greatly impressed
that all I needed was a screwdriver."—Christopher
Spencer, inventor of the repeating rifle bearing his
name, describing a test of his gun by President
Lincoln in 1863. Like most of the eminent 19th
century gun designers, Spencer was a civilian.

HOW MANY YOUNG AMERICANS ARE BEING UNNECESSARILY KILLED OR
maimed in brushfire or rice-paddy wars because of the shortcomings of our current military small-arms system?

And is stringent legislation on military-type arms—specifically
the National Firearms Act of 1934—stifling civilian genius that
could provide us with much better small arms?

The Defense Department has not dealt with the problem. It
appears more preoccupied with the fate of a few men in costly
super-equipages—the F111 fighter-bomber, for example—than
with what happens to many men wielding the most basic and still
very necessary tool of war, the rifle.

Where are the potential John Brownings of this era, the
geniuses who might have developed rifles and other small arms
that would make the current M16 controversy impossible—because
they would have devised weapons far superior to the M16?

The National Firearms Act could be a culprit in this. It levies
an almost prohibitive tax of $200 on the possession of a fully

automatic weapon (exactly the kind of weapon which is the basic tool of most war today). This puts the average young American tinkerer with a mechanical bent right out of the gun-design business, unless he is content to tinker solely with sporting arms. Yet the emphasis on fully automatic weapons has been escalating since the First World War.

How many young American tinkerers—potential Brownings—have produced super plastics or new television tubes or computers instead of a far-out new rifle because of that $200 tax and attendant red tape before they can own a fully automatic gun? The $200 must be paid to own even a prototype weapon—submachine gun or automatic rifle. In most cases, the tax is valid for just one gun. Amassing a number of different types for comparison, firing, tests, and experiments means $200 per gun!

One wonders how many advanced models of firearms Browning and his peers—Borchardt, Berdan, Henry, Colt, and Remington—would have produced if required to pay some prohibitive ownership fee to possess prototype arms of their day.

For that matter, how many cars could Henry Ford and his peers have invented if payment of some exorbitant government tax had been prerequisite to owning models of the early motor cars?

Interest in small arms among young Americans has declined steadily since the 1890's. The end of the free-land, homesteading, venture-West era was probably the major cause. An increasingly urbanized society has turned the curiosity and inventiveness of its youth to other fields—electronics, computers, mechanization, luxuries. Yet the need for small arms persists, as wars in Korea and Vietnam and many other places clearly show. The need for skill with small arms (an entirely separate and enormous area of discussion) persists too, as the Little Report and testimonials from the battlefields establish—without *competent* challenge.

Then why our continuing, senseless de-emphasis on the scientific, mechanical, and other thinking required to produce better small arms for our troops?

In most of the 19th century, American eminence was unrivaled in the design of small arms. Not just Browning but a dozen or more inventors and outstanding mechanics produced an amazing and seemingly endless diversity of fine rifles and other weapons, most of them geared to mass production. First our military and then our civilian achievements set the world pace in small-arms design; Germans excelled in military weapons and Britons in high-class, hand-made sporting arms, but the United States was the world's leading creator of mass-produced sporting weapons within the price reach of almost all citizens.

With the end of the frontier in the 1890's, and attendant urbanization, common interest in guns declined over the country. What interest did survive was preserved in rifle and shotgun groups (notably the National Rifle Association) and was stimulated by the two world wars when large numbers of young men were exposed to rifle training. But after the National Firearms Act was passed to make machine guns and sawed-off shotguns more difficult for gangsters and bandits to get, the little remaining interest in owning and experimenting with fully automatic weapons was forcibly restrained (killed outright is a better way of stating it). Most work in military automatic weapons was confined to a few government arsenals. The broad area of civilian interest, the field from which most of our mechanical and inventive genius has flowed since the colonial period, was out of bounds by Act of Congress.

Has government a duty to generate interest in the development of small arms as part of the military effort? Shouldn't the civilian mind be cultivated and encouraged in this area as it is in so many others?

If so, adjustments in the National Firearms Act could be made to allow for the reasonable ownership and experimentation with fully automatic weapons. Certainly other nations manage this. Sweden and Switzerland are prime examples. While they may regulate the possession of all firearms to a greater extent than the United States, they do not do so prohibitively and punitively—and they do much more to encourage developments with military small arms. They do not limit experiment with such arms to military and arsenal personnel. They also issue fully automatic weapons to militia forces and allow possession and reasonable latitude in the use of such weapons.

Ownership of fully automatic weapons may need more control than ownership of sporting rifles, shotguns, or pistols—but to levy a $200 tax or otherwise stifle embryonic genius in bureaucracy is simply silly. A tinkerer or ordnance buff who wishes a Uzi burp gun or AK 47 or the like for fully honorable uses should be able to get such guns without harassment. The current course retards advances in small arms that our troops need to do better (and live longer) wherever they are committed. To paraphrase a current tune, it's a strange, strange world we live in. We send into battle the world's best-paid, best-fed, best-uniformed, best-doctored troops—equipped with small arms that range from obsolescent (the Model 1911 .45 pistol, M1 and M2 carbines, M3 submachine gun) to controversial (the M16 and M14 rifles). It is a peculiar standard for the world's most technologically mature nation.

The Russians, employing incentives and driving forces peculiar to their totalitarian system, have for the last fifteen or twenty years possessed the world's best small-arms "family." It looks rugged and unlovely, but their small-arms grouping works quite well, as we keep discovering anew in various paddies and jungles. The Russians have outfitted their own forces and those of their satellites with the weapons—much to our detriment. We have yet to even start tapping our own huge reserve of creative individual genius in the small-arms realm. As long as we stupidly exert bureaucratic limits on this ability, we are not likely to do any better than we have in the last 25 or 30 years. We need to surpass our potential foes, not just try to stay abreast of them in this vital competition— the message of which is spelled out in those stark casualty lists from Asia every Thursday.

J. Frank Dobie, a Texas folklorist and teacher who would be

among the last to bless the military or making war, said something that may have a certain strong application to late 20th century America, the courses which face it and the forces that tear at it: In his *The Mustangs* (Little, Brown & Company, 1952), Dobie said, "The breed [mustangs] did not disappear from the land . . . through being driven away, but through castration."

Chapter 11

Communications

✳ ✳ ✳ ✳ ✳

"The National Firearms Act . . . was the outgrowth
of a number of bills intended to regulate firearms
. . . introduced in the Congress following the
attempted assassination of President-elect Roosevelt
in February 1933."—the Associated Press perpetuating
the factual error in a Justice Department brief, which
was itself based on an incorrect statement in an
anti-gun book.

THE GREAT PROBLEM AFFECTING GUN LEGISLATION IN THE U.S.
has for several years been one of communications—a gap between
the shooter-sportsmen element of the population and the large
remainder of the public.

The gap has been caused first by a gradual tendency among the
majority of urbanized citizens to have less and less exposure to
firearms, second by the din of propaganda and distortion raised by
those who seek strict gun controls and those who subscribe to this
goal without understanding the situation or the consequences.

It is very chic, especially in the urban centers where gun ownership is slight, to link crime with access to guns. However, there is
absolutely nothing to warrant this idea in any consistent, substantial way. In Chapter 8 readers can determine how strong such
arguments really are when the full body of facts is analyzed—not
the highly selective figures juggled by the Justice Department,
Lyndon Johnson, and the rest of the sob mongers.

But the hurdle is that those who would (and could) rout such distorted arguments have had almost no chance, especially in the mass media. The national television networks, the major metropolitan dailies (with a few singular exceptions), and the more popular magazines (some of them owned or manipulated by powerful anti-gun interests) have been approximately as objective on the gun-law fuss as Adolf Hitler—as representative of a free press as Dr. Paul Goebbels, Herr Hitler's late lie-master. The tactics of those urging stiff controls have been to literally screech murder; to make flat and false or juggled statements; to imply that adherents of civilian marksmanship are somehow unstable or extremist and to disparage the Second Amendment to the Constitution while indulging in all kinds of flag-draping and fertility rituals to keep the First Amendment sacrosanct. None of these claims has any validity, but they remain persistently popular and have been all too readily seized on by other members of the journalistic business on most levels. The exception has been a certain tendency to insist on objectivity and honesty at the local level among some radio and television outlets.

The only publishing element where the shooting sportsman's case has been faithfully presented has been in his own field—gun and hunting publications. These have strained to do an objective job to the extent of even citing the opposition's chief points, something the mass media have failed to even approach. The *American Rifleman* has played a significant role here, along with *Gun Week* (a tabloid newspaper), assisted and occasionally embarrassed by other publications in the same field. The three old, established all-round outdoor magazines—*Field & Stream, Sports Afield*, and *Outdoor Life*—have to a major extent joined the fight in behalf of responsible gun owners, with especial emphasis on writing by Richard Starnes in *Field & Stream*. Starnes's dissection of the Philadelphia city gun ordinance of 1965 demolished its value in the view of any but the hopelessly bigoted.

One or two gun publications have gone a bit far. One magazine's editor was embarrassed when quizzed about alleged misrepresentations before the Dodd subcommittee in 1965. But other witnesses opposing Dodd's thesis were so rudely treated or subjected to such endless delays or harassments that one or two cases of misrepresentation in the anti-Dodd corner hardly seem worth mentioning.

One prominent editor, Ashley Halsey, Jr., of the *Rifleman*, debated the issue with Teddy Kennedy for a British Broadcasting Corporation audience, showing that a few media at least pay some sincere regard to objectivity. Halsey, a former *Saturday Evening Post* editor, is far more sophisticated and erudite than most gun magazine writers or editors and was more than a match for the youngest Kennedy politician. Kennedy, who may have marched to the microphone thinking he was to debate some graduate gunman who dealt in four-letter expletives, rarely afterward accepted the gage of battle from *Rifleman* or NRA adversaries. He failed to show up for a spring 1968 debate with the NRA, in fact, in Boston, his own bailiwick. His foe on that occasion was to have been Representative John Dingell, Michigan Democrat, who went right ahead and stated his case, unopposed.

Harlon B. Carter, former Border Patrol head and former NRA president, said, "I have never heard anything like it in the Congress of a free country"—citing how Dodd mistreated witnesses and how his top inquisitor, Carl Perian, tried to shake all opposing testimony. "I have talked to respectable, reliable citizens who testified against Dodd's bill. They told me they were cursed, cut off, interrupted, not allowed to resume, granted a time to appear, and then repeatedly stalled—every trick in the book." So far as the writer has been able to find out, no major network, wire service, or other mass publication carried any account of this behavior toward witnesses who didn't agree with Dodd.

The distortion of the valid role of guns has carried over to the Vietnam war, ridiculous as it appears, and to other wars. In the United States' intervention in Santo Domingo, newsmen—bred in the urban folklore tradition whereby murder by knife or bludgeon or throttling is somehow less heinous than by gun—were constantly guilty of disparaging the solid role of enemy-killing marksmanship. When Charles Whitman went on his murderous sniping rampage in Austin, endless copy was ground out telling how his father made a "sniper" out of him (most of the sources wouldn't know a genuine sniper from some fool on a roof), how he was excessively fond of guns, how there must somehow be a relationship between skill with weapons and the murderous madness that led Whitman to take fourteen lives with guns.

After Whitman's terror and the Kennedy and King assassinations, a heedless, blatant minority worked overtime to associate marksmanship with violence. The Marine Corps in particular drew opprobrium, although Whitman did not make the top Marine classification with a rifle and Oswald was an indifferent shot. But the anti-marksmanship, guns-mean-violence element managed to cast doubt where they wished, at least to some degree. Not many thinking citizens reflected that the vast majority of shooters, in and out of service, have made invaluable contributions to the nation from its inception to now and have not been menaces to the republic at all, but rather leaders and defenders of what we most revere.

When the rampages occurred, the Kennedy-Dodd element joined the pack straightaway. So did most broadcasters and publishers. A few stout voices in public and journalistic life urged a go-slow attitude—led by Governors John Connally of Texas and Ronald Reagan of California, Senator Roman Hruska, and a few others. A few Western and Southern newspapers helped resist the senseless pursuit of punitive legislation—laws to restrict 20 or 30 million citizens because of the idiocies of a few. But on the two coasts and in the urbanized sections generally, hysteria was hell-bent to override whatever constitutional roadblocks remained. It was journalistic mob spirit, written or uttered by those who wish to preside over the free news dissemination of a free people but who like to exercise that freedom most selectively—only in their own causes or those they adhere to. The spirit of editorials and even of news "reports"—piously wrapped up in a word falsely connoting honest objectivity—was the spirit of some Baghdad mob. Yet the eminently respectable news managers would be the last to concede the injustice and hysteria of their campaigning.

It became impossible to elicit any kind of major-medium rebuttal. After *Harper's*, in late 1964, ran an article by a paid public relations man, Carl Bakal, disparaging gun ownership, even established writers were rebuffed when they tried to reply. James E. Serven, one of the world's top authorities and writers on firearms collecting, was told by one publisher: "The only pro-gun article we might look at would have to be from someone prominent, like General Curtis LeMay." When one author told a Dodd press aide he was preparing an article exposing the more ludicrous and criminal aspects of New York's Sullivan Law, the aide demanded to know who the publisher would be. The not-too-subtle implication was that publication just might be sidetracked. A well-known writer on infantry war and weapons, dedicated to marksmanship because he had seen its lifesaving effects, was told in effect to forget it when he tried to sell a pro-gun article to several major magazines. Those preaching or paying for the curb-guns message felt they had dominant influence to stop most such articles, except in the "gun" press. Very often they did.

All three major networks have done one or more "reports" on the gun-legislation controversy. They were obviously done to drum up anti-gun feeling, and they were as lopsided as the producers and writers could make them. The two main violators of normally objective treatment were "CBS Reports—Murder and the Right to Bear Arms" in 1964 (re-run after Whitman in 1966) and NBC's "Whose Right to Bear Arms?" dolled up as an "inquiry" in the spring of 1967. Loud and angry complaints to the Federal Communications Commission that these and other network shows outraged objectivity got absolutely nowhere. Barry Goldwater remarked that as long as Lyndon Johnson was both President and involved in making FCC appointments and was interested in advancing anti-gun legislation, the FCC was not likely to take any action whatsoever. The prediction proved remarkably accurate. The FCC did not even answer some formal complaints; when it did, it worked hard at obscuring issues and facts in legalese.

Not satisfied with discrediting marksmanship, disparaging gun clubs, and linking almost any gun ownership with criminality, the major networks went on an anti-hunting tangent. Such shows as "Cowboy in Africa," "Gentle Ben," "Daktari," and the Disney productions were primarily dedicated to orienting the public against hunting. *None* ever gave shooting sportsmen credit for the basic, irrefutable, and central fact that most wildlife programs would not even exist without firearms-hunting revenues. Complaints to the producers and others about this gross unfairness elicited either no response at all or vague replies shrouded in incomprehensible platitudes. Later, an ABC-TV "talk show" sprite, Dick Cavett, joined Cleveland Amory and David Susskind in renewed and bitter attacks on the NRA and hunting, along with the state game departments. Amory's diatribes drew objections even from non-hunting viewers in such publications as *TV Guide*. Amory's chief qualification to criticize game management proved to be high office in the Humane Society, which is a long way from a degree in wildlife management or related subjects.

The list of those raping objectivity on the gun issue is virtually endless. It would be far easier to cite those who *have* been objective. This would include the Phoenix and Indianapolis dailies, the *St. Louis Post-Dispatch*, the *Wall Street Journal*, the *Dallas Morning News*, and a few other Western and Southern dailies. One prohunting television show is ABC's "The American Sportsman," which upset Cavett and Amory almost to distraction on one talkfest. NBC-TV tried hard to limit its "Sportsman's Holiday" gunhunting exposure to the shooting of birds, not larger game which the more sensitive might endow with semi-human qualities. The NBC show settled for extensive fishing, camping, and nature-study coverage, a few flings at upland-bird shooting and a considerable amount of pure drivel about the pleasures of photography afield.

No one ever measured the financial support provided wildlife management by camera fans compared with that of sportsmen.

An excellent example of the reasonableness of newspaper-television exposure was the Little Report. When the civilian marksmanship program was challenged for its value and integrity, this made headlines all over the country. The resultant dispute triggered the Little study. But when the almost entirely favorable Little Report was delivered to the Defense Department, it was strictly back-page. The few papers that did set it up front seized upon the one or two mildly adverse points, ignoring its great preponderance of favorable findings.

When the assassination of John F. Kennedy took place, no objective examination found its way into news treatment. The notion that right-wing gun fanatics did Jack Kennedy in persists, half a decade after Dallas, because the press somehow subscribes to Earl Warren's initial reaction (he felt sure it was a gaggle of "ultras" who did the deed). Somehow the fact that JFK was done in by one demented leftist, or perhaps more than one leftist, never gained the acceptance that the evidence warranted. In the political climate of the 1960's, the image-makers simply did not want to expose the probabilities—not when these disagreed with prevailing sociology.

The same occurred after the Martin Luther King and Robert Kennedy murders. A large percentage of headline writers and reporters depicted the King killer as a murderous Klansman—which he may have been. But there was and still is powerful indication that the King killing was cleverly set up to make it appear the work of a radical rightist in order to best serve the political goals of the left wing elements which may well have actually been responsible. It is entirely possible the King killing was bought and paid for in Havana or Peking. Nothing would better serve the purposes of Havana or Peking or both than to make King's death seem due to right-wing extremism—racism of an altogether different kind than that preached in Havana and Peking. Bobby Kennedy's murder bears traces of the same origin, but it has been either unfashionable or politically troublesome to suggest this. It is far easier to blame the King and RFK murders on "society." The patient, long-suffering American middle class, punching bag for a generation of ideologues who happen to hate stability and decency along with firearms and order, remains the best scapegoat for the failures of the sociologists. Lyndon Johnson, willingly abetted by wide television and radio exposure, managed to convince some people at least that somehow guns did Bobby in, not someone using a gun.

When marksmanship was being disparaged while it was severely needed by Americans in Vietnam, no major news service or network went to responsible persons to show the program's worth. No service leader or veteran noncommissioned officer with real credentials was interviewed. The press gave great attention to the highly questionable criticism of Senator Stephen Young of Ohio and Congressman Henry Gonzalez of Texas (who may see Minutemen under his bed and elsewhere). There was and is a lengthy list of retired servicemen from generals down through privates who could attest to the real worth of good shooting. Except on occasional local levels, no such experts were interviewed. Headline-seeking politicians with peculiar grudges had carte blanche in the press and on television.

One sideshow came in the journalistic dispute (a very one-sided dispute) over gun laws and how they affect the legitimate shooting sports. *Saturday Review of Literature* critic John Barkham wrote the author that he felt strict gun controls did not have any adverse effect on international target shooting. He said Australian, English, and other shooting teams did not seem fettered by such controls. But Franklin Orth, NRA executive vice president who has worked a large part of his life to improve United States shooting performance, disagrees quite strongly. Orth and other officials close to American target shooting think that in a free society beguiled with all kinds of competing recreations, something as elemental as shooting should not be unduly fettered, as it would be by stringent regulations which tend to discourage participation. Orth, now president of the United States Olympic Committee, and his partisans argue that in police or totalitarian states, shooting is often a directed part of a maximum-effort sports program in which participants are subsidized to a much greater degree than in free nations. Neither this view nor the agonizingly slow but firm return to eminence of United States international shooters has ever had even reasonable exposure by the mass media. Most newspaper readers and television sports fans simply don't know of our immense success in recent international shooting events—after frustrating years of rebuilding, much of it underwritten and guided by the NRA. The chapter (7) on target shooting tells more about this. Suffice it to say here that the national press has ignored it with steadfastness. So much for journalistic sportsmanship.

Most real knowledge on sport shooting has been unprinted or unspoken at a crucial time, when all the arguments for it should have been marshaled with telling effect. No member of the administration in Washington showed the courage to say that marksmanship was vital on the battlefield and important for our international sports posture. It was fairly easy to guess that orders from headquarters were in effect requiring no positive advocacy of the general case for the shooting sports or the specific value of civilian marksmanship. This made even more remarkable the reluctance of the mass media to state such cases; normally the major press and television outlets are dedicated to finding dishonesty or deviation from fact in government and ruthlessly exposing it. With the gun-law argument, dishonesty passed as gospel, especially in the upper levels of news dissemination. There appeared to be some kind of unformalized code granting license to distort fact about gun ownership and to prevent reasonable rebuttal.

This situation isn't getting any better with the passage of time, as the glut of anti-gun distortions after the Bobby Kennedy killing shows very clearly.

✳

Philosophy and Legislation

✳ ✳ ✳ ✳ ✳

"Kids who have been exposed to rifles or other guns before coming into service made better shots because they did not freeze [at] their first contact with the enemy."—Lieutenant Colonel Frank Muñoz, USA (retired), speaking in 1968 on values he learned while leading troops in Korea, 1950–1953.

SOMETIME DURING THE LAST GENERATION, THE ROLES OF THE LIBERAL left and conservative right with respect to the private ownership of guns have become reversed.

In our earlier history, most American liberals associated an armed citizenry with a secure base for democracy. Armed citizens, they seemed to feel, constituted the last, best defense of individual freedom and an ultimate citizen militia reserve that made representative democracy more stable. It used to be the typical conservative who, however quietly, nursed a vague fear of an armed citizenry—perhaps because he tended to think of it as a mob.

But since 1955 or 1960, the fear of armed citizens appears to be rising among liberals and too rapidly receding among conservatives. Perhaps this may be because in the latter half of the 20th century, most conservatives in our politics represent areas which are still basically rural. In these districts, many citizens still grow up using firearms, often for hunting and on occasion for defense. The urban constituency has largely grown up feeling that guns are primarily dangerous weapons of death, terror, and crime—and thus should be limited to the very few. This is an attitude much like that prevailing in Britain and across most of Europe. It is one, as shown in this book, for which the British public and other free nations pay in blood and tissue from time to time, when an unarmed citizenry is abruptly called on to defend itself against well-prepared and intolerable aggressions.

Perhaps, too, a big reason why urban liberals fear guns and those who own them is the increasing satisfaction of liberals with greater centralization and a more powerful government. The 1970-era liberal, whether or not he realizes it, has inherited the fear of the mob that once characterized Hamiltonians (although as Chapter 3 indicates, not Hamilton himself). The liberal is increasingly preoccupied with making man safe against himself—to pad him with proofs against all the human frailties. Carried to its logical reach, this means that many of those who believe in modern centralized government and attendant planning would also like to insure that government against disruption by an ungrateful public—by a public enraged at encroachment on or losses of its individual liberties. Thus the liberal of our time, if he isn't more conscientious than some of his leaders indicate, may be building the foundation of police statism. He says government should trust in the people, but in fact he often fears the people.

The gun-control syndrome is an example. For 50 or 60 years before John Kennedy's assassination, the leaders of liberalism had been losing touch with the realities learned so bitterly by their antecedents. When John Kennedy was killed with a rifle, most of the drive for sweeping gun-control measures—a form of expiation of guilt for something beyond the control of any of us—drew its support largely from the urban, liberal-left, and humanist side of American politics. The same pattern was followed when Bobby Kennedy was killed with a pistol.

Most of the caution and skeptical resistance was led by conservative or moderate political spokesmen like Senator Roman Hruska of Nebraska, Congressmen John Dingell of Michigan, and Cecil

King of California. This is of course not a sweeping classification, and there are plenty of exceptions. Thomas Dodd, nominally a moderate Democrat from Connecticut, spearheaded the anti-gun effort. He had some support from conservatives with his original bill but lost much of this when he switched to the more punitive Justice Department proposal. Perversely, liberals like Westerners Frank Church of Idaho, Lee Metcalfe of Montana, and Fred Harris of Oklahoma opposed Dodd more on a regional basis than from partisanship. But essentially, resistance to Dodd's goals and those of his political allies in this fight has been a rural-regional grouping that cuts across all other lines. Most conservatives, including Eastern and Southern ones, lined up with the Westerners against Dodd because that is what their constituencies desired.

Oddly, Dodd and Ted Kennedy come from states with many manufacturers of sporting firearms. Both have so far managed to ignore this hazard. Dodd's "crusade" against guns started as a primarily economic one—to curb the importation of cheap foreign war-surplus guns that were literally killing competition by reputable United States (and especially New England) plants that had to meet high payrolls.

Most opposition to guns, stimulated by the Kennedy and King shootings, derives from the passive, apathetic state of mind in the nation. When physical educators fret about our lack of exercise, they are directly referring to a state of body, but what is basically at fault is a state of mind. Many of our people are offshoots of a vigorous European peasantry or of one of the most individualistic, self-reliant, and combative racial blocs in history (the old Scots-Irish and Anglo-Irish stocks that pioneered our frontiers). But they have become a static, passive society that prefers to watch a few gifted athletes perform in some packed arena before television cameras. This in turn has led to a let-the-government-do-it attitude toward almost everything. On crime, it is a let-the-police-do-it philosophy. This has much to do with the reluctance of citizens to try to deter crime, even violent crime in agonizing progress (like the 40 New York suburbanites who were spectators to the knifing to death of a woman named Kitty Genovese—whose name may yet make the dictionary as a synonym for public apathy).

Citizens who fear guns or are conditioned by a passive and fearful society to avoid them, who are not trained in their use, are indeed safe candidates for victimization. Most city dwellers fit the category. They tend to think guns are for the police (most of whom are not nearly as capable with firearms as the average civilian target competitor) or the military (only about 10 or 15 percent of whom are really adept with small arms). As Scandinavian writer Nils Kvale said, the average Swede would be horror stricken if a citizen shot and killed a criminal. It would produce newspaper headlines. Even a police shooting of a felon upsets such a highly urbanized society. This attitude is certainly not limited to Swedes. It's common to most persons living in Europe and along our own Northeastern and Californian coasts. Much of this is evident in the disapproval shown when some rare citizen does take individual, on-the-spot, forceful action to stop a crime in motion—even if he is preventing the homicide by which some other innocent citizen's life is menaced.

Many attorneys look with disapproval on even straightforward and justifiable cases of self-defense killing. Courts in some jurisdictions are constantly making it harder to get off even on open-and-shut self-defense taking of life. The use of firearms to prevent serious crimes against persons is becoming distasteful. Not at all untypical is the attitude of one big-city criminal lawyer: "I'll defend you for a self-defense homicide shooting, but I won't like it. And you'll pay like hell for it." This same individual is in the front rank of various crusades in his area and frequently goes out of his way to be identified with various "causes"; he would battle to the end to defend a client who flew a Red flag on a campus or precipitated a riot at some sit-in, or assaulted a police officer. But he balked at defending an elderly citizen who used a gun to oust an intruder—an intruder with a long police record who had made repeated assaults on an old man in his own home.

Along with this attitude is a sentimental hope among some

penologists and sociologists (most of whom have faced only the locked-up or subdued criminal) that if guns weren't obtainable, felonies wouldn't happen. Their charges would not get involved in holdups, rapes, killings, arson, or the like. The gun, this permissive reasoning (for lack of a better word) insists, causes much of our woes. But statistical evidence cited in this book and available to the unbiased person anywhere does not support this soft view. And the insanities we have committed as a nation at peace, destroying and vilifying our military preparedness, reinforce the evidence in spades. Such soft thinking simply gets more people killed. It doesn't stop war or crime—it simply accelerates or broadens them, by making the victim all the more easy to assault.

Tom Dodd may back gun-control proposals from conviction, but if so it is a peculiar conviction for a man with essentially moderate views on most matters. The writer has interviewed Dodd, surrounded by his press agents and inquisitors. Dodd's method of operation on the gun argument is a mixture of showmanship, cavalier treatment of opposing witnesses, high-class press agentry (his aides Gene Gleason and Carl Perian are genuine professionals), and emotion. I am convinced that he wants to go to his Destiny, wherever it is, with some major bill named after Tom Dodd. He happened to make the perhaps injudicious decision to grab the "gun bill" ploy. He plucked off one with more thorns than roses. It might have been a bill to police privies or control the interstate traffic in hairdressers of confused gender. It would have been better for most of us if he had gone elsewhere to seek his immortality, in some better cause.

This is a strange country for Dodd to inflict his oratory and emotion on. Because as T. R. Fehrenbach said in *This Kind of War*, we are people whose troops will blow apart a Louvre to save the life of one man. We decimated villages all over Korea to save American GIs' lives—*rightly so*, however horrified allied observers may have been. We have done the same in Vietnam and will do it again if necessary. This is humanitarianism in its genuine form—concern for life where it can be exercised with any justification at all. "To Americans," as Fehrenbach (who in this writer's opinion is the finest author on war this country has produced) said, "flesh and blood and lives have always been more precious than sticks and stones, however assembled."

Yet we balk at teaching young citizens—whether black or white—how to shoot rifles before they are called on in earnest to do so in defense of us all and themselves. Is that humane? It may rather be delusion in a form approaching idiocy. It is at the very least extreme short sightedness by a people who would blow apart a Louvre to save a life.

Most authorities disagree to some degree on the best form, if any, for firearms legislation. Some oppose any, others propose too much. Certainly laws aimed at curbing criminal misuse of guns—by imposing more strenuous punishments—are acceptable to most people if they do not infringe too much on reasonable sporting and self-defense use of guns. History has shown complete disarmament is impossible. Disarming the public, it has been shown, would be ruinous to peace and order and would accelerate further the decline already evident in a shooting craft that is very important to free nations (even nations that don't appreciate it during spasms of self-doubt). Depriving citizens of guns to hunt with would wipe out the carefully built wildlife management techniques and systems—research, experimentation, restocking. These must have hunter-license revenues for wildlife to survive.

Administration spokesmen have failed to gauge the strength of opposition to their words and plans about restricting the access of free citizens to firearms. No one is sure of the numbers of votes shooting sportsmen, as such, can muster. It probably ranges somewhere between three or three and a half million to four or five million. It could amount to that much or a bit more if the wives, relatives, and close friends of sportsmen were to become deeply concerned about the course of firearms legislation. The sportsman vote as such was split in 1964. It was not then especially attentive to the plans for firearms legislation of various candidates, at least not at the presidential level—where gun controls were not an issue.

But in 1968, with an outgoing president who had endorsed the Justice Department's strange sociology on gun legislation, very few aware and thinking sportsmen went to the polls without being informed beforehand where each major candidate stood on the issue. They were tired of being blamed for the misdeeds of a handful of lunatics, a small proportion of the irresponsible, criminals who might better be in jail rather than undergoing on-the-street rehabilitation—and a couple of mindless or subsidized assassins. They were not and are not guilty of any of those misdeeds.

Administration supporters have not helped when, almost invariably, they referred to the Dodd-Justice bill as a "first step." A first step to what? Confiscation? Stringent registration that may be unconstitutional or oppressive? The language used by Dodd, Clark, Katzenbach, Ted Kennedy, and others has been unusually ill-chosen if they wanted to dispel doubts or abate fears about the real intent of their legislation. Unfortunately, if intransigence persists, so will fierce resistance. What would work is for those seeking legislation to call in a genuinely representative cross section of involved citizens, not just accept as oracular inspiration the schemes of a few social workers, criminal lawyers, and urban policemen. That was the makeup of the President's Crime Commission—and most of its recommendations have got us nowhere. When Ted Kennedy said the Dodd-Justice bill was drawn with sportsmen's considerations carefully in mind, he didn't mention that not one representative of the lawful, recognized shooting sports sat in on any phase of the bill's formulation. There is much more at stake than simply trying to gratify the wishes of *one* sociological school of thought. It should be evident that there are vast conservation, constitutional, military, and other issues, too. If dealing with a few thousand criminals is important (and it is), much more important must be the thinking and future and welfare of the 20 or more million sportsmen who provide this country with so much—led by their enormous contribution to wildlife management and conservation—and the 20 or so million other

Americans who feel they have a right or a duty to safeguard their homes and their persons in a time of admittedly wide peril.

The National Wildlife Federation, the Izaak Walton League, the National Rifle Association, the 50 states' conservation departments, the Wildlife Management Institute, the Audubon Society, the American Ordnance Association, the Association of the Army of the United States—all these and many more major elements should be adequately included in any body evolving a realistic program for practical firearms legislation, rather than the same old and tired social soothsayers whose advanced notions can be reconciled with no one else's. Veteran, off-the-battlefield testimony on marksmanship should count for much more than the prearranged prattle of the political, civilian chiefs of the Defense Department whose war experience is remote control. So should the ideas of policemen who do not necessarily sound like a Greek chorus for Tom Dodd.

The writer thinks there are two alternate approaches to firearms legislation which are worth considering. One is simply to adopt reasonable, workable controls—not an all-out-ban—on the interstate sale of firearms. This would probably get into the area of requiring a form of affidavit on mail shipments to ordinary citizens. This was the essence of the original Dodd bill. While some shooters and others disliked this, it probably had merit and would make sense. Under this approach, the states' own laws would continue in force, with the federal government supplying only a little framework. The last Johnson administration bill put age limits on the purchase of shoulder weapons (18) and handguns (21). Few quarrel with this provided the law is written so that it does not interfere with junior gun-club training, reasonable hunting and target exposure for younger teenagers, and a parent's right to guide, teach, and provide guns for his own offspring. A great many gun collectors currently buy dealers' licenses. It would make much more sense for the Treasury Department to create a license category for collectors, probably priced about the same as a dealer license, at $10 or $15, and remove the persistent confusion about the status of both classes of persons. Some Treasury Department agents have been guilty of downright harassment of collectors, only to prove some obscure point or set up a test case. This would be stopped by the institution of a reasonable collector-licensing program. Ordnance experts, those who have a genuine need or interest in the lawful use and development of heavy ordnance, should be licensed, not persecuted because they find the insides of an anti-tank rifle or a Bofors gun intriguing. Care can be exercised to insure the licenses—dealer, collector, ordnance—are not issued to persons with undesirable backgrounds—felonies, insanity, addiction, political subversion, and so forth.

However, when the Johnson Administration's final gun package evolved in mid-1968, it banned virtually all interstate gun sales between or to individuals, (even hunting and target rifles and shotguns. It had been preceded by federal legislation (following the Martin Luther King killing) which banned interstate handgun sales. There the effort to get new federal laws had rested on a sort of sullen compromise basis until Bobby Kennedy was shot with a .22-cal. revolver. The resultant Johnson proposals escalated; first the President sought a total wipeout on interstate gun traffic among individuals—i.e., among all who were not licensed federal dealers or manufacturers. Then he pressed for nationwide licensing of all gun owners plus registration of all firearms. The Johnson licensing approach would have been especially restrictive, requiring enormous red-tape clearances, periodic medical and police approvals, etc. It was never even seriously debated; a milder form, proposed by Maryland Senator Joseph Tydings, was defeated in both houses of Congress.

Even the Tydings form was resisted strenuously by sportsmen and some others. Most senators and congressmen who made a *cause celebré* of opposing licensing and registration were helped politically by it at the fall elections; most who backed Tydings' or the sterner Justice Department's method suffered for it. This was generally true outside of the states where anti-gun crusading proved either malignantly profitable (New York, Massachusetts) or where the issue was swamped amid more demanding or louder ones.

The 1968 Gun Control Act, as passed in the emotional pre-election wringing-out process that followed Bobby Kennedy's murder, was far stiffer than anything Johnson, Ramsey Clark, or Dodd would have dared submit before the two 1968 assassinations. They recognized the chance to cash in on the murders and publicity and public mood, and moved to do so. But in pressing for far more restrictive legislation on such an openly opportunistic basis, they lost all claims to honesty of position by asking for what they had previously said they did not want—i.e., registration, a full ban on interstate purchases, etc.

The 1968 act as finally resolved not only erased almost all out-of-state purchases, even of hunting guns; it put under full federal regulation such matters as the sale of sporting-gun ammunition and reloading components and the so-called destructive devices—principally heavy, crew-served ordnance like bazookas, anti-tank weapons, mortars, and rockets. A limit or prohibition on general sales of these heavy ordnance weapons had long been agreed to and even sought by the majority of sportsmen and shooters (although when one considers how few heavy weapons appear in crimes of any nature, shooter-sportsman accession to rigid control on such weapons appears to be mainly a placatory and meaningless gesture to soothe fools who confuse gun collecting with crime).

The new act raised the dealer fee from the admittedly too low $1 annually to $10, also something most legitimate gun organizations had sanctioned. There was, however, one predictable political ploy in this. The House of Representatives sent over to the Senate a provision for a fairly reasonable collector licensing which would have enabled legitimate collectors to operate under federal control by paying their own $10 annual fee. Under the House version, there were not too many harassing strictures that could have been abused by an overzealous Alcohol and

Tobacco Unit (Treasury showed its hand by renaming the unit the Alcohol, Tobacco, and Firearms Unit as soon as the bill became law). But the Senate, led by Tydings and others carrying the banner for anti-gun thinking or non-thinking, managed to get the language eventually changed so that the collector license was restricted to accumulating curios or relics. This was nonsense, since the act had already exempted guns or replicas thereof dating prior to 1898 from its provisions. Such weapons would not even be involved in applying the 1968 act. So the collector-licensing provisions, while they sound good, are meaningless. They make the uninformed believe that all those good, grey types in Treasury, Justice, and Congress have the best interests of gun buffs in mind, along with everybody else we must consider when we redesign the world. But the provisions actually do almost nothing for anyone genuinely interested in or concerned with gun collecting, since most collections today, at least among the middle and lower-middle income brackets, involve weapons dating after 1898. Only the very well-fixed can afford to collect genuine antique guns—and such people can afford to hire the same legal and other manipulative talent that the Kennedys and other anti-gun elements retain, in order to frustrate the gun laws as they do the tax laws. Modern gun collecting increasingly is becoming a matter of weapons made for the Spanish-American, Boer, 1914–18 or other post-1898 wars.

The 1968 act does make being a gun dealer a much more involved procedure than it was, what with additional record-keeping and requirements that dealers obtain definite identifications from persons buying guns or ammunition. Much of this is post-enactment interpretation by Treasury; the gun-law subcult within Treasury applied its own freelance interpretations, citing intent of Congress, clear purpose, and other majestic divinations of mind that rival the Ten Commandments in mysterious acuteness. Just as some had feared and predicted, the ATFU legislated by executive fiat—divination—in areas where it seemed to feel Congress had been lax or left a gap that didn't suit the AFTU or its allies on Capitol Hill. The outstanding example of this mysterious gift was a ruling on interstate purchases of rifles or shotguns by individuals in contiguous states. The bill itself had created an affidavit procedure and specified a seven-day waiting period for this. But when Treasury and its supplicants were done with this, the AFTU said it was rather clearly the intent of the law to forbid such sales, even under strict control, unless both states involved had enacted enabling legislation. That was the most flagrant but far from the sole instance of bureaucratic power-grabbing by the AFTU. It was in effect legislating to suit its own purposes in areas not spelled out by Congress, or where Congress had not posed roadblocks. Thus Dodd, Tydings, & Co., who lost the big game in Congress (registration and licensing were spilled by about 2-1 edges in both houses), prevailed in getting their philosophy included in Treasury interpretations of the new law. Whether this will continue under a Nixon administration that owes much of its very existence to shooting sportsmen and gun buffs can only be told with time.

The same new law also requires the strictest kind of identification even for persons buying ammunition. It forbids those under 18 to purchase rifles and shotguns or even shells for them, and persons under 21 are banned from buying handguns or handgun ammunition. The prohibitions on sales of ammunition often amount to ridiculousness in practice, and copious record-making is attendant to all such sales. This is in rather sharp contrast to the preamble to the act which says it was not intended "to place any undue or unnecessary federal restrictions or burdens on law-abiding citizens with respect to the acquisition, possession, or use of firearms." Shooters who remember 1965, 1966, or 1967 pleas by Tom Dodd and Justice that they did not seek registration of guns are permitted snide asides in evaluating the application of the preamble's words in everyday practice.

The mood of mid-1968 which led to the passage of such a law and to the aberrant interpretations of it by bureaucracy might best be shown by two side-effects:

1. The Department of Defense, in the post-assassination mael-strom, forbade the shipment of sporting arms to military post office addresses abroad. This ban was rescinded after a while as matters returned to sanity. But it demonstrated the length to which a Lyndon Johnson-spurred bureaucracy would reach to implement the fetish against "guns."

2. Postmaster Marvin Watson without any legislative basis in-flicted rather strenuous new gun-shipment rules in midsummer 1968, long before enactment of the gun-control act. He left it up to local postal authorities to handle matters after issuing some sonorous but nebulous regulations (which his own departmental legal officers said were probably invalid if put to a test). The varying local-level exercises of this authority might have shamed even the Treasury for sheer confusion and arbitrariness.

Some postmasters used their own personal criteria or views (most of them backed by a typically bureaucratic ignorance of their own laws); some did nothing; some behaved as though personally connected to Tom Dodd. When not guided by higher officials, certain postal clerks applied their own codes or notions, which included requiring presentation of all kind of irrelevant documents to ship or receive a gun. Dealers were sometimes ignored, sometimes well served, sometimes treated as though they were carrying the plague. . . . More than a few gun buffs, hos-tilely or arrogantly treated at a post office window, eyed the picture of Lyndon Johnson on the wall and went home, brood-ing, with the vision of his Vice President in their minds, to await Nov. 5.

Many exposed to the 1968 act, even some of those called on to enforce it, have termed it poorly drawn, vaguely written and illogical—perhaps more so than any major legislation since the Volstead Act converted us all into paragons of non-alcoholic morality and created such a new and high respect for order and authority. The condemnation is neither inaccurate nor unfair. The act does succeed in a few good causes. It sets up conditions ending the importation of cheap foreign military and other low-quality weapons, notably the so-called Saturday-night specials that contribute to gun homicides in a way far surpassing sporting handguns or other guns. A group of respected shooting-hunting authorities was impaneled to pass judgment on imports to determine which ones were indeed desirable—sporting rifles, shotguns, and pistols—and which ones should be banned. This was one of the few positive and widely acclaimed accomplishments of the law. The age limits on gun sales received wide acceptance, but not the similar minimums set for buying shells. These seemed aimed more at discouraging legitimate target shooting and hunting than at curbing misuse; if not so aimed, the regulations were accomplishing that goal anyway. Dealers raised objections, many of them valid, about complex record-keeping. There is not much doubt that many marginal sellers of guns and shells will quit it, sooner or later, to get rid of the encumbrances imposed by the 1968 act. There was not much of a stampede in that direction at first (nor was there really big or widespread quitting of the gun business after the Robert Kennedy killing; a few trumpeted cases went a long way in news stories). But a small, slow movement in that direction is recognizable. Many dealers have been selling shells or hunting guns as a come-on for other sales or as a convenience for customers who spend largely for other goods. Many even stocked up on shells and sold them at cost or near cost during peak hunting periods in order to expedite sales of groceries, camping equipment, beverages, or the like. Others are small rural storekeepers who handle ammunition and a few staple guns as part of a general store operation. Most of these and some other marginal dealers will probably conclude, sooner or later, that the bookwork required by the 1968 act simply isn't justified by a few sales or scant profits. The Gun Control Act of 1968 may turn out like some New Deal programs to "save" this segment of society or that. The Small Business Administration, birthed to rescue small business from the Great Depression, succeeded in accelerating the decline and disappearance of that economic class—a deterioration still in progress. Likewise, huge, groaning, and heralded programs to save the small farmer resulted in his rather rapid eviction and the consequently faster growth of the big, mechanized, absentee-owned cash-crop "industry" farm. The 1968 gun law will very likely crowd the smaller gun and shell vendor out of existence, eventually, and replace him with more large-scale, specializing guns-and-ammunition-plus-accessories dealers. What relationship this may have to deterring crime is something beyond explanation in Washington, and beyond rationalization in Johnson City.

The 1968 gun law can and should be amended. It should not require elaborate record maintenance for the sale of ammunition or reloading materials. It most emphatically should not require extensive identification for such purchases—not unless the goal is to discourage target shooting or hunting, which we are all piously assured is not the case. It is much different to forbid a 16-year-old boy to buy shells than to ban his buying a rifle or shotgun. A parent or guardian rather logically should preside over his buying a gun, but once he has it, granted proper permission, it is rather silly to prevent his buying shells for it.

Moreover, there should be clear provision for licensing persons to collect modern as well as antique weapons, so that these persons can conduct their entirely legitimate affairs interstate as well as intrastate. The $10 fee for dealers and collectors seems about fair, but there is an overlap between the two classes of licensees that should be more clearly defined and corrected.

Then, too, ordnance experts and students—those who have a genuine interest in or need to develop, study, or use crew-served heavy weapons—should be reasonably easily licensed, not persecuted because they find the insides of a 20mm. pom-pom or anti-tank rifle intriguing. Licensing fees and procedures should be priced within reach—not the $200 that Treasury now levies for each restricted weapon. Care can be exercised to insure such licensees are not persons with undesirable backgrounds—felonies, insanity, addiction, political extremism.

It was from curiosity and interest in guns, remember, that the nation drew the gun-designing genius of ordinary citizens like John Browning, Maxim, Pederson, Borchardt, Berdan, and many others who gave us a preeminence in arms design unequaled for nearly a century.

Carrot-and-stick coercions on the states to enact strict gun controls—a ploy Ramsey Clark sought to use but which was denied to him by Congress in 1967—are probably perversions of a federal system. The gun-law requirements of the various jurisdictions differ. In a country which ranges from glare and blare to deserts and ice fields, local option is probably the right idea. But an Arkansas or Utah resident with a valid use for a handgun, for example—target-shooting, protection—should have as much right to it in New Jersey or New York as he does at home. He is, after all, a citizen of the same nation, living under the same federal constitution; he is a citizen in all 50 states, and if the Second Amendment to the Constitution is valid in one state, it has to be valid in all. This is why, as Judge Rummel pointed out, we have a 14th Amendment. However diverse the gun statutes, there will have to be some decent standard set. There is one way to accomplish this, but it would take some acceptance and some judicious planning to gain acceptance.

A uniform, federal gun law could be written with adequate safeguards for both individual and community. Licensing of individuals would be set up, with license eligibility for adults based on just two qualifications:

1. Whether the applicant has a record of felony *convictions* (not arrests), medically documented mental disturbances, narcotics addiction, or medically defined alcoholism;

2. Demonstration of moderate ability with and knowledge of firearms on a range or in the field or both—including a fair knowledge of the game codes and firearms laws that pertain.

Would it work? Yes, much more effectively than the concoctions advocated by Dodd and others at the Washington level. It would bear some resemblance to a gun owner licensing system approved in Illinois with fairly wide acceptance by shooters. If the Illinois bill, which appears to be more carefully drawn than the New Jersey version, should look good after some exposure, it might have long-range impact on other legislation. Certainly a fair, adequately proved bill of this general type would do more good than would Dodd-Justice or Sullivan—for *all* parties.

Once a standard of qualifications has been set, certification of fitness to own, carry, buy, and use sporting firearms (or in the case of handguns, defensive firearms) should be automatically valid in all 50 states and for all uses except carrying concealed on the person. Any such licensing law should be written so that police would be prevented from rejecting applicants for any reason except those specified in the law. There should be no escape clause allowing rejection for "poor moral character" or "lack of proper reason" or other loopholes allowed under some statutes. Whim, bureaucratic arrogance, or vague stalling tactics should not be tolerated. The law should spell out exactly who may be turned down and why. Those whose backgrounds cause them to be rejected at one particular time might be entitled to review after a certain number of years. There should be a certain *maximum* allowable time for police checks.

The conservation officers of the states are better geared to train people in firearms than some police officers. But both could, if willing, handle the training of those who require it before being licensed to own and use firearms. It is more likely that conservation officers would be available than policemen—particularly if some revenues from the licensing program were to go to the states' conservation agencies for the purpose of implementing the program (surpluses, if they develop, could go into wildlife management funds). The funds might enable agencies to hire more wildlife managers and other conservation officers, for training and certifying applicants and for other duties.

Once an applicant is licensed, it should be for life unless the license is revoked for good cause. This would include conviction of a felony, alcoholism, narcotics addiction, and other disturbance. Individuals guilty of hunting-field misdemeanors could be suspended; revoking their licenses for a first-time minor offense would be arbitrary, probably. The age limit should be tailored so that youngsters fourteen or sixteen, if properly trained, could hunt or shoot in target matches with adult supervision. A reasonable firearms-law approach of the type sketched here would accomplish most of the *honest* objectives of both foes and proponents of additional legislation. Certainly the public at large would benefit, in many ways. It would be no absolute panacea. But it would help curb crime, stimulate better and safer hunting, increase wildlife revenues, provide a more solid, sounder base for the citizen marksmanship program, and reduce many of the fears of a citizenry which has been the target of so much fabricated fearmongering.

It wouldn't satisfy the sensation seekers and issue grabbers, who prefer to keep screeching rather than reach solutions. Nor would it soothe the malignants who would like to lock up all guns, or those irresponsible people who oppose all legislative ideas—who insist no legislation at all is the best and public opinion be damned. A few sportsmen of the extreme persuasion and their opposite numbers in the Bakal camp try to undermine the position of the reasonable majority.

For, unschooled or self-elected experts to the contrary, the shooting sports are critical to the nation, and as needed as ever. Whatever legislation is evaluated might be considered along two lines: (1) Is it workable? (2) Will it harm the shooting sports or hamper reasonable self-defense? Concerned citizens, those worried about the nation's defense and safety postures as well as recreational conservation and urban safety, should be very careful about those two points. They're basic yardsticks for sanity in an argument of long-reaching concern—not to be dealt with for emotional reasons or for reasons of personal or partisan politics.

All this should be known and considered in any argument about gun controls. Those who blast good shooting were a long way from Korea and Defense Secretary Louis Johnson's soft, dumb young troops—whose elders would blow down villages but refused to teach them to shoot!

Former President Lyndon Johnson's Commission on the Causes and Prevention of Violence has considered, among other legislative "solutions," requiring citizens to store their firearms—even hunting and target arms—in "arsenals." Presumably these guns could be withdrawn for brief periods for sporting uses if and when some authority deemed it permissible. This Draconian solution would not *be* a solution, for crimes with firearms would most certainly continue to flourish.

It remains oddly characteristic of groups studying guns vis à vis crime—in this latest case the commission on violence's task force on firearms—that none includes anyone with a practical or realistic everyday exposure to sporting uses of guns. Such task forces are always made up of all kinds of *other* people, representing every group except the "victim" public and those who use sporting firearms. Most of the key advisory, "expert," or "technical" consultants tend to be persons very long on theory—for example, Franklin Zimring, a University of Chicago assistant law professor, who helped head the violence commission's gun-control staff. They are chronic solution seekers of academic distinction but with little or no practical experience in most of those matters which they are appointed to advise about. A quail- or deer-hunter, a skeet or target shooter—any experienced handgun user—is very hard to find when you comb the ranks of such commissions or their advisory units.

What anti-gun crusaders suggest concerning storing guns in arsenals would almost certainly lead to exactly what they were asked to help prevent—a genuinely skyrocketing rise in the incidence of most violent crimes. What they would achieve in requiring law-abiding Americans to store all guns in arsenals is simply the declaration of most homes as open cities—places where forced entry and the commission of all manner of indignities, crimes, and intrusions would be virtually unchallenged. Most Americans have no knowledge of what happened in the unprotected ghettos of Europe when Jews and others were the sudden victims of calculated cruelties—pogroms that were prevalent and even popular long before Hitler refined the extinction of minorities to a science. But the victims of such mass crimes—usually but not by any means always Jews—were peoples who had been taught that disarmament was a virtue, and resistance was evil. Ultimately this benign but insane attitude was paid for with the lives of millions. Similarly, national prohibition of alcoholic beverages turned America from a reasonably law-fearing nation into an anarchistic one; we rapidly escalated from Victorian strictness through neo-Edwardian laxity to near chaos in a decade—and the anarchy extended far beyond the confines of the question of the manufacture, shipment, and sale of illicit alcohol.

It is undoubtedly possible for University of This or That law professors to placidly contemplate a Utopian society in which criminals don't assault or kill people because people cannot resist beyond a certain feeble degree. But such dreams tend to make it pretty hard for the victims, real and potential, who do not yet live in such a society—nor even in the insulated theoretical pillboxes of a major university.

Aside from the very strong probability that violent crime would spiral out of sight in a society where citizens could not defend themselves against ever rising violence, there is another practical difficulty. Administration of such a program would be vastly costly, harassing, and confusing for gun owners, and it would with certainty lead rapidly to a drastic decline in the shooting sports. The deliberate discouraging of the ownership and use of guns would not be better accomplished. The revenues and other benefits for all which now come from the two major shooting sports would disappear. Certainly it would be a mortal blow for wildlife management and equally destructive to American target shooting, which must be evaluated as a matter of international status and prestige as well as on a pleasure or recreational basis.

Yet some campaigners are continuing—as this is written—to give serious attention to the proposal for gun "arsenals" and storage centers for gun clubs. It would be fairly safe to predict that if such measures were used, most Americans really deeply interested in the shooting sports would consider emigration, and the program would lead to worse than the circumvention and contempt occasioned by the passage of the Volstead Act. It would be treated with defiance in many parts of the United States.

The Zimring group, interestingly, did not start from the expected premise—that while perhaps one kind or another of legislation was needed perhaps *no* legislation would succeed. It dismissed from the outset the possibility that legislation would not work. Its spring 1969 progress report said it was "analyzing all the major and varying approaches to control legislation: prohibiting possession to felons, alcoholics, etc.; restrictive licensing, such as New York's Sullivan Law; other state, local, and federal laws now in effect; use of scientific detection devices where firearms are prohibited, and the establishment and regulation of private arsenals or gun-club arsenals."

In other words, the very strong possibility that controls have little or no effect on crime—or even contribute to crime—was never even considered. But less than a year after permitting this group to be selected to "evaluate" gun control, former President Johnson was back at the ranch—hunting, according to the wire services. The necessity for him to pose as gunless and ultra-humane had ended, and he was shooting deer from a comfortable stand in a grain field again while America's ordinary sportsmen—who might well be disarmed or turned into bootleggers by commissions he ordered and appointed—trudged around sweatily on steep slopes or waded through swamps in much less grand-seigneurial fashion.

About the time Zimring was deep in task-force studies, he was showing his objectivity by arguing before Illinois criminologists that handguns should be removed from private ownership. Most people missed the bizarre absence of objectivity in this, and almost certainly when the task force report and recommendations followed, they would be wrapped in verbiage of objectivity and integrity.

Yet one wonders how the anti-gun commission business can so

prosper, even with awe-struck acceptance by a strikingly unincisive press, when an anti-gun propagandist of the scale of Zimring can be appointed to a task force which is supposed to make an honest study. And one wonders more about the integrity or duplicity of key commission officials who make such appointments. Members of the commission seemed blissfully unaware that their gun task force was led by a man of distinctly lopsided and even bigoted views on the basic subject. It is about like naming Stokely Carmichael to serve as movie critic on "Zulu."

The writer will be accused of ranging from fascism to anti-Semitic views because in this book he holds in some contempt and exposes to certain sarcasm the historically untenable position of many American liberals. But it is because they advocate senseless, destructive pacifism in the face of all reality, not because they are liberal or Jewish or whatever. The writer holds modern Israel in high esteem. It has survived all by itself, except for the protective covering the United States has provided against the Soviet Union. Israel has shown how a pacific, long-suffering people can adapt themselves to a hostile and unfamiliar environment and bend it into shape as their shield. Many of the refugees who built the new state of Israel are or were as urbanized as most of our metropolitan populations—but they have adapted to conditions that may very well one day be inflicted upon the United States.

It is as ridiculous to call these views fascist as it would be to call someone anti-Negro because he praises Zulus while criticizing Togolanders. The writer feels that American Jews, who bulk so largely into our opinion-shaping and information machinery, should study the lessons of Israel and apply them here at home. And so should other Americans, because however cruel it may sound, the free world, if it had to, could get by without Israel—but it cannot get by as we know or want it without a United States.

Castro's subversions, Russian and perhaps other great-power sophisticated weaponry in Cuba, the possibility of a Castro-linked government in a free Quebec, the wide-open interplay of subversive and intelligence forces in Mexico and elsewhere near the

United States—these are all a good deal similar to the presence of the armed Arab mobs and agents on Israel's borders. But these menaces to us are potentially even more quickly lethal than the Arabs—and far more efficient. Because what the perhaps inept or temperamental Cubans cannot do in a clutch, the Soviet Union will do for them. The United States-Russian showdown is the ultimate one; that of Arabs against Israel is at most a sideshow or a preliminary skirmish if viewed from the long and worldwide perspective.

We don't need Moshe Dayan. We have our own good generals, many of them faced with tasks and options that dwarf Israel's problems. But we do need the latitude that Moshe Dayan and his colleagues have in planning for their own salvation. One does not have to turn the warmaking policy over to the generals; one should, however, let the generals have full charge of the nuts and bolts jobs of national defense. No one else really knows much about this, frankly. There is a highly dangerous trend in our military system to allow political figures to dabble in such matters as whether to use live ammo in basic training, whether Junior should get his feet wet, whether a DI went a little too far in stiffening some bolo. None of this is really pertinent to politics. It should be left to the professionals. How to use those professionals, where and when—*that* is the province of the politicians and the diplomats.

Chapter **13**

✳

Certain Historical Probabilities

(War is a Set of Surprises)

✳✳✳✳✳

"Tenno heika banzai!" ("Let us die for the Emperor!") —Japanese war cry

MUCH ADO THE PAST FEW YEARS ABOUT LESSENING TENSIONS RAISES all kinds of new perspectives—and some haunting old ones.

Consider the historical probabilities latent in accepting as genuine the desire of recent Russian political leadership to reduce tensions—and on whose terms these tensions will be reduced. There are certain hard historical judgments that persist—chronically—to nag our new perspectives on foreign affairs. Or are they new? It is modish just now to forget the criminality of appeasing Hitler and Mussolini and Tojo a generation back. But the people who have declared the vogue are hardly those who suffered or even remember the real consequences. Those who are old enough and fail to do so treat history with a senility that chills others with apprehension.

It hardly requires a geopolitician or political-science graduate to realize that diplomatic manipulations are as much a tactic of totalitarian states or blocs as the secret-police chamber, starvation, or news management. All such tactics are used to utmost advantage when an all-powerful state is in charge. A ruthless but coolly restrained state may exploit, for example, all the advantages of what we are currently calling a lessening of tensions.

Easing tensions for propitious reasons is as much a tactic—as the reader of any Ciano or Hitler account may attest—as over-flights of enemy territory and bases by high-altitude reconnaissance craft, or the pursuit of naval espionage by "trawlers" and other electronically rigged spy vessels. But because this lessening of tensions occurs in politico-diplomatic spheres where pragmatic and skeptical people may not be in command, this sort of maneuver often passes as sincere, genuine. Idealistic, often foolish political speculators and diplomats, who seldom have to exist in a world of head-on human combat, wield great authority and their judgments are usually the ones carrying the greatest weight. Most of the time moves by a monolithic state like the Soviet Union can be considered as much a warlike ploy as the shifting of forces or the conduct of espionage. All too often, realists are dismissed as "hawks" or intransigent warmongers simply because they caution against putting much faith in the latest diplomatic pose.

The Red bloc nations, especially Soviet Russia and Communist China, have been ruthless throughout their histories. The burrs have been honed off since Genghis Khan's times, but the skulls will still be stacked in barbarian fashion when the time is right for one or the other to make its move. History should have taught us to expect only pragmatism, never altruism, from the government of a Russia or a China (though in China, Marxist pragmatism is often diluted with madness). Many of the same aims have been shared by the rulers of Russia since the time of Ivan the Terrible. Over the centuries, it has been contained only by shrewd and strong neighbors—at various times, the British Empire, Poland-Lithuania, the Cossack brotherhoods, the Tartars, Turkey, Prussia-Germany, the Austro-Hungarian Empire, and Sweden. Today, Russia is constrained on its west only by the relatively distant menace of United States power. All the other, older barricades are down.

The last example of altruism in Soviet state policy, and perhaps the only example, came during the 1930s when Premier Stalin made overtures to try to save Czechoslovakia from Nazi domination. Winston Churchill wrote that Stalin felt gratitude to the Czech government for tipping him off about a rumored pro-German, anti-Stalinist conspiracy deep within his army's high command. This magnanimity, if it genuinely occurred, was a failure. It was much more characteristic of Russia and Stalin (as it might have been of Ivan or Peter and their Russia) that later when there was opportunity, the Soviets seized military control of the Czech state during the demise of Nazi Germany. This was an act Ivan or Catherine would have understood—and approved. It was repeated in varying form and degree all over Eastern Europe in the post-1945 years. It gave Russia advanced frontiers and empire that Catherine and her heirs had only dreamed of. The U.S.S.R. repeated the same brutal performance in 1968 as the U.S. sat guiltily idle, unwilling to play a role in helping keep Czechoslovakia alive.

The danger of overrating Communist sincerity is that in any Third World War, Russia will almost certainly have to mount a sneak-punch attack against the United States in order to insure success. People who think of such an attack in Pearl Harbor terms are guilty of doing just what politicians say professional soldiers do—prepare for the last war. To succeed in the 1970s, a Soviet sneak punch must be mounted with an intensity far beyond December 1941. The Japanese in the arrogant blindness of a rigid military caste underestimated our will and force; the Communist enemy, at least the Moscow version, is in all probability too clever to do this. The Communists, after all, have had a generation to study and improve on the awkward techniques of the more primitive older totalitarians.

It should be remembered that the Communists have not lost a major military effort since Republican Spain collapsed in 1939. They have been checked or stalemated here or there, forced to compromise or make truces—but they have not been humbled in 30 years. The almost paranoid air-sea banzai at Pearl Harbor was a crudity no sophisticated Soviet high command is prone to repeat. The Russians in the maturity of their ideology and the pursuit of their long-nursed ambitions to dominate the world may be boorish, but never crude. And in a cold-blooded way, the United States at Pearl Harbor got what its laxity and disjointed military posture deserved. Our political chiefs more than half knew the blow was coming in the late fall of 1941.

The appearance of Soviet naval strength at Egyptian, Algerian, and other naval bases on the Mediterranean means much more than a new menace to Israel, although that is the first implication. It means the USSR has emerged from the Black Sea to stay unless unforeseen overwhelming force requires a tactical retreat. And the mood of the United States hardly augurs that we can or will exert the power in hardware and will to cause such a withdrawal. The British Institute of Strategic Studies in spring 1969 remarked after careful analysis that the United States seemed to no longer possess either the willpower or the ability to rank as the world's first power. It was an apt capsuling of the mind and mettle of American leadership. Meantime, while Russia poured new, high-quality naval craft through the Dardanelles into what had once been the British Navy's jurisdiction, the North Koreans were committing their second act of piracy in less than 18 months on United States naval forces—the shooting down of an unarmed reconnaissance airplane following the unrequited and shameful seizure of the spy ship *Pueblo* and its crew. While most of the public sputtered or went on apathetically in quest of various irrelevancies, the more vocal Senators bleated for caution and new peace initiatives.

Soviet Russia, established in former French and British naval bases on the Mediterranean's southern shores, was also busily building up its naval presence in what had been virtually an American lake after 1945, the Pacific. It was not altogether in exaggeration that a Latin-American *jefe politico* observed that if Castro kept fretting Washington's more strident peace-seekers, we might give him Florida so he would go away for a while. In the same spirit Britain and France condoned the dismemberment of Czechoslovakia in 1938 and 1939.

One American news medium, noting belatedly how Russia's masters had schemed, fought, dissimulated, and committed every crime and hypocrisy to win a warmwater presence on the Mediterranean for hundreds of years—and then gained it in less than two decades—seemed to feel that somehow we had to recognize this without demur and make a new peace with the Soviets. It was pronounced just as though Russia had a historic right to dominate the Mediterranean in the way the Jews possessed a valid claim to Palestine or the Germans to Silesia or East Prussia.

Much the same sort of posing for peace was rife all over the nation in the fall of 1941—while the Pearl Harbor task force gathered in Japan's Inland Sea and the expeditions for Malaya, the East Indies, the Philippines, and other conquests were fitting out or in the later stages of planning. But the Japanese, led after 1940 by an insular military caste of small gentry and peasants, never mastered the long-range plot. Too many of Premier Hideki Tojo's associates looked on the mounting of a banzai charge as an end unto itself. It was in reality only a tool of the overall job, and if we failed to scare away as easily as the Japanese militarists expected, it can be blamed on their gauging us by all those frilly tourists and deprecating missionaries their spies observed on the gangplanks at Shanghai and Hong Kong. But more disastrously for their cause, the Japanese lost sight of the central fact that the goal of assault must be to achieve maximum return for costly losses— and if maximum potential results in return for calculated losses are not obtained, then lives and hardware are hopelessly and bloodily wasted. This the Japanese did over and again in 1941–45. This the Communists will never be so intemperate as to do. The Reds, for all their bluster about power primacy, are essentially a cautious people, not prone to undertake reckless military adventures—and not geared to offensive war. They will take great risks only when great gains are either certain or very strong probabilities. It is a characteristic of Russian policy, and it became particularly apparent during the Stalin regime. Khrushchev owes much of his fall from power, in all likelihood, to his gambling and losing on the Cuban missile adventure.

The likelier possibility is that the Soviets' short-term behavior patterns will continue to be predictably unpredictable. They flip-flop between overtures to reduce tensions and the unleashing of carefully plotted wars of national liberation—wars of meticulously phased infiltration, sabotage, terrorism, subversion, and political manipulation. If and when a major thrust at us is decided on, it will probably be delivered at a time when matters East-West appear to be getting more pleasant. It will hardly come at some time of strained, taut relations as did the Japanese strike at Pearl Harbor. A characteristic moment for the Russians to unleash all-out war might be when they seem procrastinating or indecisive, or even amenable. They may seem to be deliberating some slow, cautious follow-up move. Then they will strike with all weight and fury, all the ruthless and single-minded destruction within their capacity.

They will seek to extract the utmost toll in life and will use panic, sabotage, confusion. They will in all probability sacrifice many troops—paratroops and other elite assault units and infiltrators—as well as their agents within the United States and whatever material is required to achieve a devastating first-strike effect. They will know it is necessary to destroy our capacity to react and our ability to recoup within the nation. One requires no access to confidential channels—indeed, one may be better off without these—to realize the amoral quality that guides both the Soviet Union and the other great Red state, China, as they jockey for world domination. An ability to read history is judgment enough on Soviet morality—or lack of it.

Those who find comfort in Soviet cooperation with the United States in some limited, harmless, and propaganda-exploitable fields (like rescuing each other's sailors) lose sight of the continuity of Soviet policy. It suited Stalin, after all, to cozy up to Hitler in

1939—even though both tyrants knew they were partners in one of the monumental hypocrisies of history. More recently it has suited Soviet policy to try rapprochement with the United States in order to allow greater strategic attention to the long and potentially explosive Sino-Soviet border. The United States, rather predictably, has almost groveled in response to even the shallowest advances—lapping up Russian overtures and panting for more, totally oblivious to the cynicism and self-interest behind the Russian gambit. The Soviets, like Germany from the Great Frederick to modern times, are obsessed by the menace of a two-front war; they waited until Hitler was crushed and the United States and its Anglo-Saxon allies had destroyed Japan's empire before moving against the Japanese in 1945. They then trumpeted loudly for a major share of the credit in the defeat of Japan.

Obviously the USSR would like to reduce—however briefly—the dangers and tensions in its relations with the West as long as the Chinese border threatens to flare up. The same fear of a two-front war preoccupied the Kaiser and Hitler, who failed to avoid it nonetheless. Our ready reach for better relations with the USSR simply indulges the Russian desire to concentrate momentarily on Asia. The Russian ambition for better relations with the West could be better exploited than we have done.

As for Red China, look sometime at the United States the way it sees us, from its intellectual yet insulated isolation. It is an hysterically warped view, much like Premier Tojo and his military clique viewed us in 1941—credulously seeking to justify its maxims and slogans in an ideological straitjacket far more limiting in some ways than was Japanese militarism. Sized up from Peking, we seem obsessed with artificiality, gadgetry, pretense, flabbiness, and confusion (as indeed we are, to a dangerous extent). With less dogmatism and less reason, the Japanese warlords drastically misjudged us in 1941. But China's new breed of leader has had a generation to study and improve on the military and diplomatic errors of the Tojo regime. And in Red China, there is no liberalizing influence now like Japan's world-faring navy in 1940 or so.

The Japanese navy played a devil's-advocate role in diplomatic counseling before Tojo's army clique came to power; it argued against the narrow provincialism and fanaticism of the gentry-and-peasant army, which held the United States in contempt and worried about Soviet armies along the Manchurian border. The Japanese navy had seen the world and the potential industrial power of the West. It did not judge us entirely by fat tourists and fretting missionaries in China. This enlightened view delayed the onset of war; to the last, the navy advised against engaging us. But in China there is no foil to argue that the U.S. is not weak, faint of heart, and short on stamina—soft-bodied and softer-headed. Anyone in Peking who knows or suggests this has long since been silenced. And the hell of it is, in 1970 or 1971, the Chinese evaluation may be right.

A Russian onslaught on the United States would have to offer preponderant odds for success. Having survived one war in which human and material losses were apocalyptic, the Russian people would demand almost certain victory in a new adventure of drastic scope. Even a totalitarian state must to some extent consider the desires of the populace, or at least the comfort and security of the populace (thus the Soviet leaders might strive to insure success, although they would feel no compunction to make the war virtuous; if the masters of the Kremlin think they can justify a sneak-punch attack with almost certain victory, they won't take it to the electorate, any more than Tojo polled the Japanese public on Pearl Harbor). Over their history, Russians have occasionally dealt furiously with errant rulers (the defeat by Japan in 1904–05 was one direct cause of the 1917 revolution). A second deterrent to unsure adventure is that Russia has failed to amalgamate its many subject peoples. The white, European stock Great Russian is still essentially the dominant element, and many other nationalities and subnationalities within the USSR are not yet fully adjusted to the idea of Great Russian domination or Communist government. Russian officialdom must still remember the welcome many Russian subjects offered German troops when the Reich first invaded in the summer of 1941. German stupidity and brutality canceled out the unexpected assistance and helped convince Ukrainians and others that Moscow was the lesser evil. Stalin discovered that as the Germans pressed deeper into Russia, patriotism crystallized the resistance, not Red slogans or posturing. He put away—for the duration only—all the shabby and false liturgy and trappings of Communism. Patriotism evoked deeds where ideology provoked sneers.

Those who like to console themselves that World War Two was the one justifiable, holy war might also evaluate the notion that we have simply exchanged one set of monsters for another. We helped Russia dismember the one great force that for generations blocked it off from European domination. Germany reunified on its 1936–37 borders would contain the USSR, but that Germany is gone, perhaps forever. Only American power now restrains the Soviets, whatever might be the delusions of the Senate Foreign Relations Committee. The pursuit of new Russian ambitions with muted bluster indicates only how much modern totalitarianism has matured since the primitive flailings of Hitler.

China is somewhat different, as more than its perspective on the United States shows. The Chinese have replaced Japan as Asia's progenitors of race war. They spell out pretty clearly what is in mind.

"It is only by the power of the gun that the working class and the laboring masses can defeat and armed bourgeoisie and the landlords. In this sense, we may say that only with guns can the whole world be transformed." That is from Chinese Communist Chairman Mao Tse-tung, quoted by *Los Angeles Times* writer Robert S. Elegant in a story from Hong Kong in early 1967.

Chinese politico-military theory (Communists do not indulge in purely military thinking; Communists generate military policy from political dictates) involves using "great masses of soldiers against modern weapons," Elegant wrote. China continues to grind onward with a militia program of 200 million people in sight. The awesomeness of this best translates by realizing there are 200 million people *in toto* in the United States. Assuming that within a few years this manpower potential will be mated with the capability to deliver nuclear missiles from long distances, one may imagine what the future holds, once the Chinese deem the odds turned in their favor.

The odds as assayed in Peking don't need to be as good as those which Russian strategists insist on.

It was a Chinese sage, Sung Tsu, 2,500 years ago, who said that "Surprise is the key to war." World War Two furnishes excellent examples, although they're far from exclusive. The war was one long string of unpleasant shocks for the free world until mid-1942, when surprises started happening to Axis forces. But from the annihilation of Poland's game, obsolete army in a few days in September 1939, until Midway, Guadalcanal, El Alamein, and Stalingrad, the surprises hurt the democracies and their Red ally because Hitler and the Japanese planned it so—and possessed the ruthless and calculating advantages totalitarian states own when wars start. Only after the free world's industrial production and superior logistics started to overtake the advantage of surprise were we able to start rolling back a Germany that sprawled across Europe, and a Japan which was in possession of most of the more strategic parts of Asia. But the war showed that surprise was and is the constant success factor in battle. The unpredictable is the only predictable. Thus Field Marshal Wavell admonished Britain to prepare for war, not *a* war. His people ignored this, as Erwin Rommel remarked; in the 1930s, Britain meticulously if sparingly prepared for 1918 (even Field Marshal Montgomery's triumph at El Alamein was in most ways a 1918-style Western Front "big show"). Free nations tend to follow such stultified thinking between wars.

Surprise struck Japan, certainly, but only after the Japanese cashed in on some very respectable thunderbolt chips at Manila, Pearl Harbor, in the Malayan-Singapore drive, and elsewhere. Midway's ruinous aircraft-carrier losses left Japan without the best of its first-line carrier pilots. Japanese air star Saburo Sakai commented afterward that one of the great flaws in his nation's war planning was failure to provide enough good replacement pilots. No Midway was envisioned as Japanese admirals carefully charted the war during the 1930s. It was a fatal flaw.

Communists have been surprised. The Finns shocked Russia's army—after much of its best leadership was purged—in 1939–40. Philippine President Ramon Magsaysay's personal attunement with peasants led them to abandon Huk "agrarian reformers" in droves. The Central Intelligence Agency's Guatemalan coup upset and delayed Red ambitions in Latin America. A few years later, now-ousted Senator Joseph Clark of Pennsylvania aristocratically sneered that the CIA was out of date, that the world has attained that amiable stage in which "a department of dirty tricks" was unnecessary. The Senator, presumably, never had to flush Huks out of a paddy. Very few of the well-bred, effete, and delicately-geared men who make United States world policy at the cerebral level ever met Huks, the Japanese Special Naval Landing Forces, or North Koreans head-on. John F. Kennedy was almost unique in his culture (and certainly so in his family) in that he had met his enemies close up. Most of his peers conducted their war by pushing buttons or drawing charts.

Surprise, too, almost evicted the USSR from Hungary in 1956. A form of do-it-yourself militia—Hungarian rebels who seized guns from their oppressors—jolted the Red world as it has seldom been shaken. Until Russia decided the United States would not interfere, the Budapest rebels had recaptured direction of their own country. But Russian armor, artillery, and terrorist follow-up assaults by unrestrained Mongol infantry caused all that valor and groping for justice to be squandered. Those who argue that armed insurgents failed in Budapest forget that first they won, when they faced decent odds in hardware. They were overwhelmed only when outside, friendly forces did not intervene to halt invasion by other external but oppressive forces. No war can succeed unless the political climate is right, as we have learned so bitterly in Vietnam, be it conventional or unorthodox war. And the political climate of the Budapest rising was determined in Washington by an Eisenhower administration which decided not to act, much as the real outcome of the French Indochina campaigns was decided in Paris, not at Dienbienphu. But the Hungarian rebels rattled the Red empire, doubtless prematurely. For once the neutral world, in its never-never land, realized that east of the Oder River, the dictatorship of the proletariat was the villain. As Charles W. Thayer said in his *Guerrilla,* the Reds were suddenly the haves, the ins; after 40 years of preening themselves and their odious system as that of the humble worker-peasant wave, the Communists abruptly stood out nakedly as the oppressors of a small nation struggling for self-determination.

Tragically the great propaganda value of this was submerged in the diplomatic threat-mongering over the Anglo-French and Israeli sweeps into Egypt. It may be said with some accuracy that in the final days of his 1956 reelection push, President Eisenhower abandoned our two oldest major allies, Britain and France; our protege and only staunch friend in the Near East, Israel, and the first people in the Communist empire to actually rise in full-scale, 1776-style revolt, the Hungarians.

For a nation which owned the precedent for ousting foreign overlords and their systems, it was not a proud time. The bill for it started to come in with the Soviet conquest of the Czech state in 1968.

Chapter **14**

Conclusions

✳ ✳ ✳ ✳ ✳

"If the Marines are ever broken up, as a lot of
characters keep saying they should be, they should
make them a corps of marksmanship instructors for
the Army. At least they prepare for a war on the
theory that someone has to fight in it."—John P.
Conlon, Ohio National Guardsman, student of ordnance and military sniping, and accurate gadfly, 1951

READ THE HOME TOWNS, SOMETIME, OF THE MEN WHO WIN MEDALS
in Vietnam. You won't find Broadway and 42nd St. very well
represented, nor Hollywood and Vine. The young men who do
the most in war come from hamlets—Forty Fort, Pennsylvania, or
Muleshoe, Texas, or Ninety Six, South Carolina. A very large
number are from small towns, much out of proportion to the
national population—which clusters ever more in urban jams.

There is really nothing wrong with New York or Los Angeles or
Philadelphia GIs. Many have made outstanding soldiers, Marines
and so on. They will continue to do so. But proficiency with small
arms and self-reliance in open country are seldom spawned in concrete jungles or suburbs. The man who stabbed Kitty Genovese to
death in front of 40 of her neighbors wouldn't have lasted that
long back in the hinterland.

The towns that top soldiers often come from are good for laughs
on the Johnny Carson show. Kokomo is laughable, even ludicrous.
West Virginia, with its high ratio of Medal of Honor winners, is

great for contrived guffaws. Joke writers from Jolson on have been sure that West Virginia and Kokomo are automatic (some prefer Dubuque). Some of those who laugh along really agree. Others snort in tune because they desperately need to show sophistication; there is a Kokomo in their backgrounds, and they must hide it to fit in with the superior urban masses they've joined.

But when some rifleman from Cross Forks or Beecamp saves a stranded platoon because he matriculated with guns back home, the laughter is gentler among the ones he saved. They might even find the humor a little thin and want to overturn a studio of people who laughed away at it all. This day could come. It came a long time ago when the legions went home to find Rome not to their liking. Nor appreciative of all they had wrought in Arabia or Africa. A small-town rifleman isn't so ridiculous when he is measured against the other side.

What happens to make the American of rural origin, white or black, a more successful and effective soldier in the field? Various people have tried to answer this. Ancient Rome noticed a deterioration in its legions as the proportion of city types grew. Ever since World War One, a similar deterioration has seemed to accelerate in the American armed forces. In World War Two, whenever GIs had to go do it on their own, when the artillery and armor and air force weren't handily by, it became a rifleman's war. The guerrilla war against the Japanese occupying the Philippines was an example. Whenever the shoulder weapon took over, so did the country boy, as guerrilla leader Wendell Fertig pointed out. The same happened, less often, in Korea. It is occurring again in Southeast Asia.

Is the rifle-oriented country youngster a happier killer? Probably not. There is less human-to-human violence in small towns and farms than in our great cities. It may be that the young man exposed to and familiar with rifles and shotguns is efficient and less fumbling with them—less inhibited, in officer language. And wiser and safer with them. He requires much less indoctrination with the rifle in basic training (Robert Henriques' sum-up of the Arab

Legion and Frank Muñoz' "They don't freeze" judgments fit in here). His rifle training doesn't escape him like some pre-exam cram session if not directly put to use. He reacts instinctively; the boy from a gun-shy environment has more to learn, and while a few become very expert, the odds are against this kind in war.

On occasion, city people become formidable in war. The hard core of Cromwell's superb New Model Army were Londoners trained and tuned to the highest level of military skill. The Union armies of 1863 and afterward were from a less agrarian milieu than their adversaries; they nonetheless did well after overtaking Southerners in basic military skills (but they paid the predictable price in bloodshed before learning the game). They were, however, fighting in a conventional war, absorbing the discipline that has always been required for such wars. Discipline begets automatic responses to drilled-in stimuli. City people respond to these stimuli. They are conditioned to such responses. Courses in formal war require time to teach. While the much-herded-about city youth may eventually take to disciplined *conventional* war better than his rural counterpart (Fertig's go-to-hell country type), when, in this nuclear age, shall we again have the luxury of time to drill great masses of men behind someone else's shield?

We are, to repeat John F. Kennedy's phrase, living in the bull's-eye. The fact that his political and familial heirs and those who agree with them have decided to ignore this isn't too surprising. Kennedy learned his lesson in the Pacific; his heirs did not. The history of great, free societies is loaded with easily forgotten lessons, learned in great bitterness and at huge cost, dispensed with as soon as expedient. Thus we shouldn't be surprised when city political leaders or late-show nabobs insist, in all their military expertise, that there is no more need for firearms in war. This same strategic insight comes with the issue of any Justice Department briefcase. It tranquilizes the mother vote and the do-anything-to-make-them-stop segment of the crime-fighting vote—the need-a-master-masses. It is more expedient—and makes for smoother politics—for these people to sit before their television sets, swill, wal-

low, and let someone else—government, preferably—do everything
for them. It is escapism in the purest form.

An Ohio woman tourist's cry when she visited Tubac, Arizona,
and danced with a wild, primitively masculine old Mexican—
"Now there's a man!" which burst out in front of her tame husband and everybody else—is a symptom of the problem. The
woman laments a dearth of old-fashioned masculinity in the
United States, yet she missed the point. Our female-dominated,
spastic, society has been working overtime for a generation or
more to discredit manhood. Men who display the qualities she
admires—and there are still such men back in Ohio where she
comes from—are increasingly regarded as primitives, anti-social,
even menaces to her society. They still like blood sports, and practice the old skills, and have a hard-cored contempt for softness and
excessive emotionalism. They prefer to kill their own snakes. The
kind of man she admires is declining because society—led by
women, and perhaps by just this woman—is, through the media,
arts, politics, sociology, and much else, busily doing all it can to
destroy such manhood. The next time some Cleveland-curried
Ohio politician wants to abolish firearms hunting, the woman
should consider matters from a logical standpoint. It is doubtful
that she will. The media won't let her thinking process reach such
a point.

People who still like to kill their own snakes bother political
leaders in our time. The politicians don't understand and thus
vaguely distrust these last traces of self-reliance and do-it-yourself
assuredness. The citizen who proposes to solve his own problems is
a primitive. Doubtless the Hungarian rebels, the East German and
Polish crowds who grew angry with police statism would be called
dangerous in this new social order we are evolving. The young
Czechs who peacefully strove to legislate Moscow-style socialism
out of their government probably disturb some of our political
leaders, and their counterparts in London and elsewhere. They
were swamped by Moscow, and it wasn't the first nor the last sellout
of a brave people by London or Washington. In the same way the

American Continentals and their Congress must have bothered a lot of people in the capitals of Europe. Fighting tyranny is very selective; you must be sure it is a form of tyranny that can't strike back, like that we condemn in South Africa. If it is Iron Curtain tyranny, which has enslaved millions of East Europeans, or Asian tyranny, which butchers entire populations, it is not quite "the thing" to get too excited. Really, though, there is no great distinction between a bullet in the back of the neck from some Communist Chinese and a trip to a Nazi gas oven. You have to be politically attuned beyond the ordinary to discern any practical difference in the ways of being enslaved or butchered.

The effort, such as our politics permit it to be, against slavery of the Moscow or Peking brands remains a pretty basic matter. Australia's late Major Peter Badcoe, one of the most eminent as well as exposed thinkers on guerrilla and counter-guerrilla war, admonished *Look*'s Laura Bergquist from his vantage point in Vietnam: "This is a rifleman's war. You need good infantrymen, willing to go out and prove to the VC that the night isn't theirs. You Americans are trying to change the war, to fight it with sophisticated technology. And so you kill indiscriminately and alienate the very people you're trying to win over."

What Badcoe was saying also might be interpreted to mean that you don't do it with pushbuttonry. The people who will do it soonest and best and on terms the Asian Communist understands are the country-boy types from all those towns that sound so silly on Johnny Carson's "Tonight Show."

Too many people equate athletic skills with warlike ones. It is a striking misconception. Great athletes do not necessarily make great soldiers. Almost anyone can probably recall some hulking football star who was deathly afraid of being drafted. Italians often make excellent athletes, but those who stayed in Italy, for the most part, made miserable soldiers (Italo-Americans have done far better in our armed forces). Negroes in this country did not soldier well until granted the pride and sense of belonging and opportunities that came with integration after 1950, but Negroes had proven themselves superior athletes for generations before that.

The little, shriveled-up, skinny, hillbilly kid very often makes a better soldier than some college football hero who may be a gentle coward off the football field—or wherever his trained muscles do not send him to the head of the class. Psychological readiness for combat has no great relationship to the ability to run, throw, or kick a ball—Douglas MacArthur's famous statement about football has only a limited relevance. The link is partially applicable but not consistent. Rather often big, sturdy, and physically capable athletes find all kinds of psychological difficulties in war because the basic business of killing with personal weapons may be wholly alien to their social background. They fail at it as often as clerks or teachers or welders—and perhaps more often than farmers' or hunters' kids.

Most platoon or company leaders who have thought about it would almost surely rather have a unit of average physical fitness with unusual rifle skills than a unit loaded with professional athletes who have no other particular aptitudes.

The qualities that have made for manhood for thousands of years don't come across well on the late television show where rampant manhood equates with a shouting scrape at the washeteria (some buck claims his wife's detergent is better than your wife's).

There may be an excuse in countries like France or England, with their enormous losses of aggressive, seed-stock manhood in 1914–18 and 1939–45 and of pride and wealth afterward. It's harder to understand here. We are supposed to be pragmatists, if forgetful. But since 1953 we have known the Russians had the hydrogen bomb, and have done nothing about it. Our first troops in every new fight die uselessly—many would live, given sterner preparation, mentally and physically, and especially on the rifle range. Our political candidates are telling us right now that panacea is right around the corner (all that is required is helping them Get Us Moving again). And they say it well now; The old, inarticulate, crude, Kelly-Nash or Pendergast bossism has been succeeded by something far smoother, done up in Ivy and prep school packaging. We have Kennedys and Rockefellers instead of Rabbits and Goats—Clark-Dilworth have dispossessed the grubby. But these new leaders, if they can genuinely qualify for the label, however glib and persuasive, owe a certain candor—on great matters, anyhow—to those who fawn on and follow them, but especially to those who don't.

They might say, for example, that in the years since John Kennedy's time we have moved from the bull'seye into the V-ring. But try to get someone to admit it. It is easier to be comforted, spellbound, told to switch on the tube and watch baseball or your pet tame politician. He prefers this, too. Yet the next big cataclysm won't be a near miss, not with this country the prime target for that part of the world which wants to own everything else and on its own savage terms.

How do you meet Genghis Khan halfway?

You don't do it with Mace—or in a prep school gym.

Appendix A

Major Conclusions and Recommendations of "A Study of the
Activities and Missions of the National Board for the Promotion of Rifle Practice"

—Arthur D. Little, Inc.

Conclusions

1. Shooting experience, and particularly marksmanship instruction, with
   military-type small arms prior to entry into military service contributes
   significantly to the training of the individual soldier.
   a. Information regarding prior shooting experience and marksmanship
      proficiency after basic training appears to have as yet unrealized
      value in the selection and assignment of trainees to combat units
      where the primary weapon is the rifle and to marksmanship training
      units.

2. The DCM programs stimulate and support broader participation in
   organized shooting activities of affiliated club members 12 years of age
   and older all over the country.
   a. The marksmanship instruction, supervised practice, safety training,
      and competitions (including club inter-club, state, regional, and
      national matches) sponsored and supported by clubs, the NRA, and
      the DCM are of particular value to the military.
   b. As of 30 June 1965, 5,902 gun clubs were affiliated with the DCM.
      Of the 417,576 members of these clubs, 58% were in the age group
      12-25 years old.
   c. Only a small proportion of Army trainees (32% of our sample) had
      any marksmanship instruction prior to entering service. Only 6.5%
      belonged to an organized gun club and only 3.1% could say defi-
      nitely that they belonged to a gun club affiliated with the DCM.
      While these are considerably larger proportions than most experts
      had predicted, in view of the substantial benefits (to the military)
      accruing to members of DCM-affiliated clubs, more effort should be
      extended to expand participation in club membership and programs,
      particularly in younger age groups.
   d. Members of organized clubs provided marksmanship instruction to
      three times the number of trainees who reported being a member
      of a gun club.

3. The primary contributions that the Civilian Marksmanship Program
   makes to the military departments in developing competitors for international competitions are many:

a. Stimulating wider interest and grass roots participation in shooting which results in a broader pool of potential competitors;

b. Sponsoring and supporting coaching clinics, Small Arms Firing Schools, and competitions for the development of instructors of potential competitors; and

c. Sponsoring and supporting state teams and a hierarchy of state, regional and national matches. Intensive competition at this level is necessary for the development and identification of international-caliber competitors.

4. Benefits to the military departments through sponsorhip of shooting teams representing the United States in International Shooting Union Championships, Olympic, or Pan American games are related principally to: international relations; service prestige, esprit de corps, and public relations; and the enhancement of the credibility, influence, and therefore the effectiveness of successful competitors who serve as marksmanship instructors. In recent years, 75 to 90 percent of the members of international shooting teams have come from the military departments.

5. Benefits to the military departments from the support of and participation of military personnel in the National Matches include the following:

a. Since the National Matches are regarded as the most important marksmanship competition in the United States, additional effort is extended in preparing for these matches by Reserve teams, National Guard teams, and Active Service teams in all branches of the military services;

b. Knowledge and experience acquired through preparation for top level marksmanship competitions contribute significantly to the effectiveness of military marksmanship instructors;

c. National Matches serve as an effective arena for testing shooting techniques and training methods;

d. Information on developed training methods and shooting techniques which has been validated by successful performances in National Matches is collected and published by the Army Marksmanship Training Unit in a series of manuals on marksmanship and marksmanship instruction; and

e. The National Matches are regarded as the culmination of the competitive marksmanship programs carried on in the various military departments. Conclusions of the Army's study in 1964 of its competitive marksmanship program were as follows:

(1) "It provides a continuing source of qualified marksmen and potential instructors in marksmanship at all levels.

(2) "The program is directly related to promoting an individual combat skill.

(3) "It presents a public image of an Army capable in the use of its individual weapons.

(4) "Individual and team achievements are a source of pride to the individual and the unit.

(5) "The program develops outstanding competitors to represent the Army in Inter-service, National, and International competitions.

(6) "It provides a means for the individual to raise his proficiency with small arms other than through the annual qualification program."

   f. Potential public relations values inherent in the performance of military personnel competing in the National Matches are not exploited nor thoroughly capitalized upon. Coverage of the matches by nation-wide news media is quite limited.

6. Other principal side benefits from the Civilian Marksmanship Program include the following:

   a. Law enforcement agencies with organized shooting groups affiliated with the DCM regard the program as "quite important" in supporting their marksmanship training and in enabling their personnel to participate in organized shooting programs;

   b. Many DCM-affiliated gun clubs throughout the country provide NRA-designed "Hunter Safety Programs" to neophyte hunters in an organized effort to reduce shooting accidents among hunters;

   c. The DCM program as it now operates contributes in only a small way to the social and cultural acceptance of shooting in America. In light of the many recent "anti-gun" articles in newspapers and periodicals in the country, the mission of the NBPRP and the public relations aspects of the DCM program take on added importance. The skills and resources allocated to improved communication with and understanding on the part of the general public should be extended.

7. The recent Civil Rights directive issued by the DCM will result in improved control over those club membership policies in order to insure compliance with Title VI of the Civil Rights Act.

   a. We found no instances in which overt discrimination had in fact taken place.

   b. It appears that only a very small number of Negroes or other nonwhites have applied for membership in DCM-affiliated clubs, especially in the South.

8. While NRA and DCM control procedures have been improved and tightened up recently, we believe that there are other areas where improvements in control procedures are desirable in order to insure that

personnel participating in the program are not members of any organization which advocates as any part of its program overthrowing the Government of the United States by force or violence, and never have been convicted of a crime of violence.

a. Control procedures in effect apparently have at least been adequate since our extensive contacts with police and civic officials, interviews and correspondence with FBI, Treasury, and State Police officials, and our contacts with several members of the Congress and their research assistants failed to uncover a single incident where a DCM-affiliated club or its members have been convicted of using firearms, ammunition, and/or government property improperly or where DCM arms have been used in crimes of violence.

b. If it can be demonstrated that shooting club officers are responsible citizens, they can be relied upon to maintain adequate controls over the club membership and activities. Therefore, the main thrust of screening and control procedures regarding the affiliation of gun clubs with the DCM should be focused on club officers.

c. There is considerable variation from state to state in the depth and effectiveness of investigations of club officers because of the varying degrees of cooperation which the NRA receives from its state rifle and pistol associations and from the state Adjutants General. These groups, in turn, receive varying degrees of cooperation from state and local police agencies in terms of their ability to obtain and convey police records to the NRA.

d. On the basis of the information now furnished the NRA (name, age, address, and occupation), it is extremely difficult, if not impossible, to be positively sure [whether] club officers do or do not have police records. Most police agencies cannot make a thorough records check without having a set of ten fingerprints for each individual or at the very minimum, information on date of birth and a full description of physical characteristics.

9. There is a need for more direct and effective communication and interaction on the part of the DCM with affiliated clubs, especially clubs newly affiliated. More attention needs to be directed toward helping clubs get organized and adopt programs which will support and carry out the missions of the NBPRP and exploit fully the advantages of affiliation with the DCM as well as to assist in the screening of club officers and monitoring club activities in previously affiliated clubs.

10. The present system of funding the programs of the NBPRP and the DCM, including the same sources of budgetary support, appears to be quite appropriate.

a. While the funding system and sources are appropriate, there is currently no means for the NBPRP or the DCM to conveniently and systematically examine the various DCM programs in detail, evaluate their benefits and costs, and consider changes or new programs in terms of the budgetary implications of such changes.

b. The DCM has little planning, budgetary, or administrative control over aspects of its programs that could generate income to defray the total program cost.

c. The DCM programs would benefit from more systematic liaison between DCM and the various agencies affected by, participating in, and having financial responsibilities for parts of the DCM program.

d. The DCM has been vulnerable to criticism in the past because of the fact that it has been difficult to document either the concrete benefits or the full and accurate costs of its several programs.

11. We consider that the requirement that clubs enrolling with the Director of Civilian Marksmanship be affiliated with the National Rifle Association is quite appropriate. The aims and purposes of the NRA are quite similar and complementary to those of the NBPRP. The network of NRA clubs is the primary vehicle through which the DCM applies its programs and benefits in stimulating shooters and shooting activities. NRA club officers and members provide range facilities, instruction, and manpower on a volunteer basis to carry out the club programs of the DCM. The NRA magazine, *The American Rifleman*, is an excellent vehicle for communicating with individuals interested in various aspects of shooting, including the advantages of affiliating with the DCM. Therefore, it is not only appropriate but essential that the NRA and the NBPRP achieve effective liaison and work closely together. It is quite appropriate that the NRA provides three members to the NBPRP. The NRA is the national sports governing body recognized by the International Shooting Union and thus it has the responsibility for sanctioning all national championships and tournaments for the purpose of selecting representatives on teams for international competitions.

12. The National Board for the Promotion of Rifle Practice should continue with some minor changes.

a. There is a need for broader representation on the NBPRP. There is a need to build in those capabilities and interests which will result in improved communication and more effective involvement with the general public in order to more effectively fulfill the the mission of creating the public sentiment which will insure continued support for and greater participation in the NBPRP programs.

Recommendations

1. We recommend that the National Board for the Promotion of Rifle Practice (NBPRP) should be continued with some minor changes in its organization and in the administration of the Office of the Director of Civilian Marksmanship.

    a. The membership of the NBPRP should be broadened to include parties-in-interest other than the NRA and the military departments. Representation of capabilities and resources mentioned in the body of this report should result in an increased capability of the NBPRP to carry out its missions effectively.

    b. The Secretary of the Army should appoint the six representatives on the NBPRP from the Country At Large after soliciting nominations from a variety of sources.

    c. The NRA should continue to provide three members to the NBPRP.

    d. The NBPRP should develop and promulgate more effective programs to facilitate the social and cultural acceptance of shooting in America.

2. The DCM should be established as the DCM Program Office and given full program responsibility and authority for all activities related to its legal mission as prescribed in Army regulations and as directed by the NBPRP.

    a. This DCM Program Office should have the responsibility to develop a five year program and a budget plan for review by the NBPRP in its budget committee. It should then make annual reviews of all existing programs or activities and assess their progress, effects, and importance.

    b. The DCM Program Office should also be given the authority to establish reporting procedures for obtaining, on a routine basis, information from the various Army agencies concerned with and contributing to the DCM program. This should also include authority to establish an active liaison program with such agencies so that all parties concerned could contribute to the formulation of policies and procedures affecting the success of the total DCM program.

    c. We recommend that a more inclusive system of accounts be set up so that the true cost to the government of the DCM programs can be accounted for on a regular and complete basis. This should entail provisions for credits to the DCM program for all revenues returned to the Federal Government.

3. The Department of the Army should provide for field representatives for the DCM.

a. Members of the headquarters staff in each numbered Army Area Headquarters might be assigned the role of DCM field representatives. This function might be added to the job assignment of the Army Area Marksmanship Coordinator or to a member of the public relations staff particularly interested in marksmanship activities.

b. These field representatives should be responsible for assisting and maintaining personal contact with clubs in the Army Area, for facilitating club use of military rifle ranges, for stimulating organized shooting programs within clubs, especially for junior age groups, and for more effective administration and liaison of the check-out procedures of officers of clubs applying for membership in the DCM.

4. The DCM should take primary responsibility for investigations made of clubs wishing to affiliate with the DCM.

a. Checks and investigations of personnel in clubs applying for affiliation with the DCM should be focused on club officers.

b. Information used in clearing applying club officers should be more complete and lend itself more effectively to efficient check-out procedures. We recommend that the DCM require each officer of an applying club to submit his fingerprints. After the club is affiliated, each new person who is elected to office should also be required to submit his fingerprints.

c. In all other respects, the essential steps of the present system of controls should be maintained. That is, the control procedure should consist of a police records check of club officers, of endorsements from two community leaders, and of a personal meeting with club officers and members. In addition, clubs should continue to be required to affiliate with the NRA to be eligible for DCM affiliation. This will insure continued club support for and liaison with the national sports governing body for shooting and the many relevant activities it promotes.

5. Those aspects of the DCM program which relate to the stimulation of broader interest and participation in rifle shooting among the youth of our country should be emphasized more and pursued even more effectively in order to reach a greater percentage of those young men likely to enter military service.

a. In designing its programs and in allocating resources, the NBPRP and the DCM should give consideration to more emphasis on club activities. This should include stimulation of membership, more emphasis on junior programs, and further extensions of marksmanship and coaching clinics, and local and regional competitions.

b. In view of the very considerable support to state, regional, and especially National Matches, the NBPRP and the DCM should capitalize further on the public relations benefits inherent in these competitions and the potential for using films, short subjects, TV coverage, etc., in stimulating greater interest and participation in organized shooting activities in the country. Since the current interest of the general public in international competitions is high, opportunities to capitalize further upon the public relations value of successful performances of members of international shooting teams should be extended.

c. Any member of a DCM-affiliated club, regardless of whether he is an individual NRA member, should be enabled to purchase government arms and ammunition through the DCM sales program. However, in order to maintain a screening and control procedure over such orders, any such member should have his purchase order endorsed by an officer of the DCM-affiliated club to which he belongs.

d. Consideration should be given to enabling clubs to qualify for additional small allotments of ammunition issue as long as they can document the use of such issue for hunter safety programs, youth programs for non-members, or for other community programs to stimulate further interest and participation in shooting.

6. Since there are no minimum marksmanship proficiency standards established for rifle units going into combat and since no one has yet been able to "price out" the value of achieving a given level of marksmanship proficiency in a rifle unit, we recommend that consideration be given to defining and carrying out needed research in this area.

a. Consideration should be given to making "quality control checks" on the marksmanship proficiency of rifle units going into combat. If data is gathered to measure the combat proficiency of units with varying degrees of marksmanship proficiency, this information should be valuable "feedback" in adjusting marksmanship training standards and in evaluating the need for improved selection of individuals who will be more effective in combat.

Appendix E

Outline For a Civil Defense or Military-Police Militia or Reserve Program.

1. *Demonstration, nomenclature.*
   a. Disassembly, reassembly (field-stripping).
   b. Holding, carrying.
   c. Care, purposes.

2. *Training handgun (.22-cal.).*
   a. Simulated (dry) firing 50 yard.
   b. Slow-fire 25-and 50 yard ranges.
   c. Timed-fire, 25 yards.
   d. Rapid-fire, 25 yards.

3. *Service handgun.*
   a. Slow-fire (as above).
   b. Timed-fire (as above).
   c. Rapid-fire (as above).
   d. Combat shooting—grip, stances, etc.

4. *Practical situations.*
   a. Combat shooting drill.
   b. Silhouette target practice.
   c. Moving target practice.
   d. Raid drill — in streets, buildings; surprise silhouette targets.

SERVICE RIFLE

1. *Demonstration, nomenclature.*
   a. Field-stripping.
   b. Holding, carrying.
   c. Purposes, care.

2. *Sighting.*
   a. Methods of aiming, sighting.
   b. Sighting-in at short and long ranges.

3. *Standard target marksmanship techniques.*

NOTES:

—Always use dead, dummy cartridges for dry firing.

—Timed-fire can be eliminated i schedule is tight.

—With handgun, can add grip an arm exercises, including weigh ed dry-firing, kettlebells, duml bells, finger flexes, fingertip pusl ups.

a. 100-yard practice.

b. Practice at longer ranges, as available.

4. *Practical marksmanship.*
   a. Trainfire techniques, theories.
   b. Firing on pop-up targets, unknown ranges.

RIOT SHOTGUN

1. *Demonstration, nomenclature.*
   a. Field-stripping.
   b. Holding, carrying.
   c. Purposes, care.

2. *Riot gun drills.*
   a. Simulated firing.
   b. Skeet or trap practice.
   c. Raid drill—surprise situations.

FULLY AUTOMATIC WEAPONS
(Light machine gun)

1. *Demonstration, nomenclature.*
   a. Field-stripping.
   b. Crew-served weapons theories, techniques.
   c. Purposes, care.

2. *Fully automatic weapons drill.*
   a. Applications of fire with this weapon.
   b. Simulated combat practice.
   c. Trainfire-type firing—pop-up targets, unknown ranges.

BAYONET

1. *Techniques.*
   a. Offensive.
   b. Defensive.
   c. Care.

2. *Practice.*
   a. Simulated bayonet combats.

FITNESS

1. *Introductory exercises.*
   a. Looseners—for agility.
   b. Wind-builders — sprint-like exercises, short *jogs* (up to 440 yards).
   c. Muscle builders — harder calisthenics.

2. *Median exercises.*
   a. Short wind sprints.
   b. Increased calisthenics.
   c. Jogging up to one mile.

3. *Intensified exercises.*
   a. 50– and 100–yard sprints.
   b. Hard calisthenics, combinations of same.
   c. Half-mile and mile jogging with gear.

4. *Routine in-training exercises.*
   a. Sprints.
   b. Strenuous calisthenics, combinations.
   c. Jogging with gear, mile and up distance runs.
   d. Judo, other defensive and disarming sports.
   e. Knife — offense, defense, disarming.

5. *Environmental adaptation.*
   a. Conditioning to peculiarities of climate, terrain, food, water, general environment. This can be expanded as needed. Basic health course would fit in.

ALTERNATIVES

1. *RCAF Exercise manual.*
   a. 5BX for men, graduated as indicated.
   b. XBX for women, graduated as indicated.

2. *Green Beret fitness program.*
   a. 6 – 12 plan.
   b. Gurrilla exercises.
   c. Combatives.

NOTES:

—Guerrilla exercises are probably the most practical package course. Should be supplemented with some running at distances, brief preliminary loosening-up session, rope climb or other additional muscle-builders.

—See master exercise list for calisthenics.

POLITICAL TRAINING

1. *Explanation of militia.*
   a. Briefing on U.S. history.
   b. Current world situation.
   c. Domestice politics.
   d. Detailed analysis of function, value of citizen militia.
   e. Emphasis on nonpartisanship within loyalty limits.

2. *Examination of probable enemy (enemies).*
   a. Enemy strengths, weaknesses.
   b. Enemy's propaganda, ideology; how these are exploited against us.
   c. War as matter of survival, rather than old-type economic competition.
   d. Evaluation of enemy's mistakes—atrocities, racism, suppression of opposition, religious persecution and how to use these against him.
   e. What enemy thinks of us— how to use this against him; how to improve our shortcomings, take advantage of his misconceptions.

ADVANCED TRAINING
CIVIL LAW

1. *Mobs.*
   a. Anticipating, containing panic.
   b. Controlling riots.

2. *Force.*
   a. Control weapons — when to use, not to use.
   b. Deadly weapons — use, don't-use situations.
   c. Lecture on general degrees of force; feasibility.

3. *Cooperation with other forces.*
   a. With police.
   b. With military.

4. *Basic civil law police techniques.*
   a. Felonies, misdemeanors.
   b. Arrests.
   c. Searches, seizures.
   d. Public relations.
   e. First aid.
   f. Guard duty.
   g. Patrolling—foot, vehicle.

MILITARY LAW

1. *Post-disaster controls*
   a. Panic control.
   b. Mob control.
   c. Anti-subversive operations.
   d. Anti-sabotage operations.
   e. Disaster-aggravated crimes of routine nature.

2. *Cooperation.*
   a. With political authority.
   b. With military authority.
   c. With police.
   d. With military personnel.

3. *Other post-attack reactions.*
   a. Fire-fighting role.
   b. Aid to medical authority.
      (1) Disposal of dead.

NOTES:
—Assumption is to be made here that post-disaster conditions will be from nuclear attack and/or invasion or similar extraordinary military reaction.

(2) Aid in wound, burn, injury treatment.

(3) Disease prevention.

(4) Protection of hospitals, aid points.

(5) Restoration of medical facilities.

c. Evacuation procedures.

(1) Traffic.

(2) Routing survivors.

(3) Arranging vehicle priorities.

d. Guard duties.

(1) Strategic locations.

(2) Shelter protection.

(3) General assignments.

e. Arrests.

(1) Political subversives.

(2) Saboteurs.

(3) Cases ordinarily under civil law.

f. Emergency facility repairs.

(1) Water.

(2) Power.

(3) Transportation.

(4) Construction.

(5) Communications.

(6) Gasoline, fuel.

GUERRILLA
AND COUNTER-GUERRILLA

1. *Training.*

a. Demolitions, explosives generally.

b. Communications — maintaining, restoring, disrupting.

c. Sabotage.

d. Propaganda, terrorist techniques; many occupation targets.

e. Raids—different types.

f. Supply; maintaining ours, disrupting enemy's.

g. Vehicles; maintaining ours, adapting enemy's.

h. Enemy's weapons; how to
convert, adapt.

i. Sanitation.

j. Use of climate as weapon.

GENERAL IDEAS

1. Basic idea of program should be to determine which individuals are best suited to special assignments and match these people with jobs to be done. First emphasis should be on getting reasonable weapons skills, awareness of general function as militiaman and fitness. *Then* specialization should start. Skills of value not outlined include maintenance of ordnance, food preparation, mapmaking, photography, languages, entertainment, tailoring, and so on.

2. This aims at providing a sample program, in the temporary absence of a more skillfully prepared outline, for training state-guard or home-guard militia. Outline is intended only as a starting point. Persons planning program should remember militia will function at times under civil law, at other times under military law; will from time to time be required to cooperate with police and/or military or in absence of either or both.

3. Standards need not be extra high. Physical requirements would not need to meet those of regular military forces. Educationally, ability to read and write and do simple arithmetic should be minimum. "Hand" (i.e., practical) skills of primary value in emergencies, disaster war situations would be of great value. Most able-bodied younger males will be subject to call-up for military service. Underage and overage men in reasonably adequate physical condition with minimum education should be allowed to qualify.

4. Participation by representative cross sections of all major racial, religious, and ethnic groups is important. Persons belonging to subversive organizations would of course have to be kept out.

5. Weapons—marksmanship being the primary skill of any militia—should be of calibers in common use and issue in United States forces, with ammunition available in military depots and arsenals. If necessary, sporting weapons of current-issue calibers could be allowed.

SUGGESTED SMALL-ARMS CALIBERS

RIFLES: .30-06 .308 (7.62mm. NATO), .30 M1 carbine, 5.56mm. (.223).

SUBMACHINE GUNS: .45 M1911, 9mm. Parabellum.

LIGHT MACHINE GUNS: .30-06, .308 (7.62mm. NATO).

HANDGUNS: .45 M1911, .38 Special, .357 Magnum, .22 long rifle*, 9mm. Parabellum.

RIOT SHOTGUNS: 12 gauge, rifled slugs or 00 buckshot shells.

* The .22 long rifle cartridge in hollow-point bullet may be considered a special-use, survival, caliber but it is inadequate in most military applications.

MASTER CALISTHENICS LIST
  (Militia)
Chinups.
Pullups.
Sidestraddle hops.
Fingertip pushups.
Regular pushups.
Handclap pushups.
Squats.
Half-squats.
Squats with leg stretches.
Squats and jumps.
Duckwalk.
Standing toe-touches.
Running in position.
Situps (toe-touches).
Cradle-rolls.
Prone leg-lifts.
Elbow-to-knee situps.
Torso twists.
Bicycling.
Arm-thrusts.
Finger-flexes.
Rifle thrusts (out, up; switch sides).

Note—On calisthenics and weights (static exercises), number of repetitions should be low at first, gradually increased as progress is made.

For militia, static exercises are not as much recommended as the mobile exercises listed under "Other."

WEIGHTS

Dumbbells: Straight-out arm thrusts Alternate standing curls Alternate sitting curls with presses Alternate standing presses
Reversed-hand standing up-sweeps

Kettlebells: Shoulder exercise (over-head-horizontal) Alternate front lateral raises Thighs-horizontal shoulder exercise Alternate standing side bends
Alternate standing curls

Barbells: Presses
Curls

> Bench-presses
> Rowing motion
> Deepknee bends (squats)
> Toe-raises
> Side-bends
> Situps (elbows to knees)

Other

Bellycrawl: (50 yards).

Sprints: Start with 30 yards, progress to 100 yards.

Jogging: Start with 440 yards, advance to half-mile, then beyond; add weight (gear, pack) as condition improves.

Skirmish Run: Start with 100-yard runway; dry-fire (or use live ammunition if possible) one or five rounds (depending on mechanism of weapon) with rifle from *sitting* position: run 25 yards, fire one or five shots *prone*, one or five shots *kneeling* or *squatting*; run 50 yards, fire one or five shots *standing*, bellycrawl 20 yards to target. If live ammunition is used, score target (suggest 100-yard rifle target).

Climbing exercise: Start with light pack, weighing 15-25 lbs. (gradually increase weight of pack); with pack plus gear on GI belt and rifle, step on and off height of 18 to 22 inches above ground; lead with left foot, then right foot, in alternation. Start with 50 such steps up and down or 2.5- to 3-minute time limit. Gradually increase, first to 100 such steps, then to 200. Eventually do this for 20 to 30 minutes adding weight.

The Armed Citizen*

Violence was averted in northwest Washington, D.C., because Mrs. Ellen Von Nardroff, an attractive brunette, took a detective's advice and armed herself with a 20 ga. shotgun. Detective L. E. Simmons gave her the advice after an intruder broke into her home, attempted to attack her and stole $50. The same man, a husky 6-footer, got halfway upstairs to Mrs. Von Nardroff's bedroom on a noisy second attempt—only to be met by her with the shotgun and a visiting girl friend with a pistol. The intruder was arrested and held.

Mrs. Von Nardroff said she had practiced considerably with her 20 ga. after the Washington detective recommended a shotgun, properly handled, as the most effective defensive arm for a "lady who lives alone." (Washington Star)

Ever since a young man with a black glove on his right hand robbed her of $150 at knifepoint, Mrs. Sue Ball, 59, a Hollenbeck, Calif., cafe proprietor, carried an 8 mm. pistol. Six months after the robbery, she said, the same man came to her rear door and grabbed at her. Her one shot killed him instantly. (Los Angeles Herald Examiner)

At Inglewood, Calif., John Bitters saw two men take a television set from a parked pickup truck and slip it into the rear seat of their car. When he confronted them, they ran. Bitters fired one shot into the ground and ordered them to halt. Police then arrested the pair. (The Citizen, Inglewood, Calif.)

Gerald Boyum, a farmer of Farmington Twp., Minn., returned from a weekend fishing trip to find 2 rifles, a shotgun and car accessories missing from his home. While he was calling the sheriff, a strange car with 2 youths drove up. Boyum held the 2 at shotgun point. Deputies arrived, searched their car, and found the missing firearms in the trunk. (Rochester, Minn., Post-Bulletin)

Restaurant owner Emilio F. Quintana waited quietly while two burglars knocked a hole in a rear wall of his Phoenix, Ariz., cafe. When the thugs finally crawled through, Quintana held both of them at gun-point until police arrived. (Tuscon, Ariz., Daily Citizen)

When a shaggy-haired young tough led 4 others in an attempt to break into a house occupied by a 14-year-old girl baby sitter, the girl's 12-year-old brother, Roy Bourgault, drove them off by firing a .22 pistol into the ground at their feet, the Palm Beach County (Fla.) Sheriff's Office reported. Returning later, the gang smashed windows with beer bottles and the leader began climbing into a bedroom. Again the boy drove them off with warning shots from the .22. Police arrested the tough, his fourth arrest in 14 months. They

* Law-enforcement officers cannot at all times be where they are needed to protect life or property in danger of serious violation. In many such instances, the citizen has no choice but to defend himself with a gun. These are accounts from newspaper clippings sent in to the American Rifleman by NRA members.

said he had been twice fined $25 and once reprimanded for driving 100 mph. in a 45-mph. zone. They identified him as John M. Whitman, 19, youngest brother of the slain University of Texas killer. (Associated Press)

Because of a burglary, Les Harris, Chicago (Ill.) homeowner, bought a .38 caliber pistol and taught his wife Auriel to use it. A few nights later, finding an intruder climbing through her window, she shot him in both hands. When a man with bullet wounds in both hands sought hospital treatment, police were notified and Mrs. Harris identified him. He was charged with attempted robbery. (*Chicago Tribune*)

When he was robbed of $125, Carl B. Peters, Long Beach, Calif., store clerk, shot and wounded two holdup men with a .38 revolver before police answered the store's silent alarm. (Pomona, Calif., *Progress-Bulletin*)

Charles Bradbury, of Miami, Fla., visiting in New Orleans, was thrown to the sidewalk by a man who leaped on him from behind a parked car and placed a knife at his throat. Taxicab driver Joseph Hirstius, passing just then, stopped his cab and with his personal pistol held the attacker until police arrived. (New Orleans *Times-Picayune*)

Donald Wayne Roach, investigating a noise in his suburban Portland (Oreg.) backyard, fired one shot over a fleeing intruder's head. While a neighbor phoned police, Roach searched and disarmed the man. Police said he was wanted as a suspect in a $12,000 bank robbery. They arrested 2 other suspects nearby. (*Oregon Journal*)

As Joseph Lobue was closing his Sacramento, Calif., tavern for the night, two hooded robbers armed with pistols jumped him. Lobue pulled his own gun and pointed it at them. "It looks like a standoff," said one robber. Both fled empty-handed. (San Francisco, Calif., *Examiner-Chronicle*)

A gang of 5 cornered Louis Rivezo, a Brooklyn, N.Y., undertaker, as he left his home. Slamming him against a fence, they robbed him of $150 and mauled him. Rivezo fired 3 shots from a revolver, for which he had a permit. One fell dead and the gang scattered. (Poughkeepsie, N.Y., *Journal*)

Receiving a sheriff's alert to watch out for an escaped convict, Max Burgh, 71, a retired mail carrier living near Nace, Va., searched outbuildings on his farm, pistol in hand. He surprised the convict there and held him at gunpoint while Mrs. Brugh called police. (Fincastle, Va., *Herald*)

Walter Pahuta became suspicious when three men walked into his Elba, N.Y., grocery store at closing time. He secured his .25 caliber pistol. When one of the intruders pulled a gun, Pahuta ducked behind the counter and fired one shot. The trio fled. All were rounded up later, one with a bullet wound in the shoulder. (Batavia, N.Y., *Daily News*)

While Nick Perciballi was transferring money to the cash drawer of his Akron, Ohio, grocery, an armed thug held him up. Perciballi warned: "I have the same thing you have." The gunman fired and missed. Perciballi shot him in the stomach and again in the back as he turned to flee. Police arrested him at a hospital, together with two other men. (Akron, Ohio, *Beacon-Journal*)

Two Sacramento, Calif., brothers, Daniel and Michael Valverde, were alerted in the early morning hours by noises at the rear of their home. Arming themselves with a shotgun they found three men loading a truck with property from a neighbor's garage. Daniel held the men at gunpoint while his brother summoned the police. Sheriff John Misterly commented: "We could use more good work such as this by citizens. I compliment them." (Sacramento, Calif., *Bee*)

Burglars plagued the Veterans of Foreign Wars Club in Winter Garden, Fla., to the point where Manager James Cothern stayed after hours on guard. When two men broke in, Cothern wounded one critically and downed the other with a pistol bullet in the arm. (Orlando, Fla., *Sentinel*)

Mrs. Donald Coughlin observed two men breaking into the coin box of an outside telephone near her home in Portland, Oreg. Alerting her husband to call police, she went outside with a shotgun and held the pair at bay until the police arrived. (Salem, Oreg., *Capital Journal*)

When David Varaday of Inglewood, Calif., was awakened by the sound of shattering glass, he glanced out his window and saw two men burglarizing a store across the street. Grabbing a gun, Varaday halted the pair as they emerged from the store with $120 in loot. He held them at gunpoint until police arrived. (Los Angeles, Calif., *Herald*)

"Give me all the money you have here," demanded a man armed with a big knife of Cleveland, Ohio, van lines clerk, Mrs. Patricia Cawthon. Mrs. Cawthon walked calmly to a nearby closet, picked up a snub nosed automatic pistol, turned to the knife-wielding bandit and said: "Where do you want it?" The thief ran out the door. (Cleveland, Ohio, *Plain Dealer*)

Service station attendant Edward Stambaugh, Provo, Utah, was counting the day's receipts when a car drew up on the drive and a man came around the car, gun in his hand. With no lost motion, Stambaugh scooped up a .38 caliber revolver and took one shot at the surprised "customer." The man fled. Station owner Al Nielson commented, "We always have the gun here just in case." (Salt Lake City, Utah, *Deseret News*)

The Russell Hagermans, an elderly East St. Louis, Ill., couple, were awakened by a knock at their door at 1:15 a.m. When Mrs. Hagerman answered, an intruder grappled with her. Hagerman, hearing his wife's screams, grabbed a .25 cal. automatic and fired one shot. The intruder collapsed, fatally wounded. (St. Louis, Mo., *Post-Dispatch*)

As customer GEORGE LOUIE was handing over a $10 bill to liquor store owner Arthur Norwitz in his SAN FRANCISCO, CALIF., shop, an armed bandit walked in and grasped Louie's $10 plus $125 from the cash register. As Norwitz called police, Louie grabbed a pistol from under the counter and ran after the robber. He fired a shot which hit the fleeing thug, who was then picked up by police. *(San Francisco Chronicle)*

NORTH BEND, OREG., cab driver JAMES A. HARTWICK picked up a fare at a night club and started to deliver him to his destination. After they had traveled a short distance, the passenger leaned over the front seat and placed a knife at the cab driver's throat. The "fare" then ordered Hartwick to take him to a secluded spot where he took the driver's money and his wrist watch. He then ordered the cab driver to take him back to town. At the intersection of a busy highway, Hartwick suddenly jammed on his brakes, throwing the robber off balance. The cabbie managed to pull a gun from his belt and shoot the thug. The man was taken into custody by police who were sitting in a parked cruiser at the scene of the shooting. (*The World,* Coos Bay, Oreg.)

Citizen JAMES KUHN, who lives above a ST. LOUIS, MO., food store, was awakened by the sound of breaking glass. Kuhn obtained his revolver and went to the store to investigate. As Kuhn arrived on the scene there was the sound of more breaking glass. He apprehended a man in front of the store and held him until police arrived. When the police searched the store, they found another intruder hiding in the basement. *(St. Louis Post Dispatch)*

When an armed bandit walked into CASIMER OLSON'S office in BUFFALO, N.Y., he laid a pistol on the counter and kept pointing at the money drawer. Olson, noting that the pistol was a toy, pulled his own gun and held the man at bay until police arrived. *(Buffalo Evening News)*

JOSEPH BAUSONE, manager of a DALLAS, TEX., package goods store, was approached by a man who ordered a bottle of whiskey. As Bausone turned to fill the order, the intruder drew a pistol and demanded that the shopkeeper open the register. At that moment a passerby looked into the store and saw the holdup in progress. The thug fired one shot at Bausone, who dove under the counter and came up with his own gun and got off 4 quick shots. The would-be bandit staggered out of the store and fell dead. *(Dallas Times Herald)*

In PONTIAC, MICH., ROBERT CLARK was working in his service station when he heard noises at the rear door of his building. Clark called his assistant, LARRY SEATON, and then phoned police. Seaton arrived on the scene armed with a rifle and spotted 2 men running from the station. One fled into a nearby field, and the other jumped into a car where he was held at gun point by Seaton until police arrived. *(Pontiac Press)*

A NORTON TOWNSHIP, MICH., pool hall owner, EDDIE MORGAN, sleeping in quarters at the rear of his establishment, was awakened in the early morning hours by pounding noises. Arming himself with a shotgun, he went to investigate and surprised 2 men who had knocked a lock off the front door. One of the intruders fled and Morgan held the other thug at gun point until police arrived. *(Muskegon Chronicle)*

MRS. BERTHA SIMMONS was awakened in the middle of the night by screams for help outside her COLUMBUS, OHIO, home. She heard a man pleading, "Don't hit me again. I gave you all I got". Mrs. Simmons, 81, got out of bed, grabbed a pistol from her dresser drawer, and ran out onto her front porch. She observed 3 men with lead pipes beating a cab driver over the head. Mrs. Simmons started firing and the thugs fled. When police arrived at the scene they credited Mrs. Simmons' action with saving the cab driver's life. Later she received a citation for bravery. *(National Enquirer)*

As CHARLES DI MAGGIO was closing his NEW YORK CITY, N.Y., grocery store 3 thugs entered and forced Di Maggio into a washroom in the rear of the store. One of the bandits pointed a pistol at Di Maggio and warned: "I would rather shoot you than look at you. We always wanted to get you, Di Maggio, and we're taking no chances this time." The stick-up men took $300, a wallet, keys, and wrist watch from the grocer and then returned, single file, to the front of the store pausing at the cash register. This gave Di Maggio time to get out his rifle which was hidden in the washroom; he inserted one cartridge and fired. The single bullet went through the upper chest of the last bandit and into the body of the second. The last thug staggered out the door and fell dead into the gutter. The second bandit made it to about a block away and collapsed at the feet of a policeman. He was taken to the hospital in critical condition. The third bandit escaped with the money. During the past 10 years, Di Maggio has had 26 attempted robberies, 11 of which were successful. He has captured 15 thugs, and killed 3. *(New York Daily News)*

HOWARD R. CHISIM, who lives behind his BATTLE CREEK, MICH., grocery store was awakened in the early morning hours by noises coming from the store. Grabbing a pistol, he went to investigate. Encountering 2 men, Chisim ordered them back into the store, made them deposit their loot on the counter, and then marched them into the walk-in cooler to await the arrival of the police. *(Battle Creek Enquirer And News)*

In bed in his ANCHORAGE, Alaska home, DR. ROBERT W. MILLER was stabbed in the chest by a knife-wielding intruder. Mrs. Miller coaxed the intruder into the living room. While they were gone Dr. Miller located his pistol and went after the armed thug. He fired several shots at the intruder, killing him instantly. It was later learned that the man was wanted by the FBI for assaulting a woman and then threatening her with a gun. *(Anchorage Daily News)*

RUDY SHARE looked out of the bedroom window of his PHILADELPHIA, PA., home at 4.30 a.m. and saw someone breaking into a neighbor's car. Getting his hunting rifle, Share drew a bead on the man and ordered him to stand where he was. He then pounded on the wall and awakened the man next door. He called police who took the would-be car thief into custody. *(Evening Bulletin)*

In BALTIMORE, MD., MISS IRENE SIMMONS discovered that someone had broken into her shop. Miss Simmons, who lived over the shop, went upstairs and got her pistol. She returned to the store and lay in wait for the intruder's return. When the man returned, Miss Simmons held him at gunpoint for police. *(Baltimore Sun)*

Two men entered FRANK MENDOZA's CHICAGO, ILL., shop, drew guns, and demanded his money. Mendoza pulled his own gun and fired once, hitting one of the would-be bandits. The man crashed through a plate glass window and fled. Mendoza held the other at gunpoint until police arrived. Later police picked up the second man as he applied for treatment for a gunshot wound at a nearby hospital. He was identified by Mendoza as the first man's accomplice. *(Chicago American)*

In MILLERS TAVERN, VA., Assistant Postmaster A. R. WATTS and store-owner S. S. COURTNEY closed their combination store and post office for the night. A short time later, Courtney, who lived nearby, was alerted by the sound of breaking glass. As he looked across the street, he observed a man entering the store through the shattered front window. Courtney phoned Watts, and they headed for the store. When they met at the building, the 2 men entered the building with guns in hand. There they found a would-be robber hiding behind some boxes, and they held the man at gunpoint until police arrived. *(Richmond Times-Dispatch)*

After DENVER, COLO., liquor store owner, KURT M. RUTZ had been forced to hand over $60 to an armed thug, he grabbed a gun, followed the fleeing bandit, and fired 2 shots at the man, who threw down his gun and waited meekly for police to arrive *(Denver Post)*

WASHINGTON, D.C., grocery store owner ISSAC JOSEPH was accosted by a gun-wielding masked bandit who shouted, "This is a hold-up". The armed intruder lined up 6 customers against the wall, stepped over and opened the cash drawer, and for a moment his attention was diverted. At this point Joseph grabbed the bandit's arm. In the scuffle that ensued, the store owner was able to get his own gun from under the counter and fired at the intruder once. The man fell to the floor fatally wounded. *(Daily News)*

Having been robbed twice previously by bandits who asked for paper bags, BALTIMORE, MD., package goods store owner LEONARD ANDERSON was wary of a stranger who walked in and asked for a paper bag. Anderson walked to the cash register where he kept his gun. When the would-be robber pulled a loaded gun from his pocket, Anderson felled the bandit with 2 shots. *(Baltimore Sun)*

LOS ANGELES, CALIF., liquor store owner JOHN LELAND was accosted in his shop by 3 bandits. Leland grabbed his pistol and routed 2 of the robbers and slightly wounded the third whom he held at gunpoint until police arrived. *(Herald-Examiner)*

Two women walked into a PHOENIX, ARIZ., package goods store and asked night clerk ALBERT E. MOOTS for a paper bag. Moots asked the women what they wanted to do with it. "I want to put all of your money in it," one of the pair replied, whereupon she raised the front of her shirttail and displayed the butt of a pistol. Moots reached under the counter and came up with his own pistol. He disarmed the woman and then called the police. *(The Arizona Republic)*

Grocer SALEM TOTAH and his son were in their SAN FRANCISCO, CALIF., store when 2 men walked in and robbed him at gun point. One robber fled with the loot while the other armed bandit walked around the counter and knocked the grocer down. Totah reached under the counter and got his pistol. The bandit fired at the shopkeeper and missed. Totah fired 3 shots at the bandit. The armed robber was dead on arrival at the hospital. *(San Francisco Examiner)*

NORTH HOLLYWOOD, CALIF., liquor store owner BROOKS BURTON faced the same gunman who had robbed him 3 times previously. The bandit ordered Burton to the rear of his shop where he took money from the safe and Burton's wallet. As the bandit turned to leave, Burton moved to the cash register and got his own gun. The armed thug fired one shot at the storekeeper who followed him out, shooting at the robber. The bandit returned the fire and then suddenly cried, "I'm hit!" He threw his gun in front of him and collapsed in the street. He was dead on arrival at the hospital. *(Los Angeles Herald Examiner)*

CARY, ILL., tavern owner KENNETH STRONER, who was sleeping in his tavern, was awakened by a disturbance behind the bar. He obtained a pistol and surprised 2 men in the process of burglarizing the tavern. One of the robbers jumped through a plate glass window and escaped, but Stroner shot the other burglar. When police arrived, they discovered the wounded man had $250 on him. It was also learned that the man was on probation. (McHenry, Ill., *Citizen Newspapers*)

WAYNE McWILLIAMS, who was sleeping in the office of his VISALIA, CALIF., automotive center, was awakened by the sound of someone prying the lock off the front door. As he went to investigate there was the sound of breaking glass and an intruder came through a window—only to be held by McWilliams until police arrived. (Visalia *Times-Delta*)

JIMMY LEWIS HEATON, night manager of a HOUSTON, TEX., produce store, was on guard in his market after having been alerted by an earlier robbery in another store. When a masked man walked in by a side entrance and pulled a gun, Heaton drew his own pistol and fired 5 shots at the armed robber. The bandit fired once and then fell dead. *(Houston Chronicle)*

BALTIMORE, MD., cab driver GUY TUCKER was delivering a fare when 2 men tried to wave him down. As Tucker's cab went by, one of the men hit the side of the vehicle and yelled: "I'm hit." Tucker stopped his cab and the 2 men attempted to rob him. The cab driver picked up a pistol and felled one of the would-be bandits. When police arrived, the other robber tried to escape and was shot by one of the officers. *(Baltimore Evening Sun)*

PLATTE CITY, MO., gasoline station operator JIM RIDDLE surprised 2 men in the act of burglarizing his service station in the early morning hours. The pair fled, and Riddle grabbed a rifle and called for them to halt. When the men kept going, Riddle brought one of them down with a shot from his gun and held him for police. The other bandit escaped. *(St. Joseph News Press)*

A prisoner who escaped from the Federal Reformatory at Chillicothe, Ohio, while serving a stolen car sentence, was recaptured without firing a shot because, Deputy Sheriff Dwight Beery reports, farmer WENDELL BRYANT, who lives near FRANKFORT, OHIO, got his shotgun out and backed up the lone deputy who answered Bryant's call and helped to trace the prisoner.

Deputy Earl Kuhn reported to Deputy Sheriff Dwight Beery, that the prisoner appeared ready to make a break at one point but did not do so "because of Mr. Bryant standing in an advantageous position. I couldn't have asked for better assistance." The Ross County Law Enforcement Officers Association honored Bryant at a special meeting. (Chillicothe, Ohio, *Gazette*)

FRANK E. PAHLER and friends were in a parked car across the street from a MOUNTAINTOP, PA., service station. Pahler suddenly noticed someone walking around inside the closed station. Going to his home and obtaining his shotgun, Pahler returned to the service station and apprehended an intruder whom he held at gunpoint until police arrived. (Hazleton, Pa., *Standard-Speaker*)

PEARL FERGUSON, a SACRAMENTO, CALIF., veteran of 4 previous holdups in her little grocery store, was accosted by an armed thug who said, "This is a stickup." "Go ahead and shoot," she replied. As the gunman edged towards her, Mrs. Ferguson reached for a hidden pistol, cocked it, and pointed it at the startled bandit. He fled into the street shouting, "Don't shoot, I give up, I give up." (Ukiah, Calif., *Daily Journal*)

In PORTSMOUTH, VA., two men walked into ROBERT H. OLIVER's jewelry store and asked to see a watch and bracelet. Oliver became suspicious and went to a back room to obtain a pistol. As he returned to the store, one man pointed a gun at him and said, "This is a holdup." Oliver ducked behind a partition and fired 2 shots at the fleeing bandits. Moments later one man was picked up by police, wounded by a bullet from the jeweler's pistol. (The Norfolk *Virginia-Pilot*)

Comments on the Report of
the President's Commission on the
Causes and Prevention of Violence

The recommendations on gun control issued in midsummer 1969 by the President's (Lyndon Johnson's) Commission on the Causes and Prevention of Violence amounted to a plaguing hangover from the LBJ era and consisted mainly of the same mindless anti-gun fixations that haunted law-abiding Americans during Johnson's presidency.

The report urged that handgun ownership be restricted to a very few citizens—policemen, security guards and messengers, a select and privileged few living in high-crime districts, and some others. The creator-in-chief of the recommendations and report on them, a University of Chicago law faculty member named Franklin Zimring, had advertised his study as the first genuinely from-scratch, objective, and unfettered approach to the matter. That was at the inception of the study. But while all this was underway, Zimring (January 1969) urged Illinois criminologists to work for banning privately-owned handguns in their state—a point of view remarkably equal to just what he dumped on the violence commission six months afterward. The much-trumpeted objectivity was notable for its absence, as it turned out. What apparently happened was that it took Zimring and confreres six months to grind out a plausible case for their predetermined position.

The New York *Times* thought that the report—endorsed by nine of the 13-member commission, including Chairman Dr. Milton Eisenhower—was designed to rally support from the National Rifle Association and other shooting-sportsman groups, since it appeared to urge repressive controls only on handguns. But it was probably in fact intended to bypass the handgun-favoring and shooting element within NRA and to deaden resistance from riflemen and shotgunners generally. It urged only "identification-card" regulation for users of long guns. The technique actually seemed to be to help split sportsmen and others who use handguns away from those more concerned with continuing free access to rifles and shotguns. The approach had a certain dangerous logic in application—much more logic, indeed, than the content of the report itself.

Zimring dismissed as "garbage" a singularly well-prepared study arguing that the presence of handguns in homes deters crime. Instead, his report insisted household handguns were risky and dangerous. This came across as nonsense to NRA Master- or Expert-class handgunners—civilian, military, police—who know from performance and exposure just how effective a competently wielded revolver or pistol can be. The Zimring report actually presented (but of course left unsaid) an excellent case for adequate training with handguns—training like that scuttled by the Defense Department's 1967–68 withdrawal of support for the civilian marksmanship program. If citizens owning home-kept handguns are at times inept or unsure, such training would be valuable both as a safety factor for them and as the deterrent to violent crime sought by so many citizens and agencies.

The report—surprisingly to those anticipating objectivity after Zimring wrapped himself in it—ignored the role of the organized competitive target handgunner and the hunting handgunner. The irony from the target shooter's standpoint is that both the International Shooting Union and the Olympic Committee have recently added *more* pistol events to an already-impressive shooting program. For the hunting handgunner (often a Westerner), the oversight was at least as frustrating; hunting even big game with handguns is a rapidly-growing sport. Today's magnum-caliber revolvers and target-tuned semiautomatic pistols are capable of accuracy that would have satisfied most respectable riflemen a generation ago. Many of these hunters use magnum revolvers by choice, for greater sport; others do so because they require a light weapon and don't want to encumber themselves with the bulk of a rifle or shotgun. This group would include many normally not thought of as hunters, including backpackers, campers, and others.

Nor were collectors provided for in the report. Whether to include them along with target shooters and handgun hunters in the proposed regulatory framework was to be left to the individual states. Zimring's report did spell out a most remarkable and extremely debatable sociological argument—that mere need for self-protection in the home should not be a satisfactory reason for ownership of a handgun.

Apparently the report was a studied and preordained effort to abrogate the basic right of self-defense in favor of a dangerous social experiment—beguiling to chronic reformers and sociological adventurers. It offered a certain appeal to politicians interested in the *volte-face* stance—or lack of one—on gun legislation. Like Michigan Senator Philip Hart (a member of the LBJ-named commission), the report allowed a politician with no particular spine to be both for sportsmen—in not seeking to restrict rifle or shotgun ownership beyond a certain degree—and to be for gun controls, by drastically curtailing private handgun ownership. Some office seekers in 1970 may find this double posture appealing if not rewarding. The outcome, if it should be put into practice, is very likely to make violent crime on the streets and against homeowners considerably worse than it already is.

Dr. Eisenhower, who has long been established as the social experimenter in his remarkable family, told the press that the report perhaps would cause President Nixon to change his administration's view that no new federal gun controls were needed (Nixon representatives had stated this case just a week before the Zimring report's release). But the chairman must not have known that high Nixon administration officials in the Justice and Treasury Departments—those agencies most concerned with crime, violence, and civil rights—were well aware of the thrust of the report at least six weeks prior to its release. The gist of the report was common gossip in gun-trade and sportsmen's publications in early June; the report was released July 28. Far from being shaken by the report, Nixon-administration leaders may have gone to Capitol

Hill to state their position in anticipation of the release and its contents. And they stated in July 1969 what candidate Nixon said in fall 1968—that repressive gun controls seemed unwise and foolish, and that decisions on virtually all new controls should be left to the individual states.

Perhaps the Nixon people felt what many other Americans feel deep down —that the right of self-defense is not negotiable, no matter how anointed the social experiment may be.

Bibliography and Acknowledgements

Anyone wishing to know about the pluses and minuses of American riflemen at war can easily find the best starting point—T. R. Fehrenbach's *This Kind of War—Korea: A Study in Unpreparedness* (MacMillan, 1963). More than just the best story of the Korean fighting, it capsules all our military history from 1775 on. Yet to this writer's knowledge, only one major United States officeholder has expressed interest in the book—that admirable exception being Senator Paul Fannin of Arizona.

The lawyers and scientists, the bankers and professors and politicians who make state policy one day force us all to pay fearful forfeits by ignoring such bitter testimonials as those of Fehrenbach's sergeants, specialists, lieutenants, and captains. Such policies and their architects have already cost us too much. Young riflemen—most of them hardly deserving the proud name—pay the standard price; they are your sons and mine.

But there is much testimony to buttress Fehrenbach, and it should be acknowledged here. All I can say to my prime source is that along with the rest of the American public—a largely unappreciative public—I owe him a big debt for writing the book (and also for his permission to quote widely from it).

Other sources which played strong parts in the conclusions reached in this book include *Operation Sea Lion*, by Peter Fleming (New York, Simon and Schuster); the Arthur D. Little Report: "A Study of the Activities and Mission of the National Board for the Promotion of Rifle Practice" (Department of Defense, 1966); the *Gun Digest* for several years, notably the 1960 and 1962 issues (published by the Gun Digest Corp., Chicago, Ill.); *Marauders*, by Charlton Ogburn Jr., a fine accounting of the deeds and tragedies of our bushfighting guerrillas in Burma in World War Two (New York, Harper & Brother, 1956–59); Charles W. Thayer's *Guerrilla* (New York Harper & Row); *They Fought Alone*, John Keat's intriguing tale of United States guerrilla tactician Wendell Fertig in the Philippines (Philadelphia and New York: J. B. Lippincott, 1963); *The Federalist Papers*, Alexander Hamilton and James Madison; *Wavell, Scholar and Soldier*, John Connell's biography of Britain's outstanding 20th century military thinker (New York, Harcourt, Brace and World, 1962).

I owe a special debt to the *American Rifleman* for permission to use voluminous amounts of material from its issues between 1950 and 1968. I leaned mainly on the skillful summaries of small-arms training, theory, and weapons by Jac Weller, who has written extensively about the sort of wars this republic has prosecuted since 1945.

Less willing sources, probably have been the news stories and columns of several major metropolitan newspapers and wire services, as well as the news treatments of the three major television networks. As I say in the proper chapter of this book, few of these sources have been objective or even rational in their coverage of the firearms law issue. Main sources of news stories cited in this book have included the *Los Angeles Times,* the *New York Times,* the American Broadcasting Company, the Columbia Broadcasting System, the National Broadcasting Company, the *Washington Post,* the *Philadelphia Bulletin,* the *Philadelphia Inquirer,* the *Chicago Sun-Times,* the *Chicago Daily News,* the *Arizona Republic* (Phoenix), and the *Tucson Daily Citizen.* The last two have been considerably fairer and more objective than about 90 percent of their fellow strivers for what passes as Freedom of the Press.

Major "slick" mass-media magazines whose material has been cited, quoted or used include *Time* and *Look.* National-scale newspapers are led by the *National Observer* and the *Christian Science Monitor.* None of these have treated the gun isssue much more reasonably than the Hollywood–New York–Los Angeles news-and-image axis.

More neutral sources have included the United States Constitution; the *Congressional Record;* Robin Moore's *Green Berets;* (New York, Crown; 1965); *The Road Past Mandalay,* John Masters' tale of Allied guerrilla efforts against the Japanese in Burma (New York, Harper & Brother; 1961); the *Journal of the American Bar Association; Army* magazine; *Combat Forces Journal;* the FBI's *Crime in the United States—Uniform Crime Reports* for various years; *One Hundred Hours to Suez,* by Robert Henriques (New York, Viking Press; 1957); *Infantry* magazine; *The Mustangs, by* J. Frank Dobie (Little, Brown & Co., 1952); *Rommel, the Desert Fox,* by Brigadier Desmond Young (Harper & Brother, 1950); *Western Outdoors* magazine; Plato; Nicolò Machiavelli; Winston S. Churchill's *Second World War,* with emphasis on Volume II (Boston: Houghton, Mifflin Co., 1953); *Samurai,* the Martin Caidin story of Japanese fighter-plane ace Saburo Sakai (Ballantine, 1968); the *New York University Law Review,* and the wire stories of the Associated Press and United Press International—though at times neither wire service seemed to quite merit the description "neutral."

In hunting, shooting, and related publications, the author owes much to *Guns and Ammo, Guns, World of Guns, Gun World,* the various bulletins and other news releases of many game and fish (conservation) departments, and the news releases of both the National Shooting Sports Foundation and the Small Arms and Ammunition Institute. The *American Rifleman* is easily my strongest source in this field, with *Gun Digest* and *Gun Week* very helpful. Also valuable have been the three outdoor "slicks"—*Sports Afield Field and Stream,* and *Outdoor Life.* Anyone caring to read what a first rate news columnist can do with the flaps and foolishness of a Senator Tom Dodd should read Richard Starnes in *Field and Stream.*

Henry Sienkiewicz (better known for *Quo Vadis*) wrote about battles of great carnage and greater impact, which most Westerners have never even heard of, in his Polish-Russian historical novels—*With Fire and Sword, Pan Michael,* and *The Deluge.* There was Berestechko, fought around 300 years

Bibliography and Acknowledgements   289

ago; how many Americans, even history buffs (including historians who have gone to Hanoi to commiserate with Uncle Ho about our barbarities), have ever heard of Berestechko? How many know that about half a million men collided in that classic East European battle—at a time when the much-trumpeted kings of France, England, and Spain had to sweat and pilfer to put 20,000 men in the field? Berestechko, unfortunately, didn't settle much as things turned out, even with such numbers and attendant bloodshed; it just delayed the partitions of Poland about a century and ensured a different cast of characters for the latest thievery.

I also want to thank some individuals whose written and spoken misinformation, distortion, and outright untruths spurred me to try this book. Heading this list have to be Senators Teddy and Bobby Kennedy, Tom Dodd, Joe Tydings, Joe Clark, and Jake Javits; former President Lyndon Johnson; former Attorney General Ramsey Clark and his predecessor, Nicholas De B. Katzenbach; Congressman Richard McCarthy and a host of others. If including Bobby Kennedy after his murder seems uncharitable, was it not uncharitable of him to conduct a full-scale vendetta against the wise, lawful use of firearms? It helped get a great many more young men killed and will go on doing this. At the time he was killed, there were over 80 Americans held under oppressive conditions in North Korea—prisoners of an act of piracy; there were several hundred American servicemen mentally and physically persecuted in North Vietnamese prison camps. Not much was done, in an honorable way, to free these captives, some of whom may have got or been kept where they were by the policies to which Kennedy contributed.

Most of all, the writer owes an ancient and great debt to three of his elders, now long returned to dust in their Ohio Valley. Two great uncles and a great aunt, they had the library and allowed the time and freedom to use it—and if this book is any good at all, it is their doing; if not, it cannot be their fault, since they gave every opportunity. They were old and gentle people—gentle until aroused. My first recollection is of my great aunt abruptly adjourning a Ku Klux Klan rally with her .22 pistol when the Klan burnt a cross on our farm. Elderly and gentle souls as they were, they were also determined and sometimes defiant people who knew how this country was won and how it could be held. Some of their deeds would scare a lot of today's softer breed right into a nervous breakdown. They happened to be a cross section of Anglo-Irish stubbornness, Huguenot French quickness, and English courage; their descendants are and will be of other mixtures, but as long as the will and the flint-and-grit soul remain, it won't make any difference. The important element is that the people of this country do not continue to ignore what made us. If this book helps even a bit to revive interest in our heritage, or show how much it is still needed—though it is being ridiculed by false prophets and fools—then it will be worthwhile.

Index

✳✳✳✳✳